Protection Against Genocide

Protection Against Genocide

Mission Impossible?

Edited by
NEAL RIEMER

PRAEGER

Westport, Connecticut
London

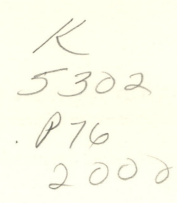

Library of Congress Cataloging-in-Publication Data

Protection against genocide : mission impossible? / edited by Neal Riemer.
   p. cm.
  Includes bibliographical references and index.
  ISBN 0–275–96515–5 (alk. paper)—ISBN 0–275–96516–3 (pbk. : alk. paper)
   1. Genocide. I. Riemer, Neal, 1922–
  K5302.P76 2000
  341.7'78 21—dc21   99–046405

British Library Cataloguing in Publication Data is available.

Library of Congress Catalog Card Number: 99–046405
ISBN: 0–275–96515–5
     0–275–96516–3 (pbk.)

First published in 2000

Praeger Publishers, 88 Post Road West, Westport, CT 06881
An imprint of Greenwood Publishing Group, Inc.
www.praeger.com

Printed in the United States of America

The paper used in this book complies with the
Permanent Paper Standard issued by the National
Information Standards Organization (Z39.48–1984).

10 9 8 7 6 5 4 3 2 1

To Hadassah Leah Riemer

May her generation see the end of genocide.

Contents

Preface

The agonizing problem of genocide challenges the conscience of humankind and cries out for a sensible solution. Events in Kosovo in the spring and summer of 1999 underscore the relevance of the title of this book: *Protection Against Genocide: Mission Impossible?* Both the urgent need to protect against genocide and the great difficulties in doing so are starkly revealed in the diplomatic and military efforts to achieve a just and humane solution in the Kosovo crisis. The problem painfully persists and continues to highlight the tragic failure of the international community to develop an effective response to the radical evil of genocide after the Holocaust. After World War II, the international community saw the passage in 1948 of the UN's Convention on the Prevention and Punishment of the Crime of Genocide, yet horrible genocides in Cambodia, Bosnia, Rwanda, and other areas of the world have still occurred. Today, over fifty years after the adoption of the UN's antigenocide treaty, the challenge is clear, but a wise and effective response still needs to be crafted.

This book is a response to that challenge. Neal Riemer, in his introductory Chapter 1, raises the central question of this volume: Can a Global Human Rights Regime to protect against genocide be put into place—or is this an impossible mission? He argues that this vital, if extraordinarily difficult, mission will depend upon whether four crucial needs are addressed: (1) to strengthen the institutions and actors of such a Global Human Rights Regime; (2) to articulate a cogent philosophy of prudent prevention; (3) to craft a policy of carefully targeted sanctions; and (4) to develop a wise theory and practice of just humanitarian intervention.

Strengthened institutions and actors include such existing organs of the
UN as the UN Security Council, the UN Secretary-General, and the UN
High Commissioner for Human Rights. Additional (and new) UN actors
would include a UN Human Rights Monitor in every region of the globe,
a UN Antigenocide Police Force, a Permanent International Criminal Tribunal, and a UN Protectorate Agency. Key regional organizations, such as
the North Atlantic Treaty Organization (NATO), and major powers, such
as the United States, must also develop a coherent policy on protection
against genocide and the courageous will to make such a policy effective.

Prudent prevention of genocide involves attention to the tough long-
range problem of encouraging the development of genuine constitutional
democracies (crucially, nations that protect basic human rights), and to the
more immediate task of shaping effective policies of deterrence and preemption. Carefully targeted sanctions rest upon improved monitoring and
early warning of genocide, and effective political, economic, legal/judicial,
and police and/or military sanctions. Just humanitarian intervention would
embody the principles of appropriate authority, just cause, timely resort,
prudent appraisal of costs and benefits, reasonable chance of immediate success, proportionate means, and long-run reasonable chance of success. Key
follow-up questions (as they relate to the institutions, actors, principles, policies, practices, and problems of the Global Human Rights Regime) are
explored more fully in succeeding chapters.

Thus, in Chapter 2, "The Evolution of the International System and Its
Impact on Protection Against Genocide," Douglas Simon asks: "Are recent
major changes in the international system causing states and international
organizations to begin taking more effective steps to confront the problem
of genocide?" His "perhaps" response (a cautious "yes") highlights the potential importance of such changes as the end of the Cold War, global economic integration, the important if uneven spread of constitutional
democracies dedicated to human rights, and the communications revolution. These are developments that hold open the opportunity for important
(if, so far, modest) movement in the battle against genocide. Simon prefaces
his analysis by emphasizing the importance of taking a critical look at the
realist paradigm in international affairs, which has so often cast doubt on
the possibility of protection against genocide. He favors an outlook more
attuned to recognition of new and changing realities in the international
system, developments that may encourage states, in their own self-interest,
to confront the horrors of genocide.

In Chapter 3, Helen Fein deftly explores "The Three P's of Genocide
Prevention: With Application to a Genocide Foretold—Rwanda." She asks
three interrelated questions: Is developing a far-sighted, coherent, and effective policy of prudent prevention of genocide our problem? Is it not only
prudent but in our interest to develop such a policy? And is it really possible,
if assisted by a paradigm that anticipates genocide, to detect genocide? She

answers all three questions in the affirmative. She argues that genocide is "an impediment to our international goals" of a peaceful, stable, and refugee-free world. She emphasizes that prevention is not only more humane but less costly than intervention. She warns about an uncritical endorsement of democracy as the answer; she is wisely leery of nations that may have elections but do not protect human rights. She argues that anticipating and deterring genocide requires us to "focus directly on protecting both individuals and groups against gross violations of life-integrity, using intelligence analysis, historical interpretation, monitoring, and warning systems." She uses genocide in Rwanda to illustrate her argument. Events in Kosovo in 1999 underscore the continuing cogency of her analysis.

In Chapter 4, George Lopez explores the very difficult question of economic sanctions. He surveys the cases in which sanctions have been imposed to halt genocide and mass murder and assesses the economic sanctions' strengths and weaknesses. He examines the claims by many in the humanitarian community that sanctions themselves have had a devastating impact on the economic and social well-being of the most vulnerable members of the targeted nations. He then explores what might be done to make sanctions work more effectively to deter or halt genocide without causing serious harm to the vulnerable innocents in the offending regime. He envisages the development of "smart" and more carefully "targeted" sanctions in conjunction with more prudent and effective diplomacy.

In Chapter 5, David Wippman critically examines the role that a Permanent International Criminal Court can play in preventing and punishing genocide. He argues that such a Court constitutes a promising, but still problematic, breakthrough. It is promising because, hopefully, it can contribute to the difficult effort to end impunity for genocidal criminals. It is problematic because of shortcomings in the treaty, the lack of support for the treaty by such crucial nations as the United States, and by the still deficient political culture of the globe. Difficulties of the treaty include controversies over the very meaning of the words "genocide" and "intent"; over the Court's jurisdiction, independence, and its amending process; over enforcement and compliance, and thus over the Court's effective capacity to deter and prosecute offenders. He is concerned that the present Court will "lack both the broad international legitimacy and the political, financial and logistical support" to be truly effective. The Court, in brief, represents a highly important step, but its fuller effectiveness may well depend on key changes that will bring the United States into its fuller support. Chapter 5 provides very valuable historical and analytical background for understanding the obstacles confronting, and the emergence of, the newly established Permanent International Criminal Court.

In Chapter 6, Saul Mendlovitz and John Fousek imaginatively and forcefully argue on behalf of "A UN Constabulary to Enforce the Law on Genocide and Crimes Against Humanity." Such a Constabulary—under the auspices of the UN Secretary-General and assisted by an International Crime Watch Advisory Board—would be a volunteer, permanent, transnational police force, under international law, dedicated to preventing and halting genocide and crimes against humanity. They maintain that such a Constabulary would not only save countless lives but also billions of dollars now spent on postconflict refugee relief and economic reconstruction. Members of the Constabulary would be recruited as individuals. Mendlovitz and Fousek contend that "the appropriate composition, mission, financing, command and control of such a force . . . could overcome many of the political obstacles that have traditionally blocked the creation" of an international police force. Readers will be challenged to ask whether a UN Constabulary—if in place— could have played a role in preventing the tragedy in Kosovo.

Michael Joseph Smith, in Chapter 7, "On Humanitarian Intervention," explores the fuller meaning, tough problems, and recommended policies facing such intervention to protect against genocide. He deftly explores key problems of "justification, agency, and capability." He argues that state sovereignty can be overridden when states commit egregious or genocidal violations of human rights. His case for just humanitarian intervention embraces security and peace as well as genocide. Reflecting upon the failure of the UN and other key actors after the dissolution of Yugoslavia, he emphasizes that force and diplomacy must be skillfully integrated if either is to work; that "a credible *threat* of force made in advance may well obviate the necessity actually to *use* force"; that "a 'humanitarian' mission cannot be undertaken in isolation from the political circumstances of the conflict." An "overarching lesson is that we can prevent genocide only if we muster the collective will and create the capabilities to do so." Again, readers will be challenged to ask if the combination of skillful diplomacy and the credible threat of force were wisely employed in the dispute with Serbia over Kosovo.

In a concluding Chapter 8, Neal Riemer returns to restate the difficulties facing the mission of protection against genocide, and to respond to the adverse critics of such a mission. Drawing on his earlier analysis and the analyses of other contributors to this book, he assesses more fully the probability of the possibility of (1) strengthening the institutions and actors of a Global Human Rights Regime, (2) prudent prevention of genocide, (3) articulation of the theory and practice of wisely staged implementation of sanctions, and (4) just humanitarian intervention. He concludes that a creative breakthrough to a Global Human Rights Regime capable of protecting against genocide is a theoretical possibility. With crucial assistance from creative leaders and creative followers, what will be tested in the future will be the probability of that possibility.

Acknowledgments

The central question of this book—*Protection Against Genocide: Mission Impossible?*—was initially explored at a Drew University Graduate School Colloquium on October 7, 1998. In connection with that event, I especially wish to acknowledge the splendid support of Dr. William Rogers, Assistant Dean of the Graduate School. The Colloquium was also made possible by the strong support of Drew University President Thomas H. Kean, Dr. James Pain, Dean of the Graduate School, and William Messmer, Chairman of the Department of Political Science.

This book is also greatly indebted to Helen Fein, Saul Mendlovitz (whose paper was coauthored by John Fousek), Douglas Simon, and Michael Smith, who joined me in presenting papers at that Colloquium and in subsequently revising their papers for this volume. It is also indebted to George Lopez and David Wippman, who kindly agreed to round out our exploration of our key problem with their important contributions.

I also want to thank the keen participants in our Colloquium for their stimulating comments and helpful insights, and the larger community of scholars and writers who have done so much to enhance our understanding of the difficult problem of protection against genocide.

Neal Riemer

1

The Urgent Need for a Global Human Rights Regime

Neal Riemer

INTRODUCTION

Can an effective Global Human Rights Regime to protect against genocide be put into place—or is this an impossible mission?[1] That is the central question—the excruciatingly difficult problem—that I shall be exploring in this chapter and that our coauthors shall, by focusing on cardinal aspects of the problem, be investigating in this book. Those concerned with the radical evil of genocide are challenged to do more than simply dream of a world free of genocide. We are challenged to see if we can break through—creatively, but realistically—to the institutions and actors, principles, and policies that will effectively ensure a genocide-free world.[2]

The difficulties here are daunting. The conventional "realistic" wisdom maintains that a breakthrough is impossible. This conventional wisdom too often "realistically" accepts the historical inevitability of egregious violations of human rights, the sacrosanct principle in international law of noninterference in the internal affairs of nation-states, the absence of a vital national self-interest (or political will) in humanitarian intervention, the weaknesses of the UN, and the costs and dangers of intervention.[3]

Yet in responding to this extremely tough challenge of protection against genocide, I would like to suggest that we can be encouraged by another, often overlooked, reality—the reality of past and present creative breakthroughs in politics. Appreciation of this reality may help foster the psychological readiness to see the possibility of a creative breakthrough to protection against genocide. In the United States, for example, we did break through to religious liberty in defiance of the conventional wisdom, which held that there could be only one true religious faith and that it was the duty of the rulers of state to enforce that one true faith. In the United States we also broke through to the federal republic—our current federal system—despite the conventional wisdom, which held that democratic liberty and large geographic size were fundamentally incompatible. In the post-World War II world, Western European nations are demonstrating through European Union that (again, contrary to the conventional wisdom) it is possible for historically antagonistic nations, which have fought two cataclysmic world wars in the twentieth century and countless others in previous centuries, to overcome their historical animosities and achieve (I believe, now, and forever) peace, prosperity, and mature constitutional democracy. These significant breakthroughs give us hope as we explore a breakthrough to protection against genocide. They also underscore the crucial importance of creative intellectual and political leadership—whether it is found in a Roger Williams, a James Madison, or a Jean Monnet. In addition, they also emphasize the importance of patience, persistence, and prudence when addressing tough problems.[4]

In this introductory chapter, the start of our book-long exploration, I shall argue that the creative breakthrough to a genocide-free world calls for addressing four interrelated, crucial needs. *First*, there is a need to strengthen the institutions and actors in our Global Human Rights Regime. *Second*, there is a need to articulate a cogent philosophy of prudent prevention. *Third*, there is a need to craft a policy of wisely targeted sanctions. *Fourth*, there is a need to develop a wise theory of just humanitarian intervention.

In this introductory chapter I can only open up our tough problem for exploration by emphasizing the imperative of addressing these four crucial needs. The authors of subsequent chapters will be exploring our book's central problem more fully.

The difficult problem to be explored here is underscored by the tragic failure of the international community to develop an effective response to the radical evil of genocide in a post-World War II world traumatized by the Holocaust, a world only now coming to grips more fully with the earlier Armenian genocide and even earlier genocidal activities. This post-World War II world saw the passage of the UN's convention against genocide,[5] *but* it is a world still, tragically, characterized by genocide.

Despite the global revulsion against the Nazi extermination of six million Jews and other target groups in the Holocaust—a revulsion that contributed to the UN's Convention on the Prevention and Punishment of Genocide—genocide has continued in the post-World War II world. It continued in Cambodia, in East Pakistan (now Bangladesh), in Bosnia, in Iraq, Rwanda, and in other areas of the world.[6] The year 1999 also saw barbaric "ethnic cleansing" on a major scale in Kosovo.

In this chapter I will focus primarily on the imperative of developing a Global Human Rights Regime capable of preventing and stopping genocide. My crucial assumption is that, if we can break through in dealing effectively with genocide, we can then consolidate that breakthrough and deal more successfully with other flagrant violations of human rights.

The word "genocide" is variously understood. Let me here define the term as it is defined in the UN Convention on the Prevention and Punishment of the Crime of Genocide (adopted 1948; in force 1951). The Convention defines genocide as "any of the following acts committed with the intent to destroy, in whole or in part, a national, ethnical [sic], racial, or religious group" by, for example, "killing members of the group"; "causing either bodily or mental harm to members of the group"; "deliberately inflicting on the group conditions of life calculated to bring about its physical extermination in whole or in part."[7] Moreover, by interpretation or amendment, it is vitally important that the antigenocide convention should also clearly protect political groups or economic classes from genocidal killing.[8]

The persistence of the problem of genocide urgently prompts us to address four seriously neglected needs and thus to outline the key features of the creative breakthrough required to attend to these needs. Whether we can address these four needs will determine whether we can successfully protect against genocide!

FOUR BADLY NEGLECTED NEEDS

Strengthened Institutions and Actors

The first need is for strengthening the ability of key institutions and actors in the Global Human Rights Regime so that they can protect against genocide. By a Global Human Rights Regime I mean all those actors—for example, the UN, key nations (especially the United States), certain regional organizations (e.g., NATO, European Union), committed nongovernmental organizations (e.g., such NGOs as Human Rights Watch) dedicated to the protection of human rights. These actors in the Global Human Rights Regime are committed to those norms, principles, institutions, policies, and practices concerned with the protection of human rights.[9] The norms, for example, are articulated in the UN Universal Declaration of Human Rights, the UN Convention Against Genocide, and other key UN documents. Here I will concentrate on key institutions and actors and, most importantly, the will to make them work effectively. Key principles, policies, and practices will become clearer as I subsequently address the tasks of prudent prevention, carefully staged sanctions, and just humanitarian intervention.

Currently, we have a number of diverse political actors who respect and try to abide by these norms: certain nation-states (such as the United States) committed to the protection of human rights, certain regional actors (e.g.,

NATO, European Union) equally respectful of human rights, most organs of the UN, a number of nongovernmental organizations (NGOs)—for example, Human Rights Watch—highly dedicated to human rights. If we focus on the UN, we find that key UN institutions and actors are weak, often ineffective, or untested. For example, the UN Security Council is potentially strong but actually weak in its ability either to prevent or intervene against genocide. The UN Commission on Human Rights lacks stronger powers to be effective. The person appointed to the recently created position of UN High Commissioner for Human Rights is untested. UN policies and practices are thus theoretically promising, but weak and often ineffective. Clearly, there is a need—especially in the most promising global organization, the UN—to develop stronger institutions, policies, and practices that could make prudent prevention, effective implementation of sanctions, and just humanitarian intervention genuinely meaningful.[10] It is tragically clear that the reality of a possible veto by Russia or China made intervention by the UN Security Council impossible in the Kosovo crisis in 1999.

Moreover, if we examine the record of the United States or of other nations in Western Europe (all theoretically devoted to the protection of human rights), whether in Cambodia, the former Yugoslavia, or Rwanda, we find that record delinquent in policy and will.[11] It remains to be seen how NATO's belated military intervention in, and occupation of, Kosovo in 1999 will finally play out. If successful, it could represent a crucial turning point for the protection of human rights in Southeastern Europe.

The breakthrough I envisage requires a UN Security Council with the requisite policy and will to act against genocide; and this, in turn, means a policy and will to act on the part of the permanent members of the Security Council, especially the United States. If the Security Council is, theoretically, powerful but often lacks adequate resources, a coherent policy, and a courageous will, other key UN institutions lack power, resources, policy, and will. The creative breakthrough proposed here envisages a strengthening of the UN High Commissioner for Human Rights and the UN Commission on Human Rights. The UN High Commissioner, in particular, working closely with an empowered UN Commission on Human Rights, would have a particularly important role to play in monitoring the status of human rights and in utilizing the power of publicity. The strategy here would be to increase the powers of these organs to investigate and publicize genocidal threats or acts. The UN High Commissioner for Human Rights, working with the UN Commission on Human Rights, would then be required to recommend more stringent actions to prevent or stop genocide to the Secretary-General and the UN Security Council. Presently, the inability to achieve unanimity among the permanent members of the UN Security Council in controversial cases, such as Kosovo, remains a disturbing reality. As the case of Kosovo illustrates, the Security Council would not have been able to engage in military action to combat "ethnic cleansing" in view of an expected Russian or Chinese veto. Hence, military intervention depended on reliance upon NATO.

Strengthening other key UN institutions calls for building on the work of the UN's Ad Hoc International Criminal Tribunals for the former Yugoslavia and Rwanda. The establishment of an effective permanent UN International Criminal Tribunal to make certain that those who commit genocide will be brought to justice is crucial here. A most significant step in that direction was taken in the summer of 1998, when the UN conference in Rome voted (by 120 to 7, with 21 abstentions) to establish a Permanent UN International Criminal Tribunal. The possible breakthrough this Tribunal represents is threatened, however, by the failure to garner the endorsement of the United States and by provisions that may limit its effectiveness in certain cases of genocide.[12]

Several new UN institutions also need to be put into place. For example, to make monitoring more effective, a UN Human Rights Monitor needs to be established for every region of the world in order to cover every country of the world. In addition, a UN Human Rights Protection Force needs to be established and made ready to move in the event that protection against genocide requires its use.[13] Similarly, a UN Protectorate Agency needs to be established to ensure temporary guardianship of a country after a genocidal regime is removed and until a human rights-respecting regime is put into place in such a country.[14] Kosovo will put the establishment of protection for the people of that terribly disturbed province of Serbia to a severe test.

As key institutions and actors in the Global Human Rights Regime are strengthened or developed, it will be most important to address more fully and clearly the broader operative political philosophy—the key principles, policies, and practices—that will guide those institutions and actors. Again, neglected needs highlight the imperative of appropriate responses.

Prudent Prevention

The second neglected need is for the articulation of a cogent philosophy of prudent prevention of genocide.[15] My argument here is simple and compelling: It is far better to prevent genocide than to have to cope with it after it has occurred.

A philosophy of prudent prevention rests on three cardinal principles. *First*, it is important to encourage the emergence of mature constitutional democracies—a challenging, difficult, long-range task. This means more than free elections (whether free or phony). It means, crucially, the protection of basic human rights.[16] Support of the existence of mature constitutional democracies dedicated to the protection of human rights is the best preventive principle, because such democracies do not practice genocide against their own citizens. Thus, with their emergence around the world, the danger of genocide would decline. Moreover, a world of mature constitutional democracies would contribute to a peaceful world because such democracies do not wage war against each other, and war is unquestionably the condition that makes possible the worst violations of human rights, including genocide.[17]

It must be reemphasized that the emergence of mature constitutional democracies that are genuinely respectful of human rights will be a long-range and difficult process. Serious and sustained efforts to encourage the emergence of such democracies must, however, be pursued, even as we focus on the immediate task of prevention of genocide (via deterrence and preemption)—in a world of nations still guilty of egregious violations of human rights.

The key actors in a Global Human Rights Regime—the existing mature constitutional democracies, regional organizations sensitive to the protection of human rights, the UN, and committed human rights NGOs—have an ethical and prudential reason to foster rights-respecting constitutional democracies. Because the protection of human life is an undeniable ethical imperative, key actors recognize that such protection makes the global climate safer for each nation's vital interests, and safer too for the vital interests of regional organizations and the UN. These vital interests are clearly served when legitimate humanitarian intervention is not needed, and when the costs and dangers of such intervention are either eliminated or minimized.

The Global Human Rights Regime would have the important, yet delicate, task of monitoring the evolution of mature constitutional democracies around the globe, and of supporting national, regional, and UN policies to assist in the healthy maturation of such constitutional democracies. The monitoring would look to the existential status of nations around the globe, with particular emphasis on respect for human rights and threats of genocide. Monitoring would also include the empirical investigation of the necessary and sufficient conditions—social, cultural, political, economic, religious—that facilitate the emergence of mature constitutional democracies. National, regional, and global policies to achieve these conditions would then logically flow from such monitoring. Such policies would stress the primacy of protection of basic human rights, genuinely democratic and constitutional political institutions, and healthy economic and social systems.

Second, it is important to develop the philosophy and practice of deterrence of genocide. Deterrence is the next best preventive medicine. It is based on the premise that mature constitutional democracies respectful of human rights will not come into existence immediately or all over the globe. Authoritarian and despotic regimes—even spurious "democratic" regimes— that egregiously violate basic human rights will, unfortunately, continue to operate for many years ahead. Consequently, a strategy of prevention must also contemplate additional ways of stopping acts of genocide before they occur. A policy of deterrence is one such way. It would warn potentially genocidal violators that they would pay a high price for such violations. Deterrence would be premised on reliable monitoring to identify potentially genocidal violations. Publicity, in turn, would serve to signal violators, as well as the global community, that the Global Human Rights Regime is aware of dangerous conditions, and that egregious human rights violations are unacceptable. The high price of egregious violations would include an escalating series of actions—political, economic, legal, police, military, and judicial. The credible threat of such actions would be designed to forestall genocidal violations.

Third, it is important to develop a philosophy and practice of preemptive action in the event that deterrence doesn't work. Preemptive action is a fall-back preventive strategy. All three principles of a theory of prudent prevention rest on the irrefutable proposition that it is unquestionably better to prevent genocide than to stop it once it has occurred.

Preemptive action could include political, economic, legal, police, military, and judicial sanctions. Police or military intervention would normally—but not inevitably—follow political, economic, and legal sanctions. Police and military intervention would be based on overwhelmingly credible evidence of a clear and present danger of genocide.

The fuller conditions under which deterrence and preemptive action can occur, as well as policies and practices of implementation, will be spelled out as I discuss the following needs, and thus speak to the issues of effective implementation and just humanitarian intervention.

Effectively Staged Implementation of Sanctions

The third need is for working out an effective policy of wisely staged sanctions. Such a policy would guide the Global Human Rights Regime, particularly the relevant UN or regional organs of that regime. Four key points in such a policy can be identified.

First, it is important to enhance effective and respected machinery for monitoring, investigating, and reporting.[18] Such enhanced monitoring would build on the important monitoring already in existence. Ideally, a strengthened UN High Commissioner for Human Rights, working with an empowered UN Commission on Human Rights, would coordinate the diverse UN, regional, national, and NGO monitoring already taking place in the arena of human rights and then report to the UN Secretary-General. Reliable information about potential or actual genocide is the primary basis for a sensible response.

Second, the power of publicity must be employed to deter potentially genocidal violations—where there is a clear and present danger of the eruption of genocide—and solidify strategic support for just humanitarian intervention to stop genocide in progress. Key UN organs (i.e., the UN High Commissioner for Human Rights, the UN Commission on Human Rights, the UN Secretary General, and the UN Security Council), effective regional organizations, key nations, NGOs, and a vigilant press, radio, and television media would publicize egregious violations.

Third, effective remedies—political, economic, legal, police, military, and judicial—must be on hand, to be prudently chosen, wisely targeted, and sagaciously employed to prevent, stop, and punish genocide. Such remedies, to have any chance of success, must have the support of UN members (especially the permanent members of the UN Security Council and, crucially, the United States) willing and able to implement recommendations and decisions of the UN Security Council. These recommendations and decisions may, for example, involve such political actions as withdrawal of diplomatic recognition and restrictions on travel abroad; such (wisely targeted) economic sanctions as a military or selective trade embargo and freezing of a country's assets; such police or military sanctions as the use of force to stop genocidal actions; and such judicial remedies as trial and punishment of those guilty of genocide.[19]

Fourth, it is vital to work out the problem of what might be called "human rights consolidation," namely, what it takes to ensure that human rights will continue to be respected after initial efforts of prevention or intervention have been successful. Consolidation might involve (1) temporary maintenance of a UN Human Rights Protection Force in the country involved, (2) placing the country involved in the temporary status of a UN Protectorate, or (3) other prudent measures. Although I emphasize the desirability of reliance upon UN organizations, I do not exclude the role of appropriate regional organizations in ensuring the success of "human rights consolidation."

Just Humanitarian Intervention

The fourth tragically neglected need is for the articulation of a cogent theory of just humanitarian intervention. Such intervention must clearly be distinguished from unwarranted interference in the legitimate internal affairs of a sovereign nation. Such a theory—easier to articulate than to employ wisely—would include the following principles:[20]

First, an appropriate authority is required to bring the doctrine of just humanitarian intervention into action. The UN Security Council, for example, would be such an appropriate authority.[21]

Second, just humanitarian intervention could only be involved in support of a just cause—for example, intervention to prevent or stop genocide.

Third, police and/or military intervention would normally function as a last resort, after other pacific means—political, economic, legal/judicial—have been tried and found wanting. However, early police and/or military intervention may be wisely dictated in those cases where it is clear that genocide is imminent or already in process and where other sanctions will not work.

Fourth, the appropriate intervening authority would be required to make a prudent appraisal of the benefits and costs of intervention.[22]

Fifth, just humanitarian intervention must be based on the expectation of a reasonable chance of immediate success in preventing or stopping genocide.

Sixth, the intervening authority must employ humane and proportionate means to prevent or stop genocide, in the interest of minimizing harm, especially to the innocents involved in the conflict.

Seventh, just humanitarian intervention must also calculate the reasonable chance of long-run success; success, for example, in putting into place a human-rights–respecting regime to ensure the ongoing protection of human rights.

These principles of just humanitarian intervention are, of course, easier to state than to implement wisely. Yet it is important to set forth the larger philosophy that guides both the deterrent and preemptive aspects of prudent prevention and the conditions for actual intervention when preventive measures fail.

CONCLUSION

I have argued that a creative breakthrough to a genocide-free world calls for addressing four interrelated needs: (1) the need to strengthen the institutions and actors of a Global Human Rights Regime, (2) the need to articulate a cogent philosophy of prudent prevention, (3) the need to craft a policy of wisely targeted sanctions, (4) the need to develop a wise theory of just humanitarian intervention. Addressing these needs will lead to a responsible, courageous, and effective Global Human Rights Regime capable of protecting against genocide.

I appreciate that the difficulties involved in addressing these needs are daunting, and that the devotees of the "realistic" conventional wisdom are very skeptical about the possibility of the breakthrough outlined here.[23] They argue that very little can be done; that the world lacks adequate institutions and actors, policy, machinery, and will; that the costs of protection are too high; that nations (realistically concerned with protecting their own vital national interests) are not going to stick their humanitarian necks out for foreigners; that the UN is ill-equipped to handle such problems; that key nations deem it unwise, dangerous, and unlawful to meddle in the internal, domestic affairs of sovereign nation-states.

Yet, despite this skepticism, and despite the cogency of some of the arguments above, which we need to address seriously, I remain convinced that we must confront the problem boldly to see whether a creative breakthrough is possible. If we cannot break through on the protection against genocide, then—clearly—the effective global protection of other human rights is placed in jeopardy. On the other hand, if we can break through to protection against genocide, we may have developed the requisite institutions and actors, coherent policy, and courageous will that can then be employed to protect a wider range of human rights.

In exploring a creative breakthrough to protection against genocide, it is also important in conclusion to emphasize several additional points.

We need to avoid the temptations of a narrow-minded nationalism, a super-skeptical political realism, and a relativistic (and, I believe, cowardly) postmodernism. We need to avoid these temptations without, however, succumbing to falsely utopian notions about the possibility of creating an angelic new person in a miraculously new earthly society where all conflict, tyranny, want, and egotism have been eliminated. We need to avoid these temptations without also succumbing to falsely utopian notions about creating a benevolent and altruistic global commonwealth where unanimity automatically prevails on all tough problems, where the will to act is magically untroubled by considerations of vital national interests, and where, miraculously, manpower, resources, and money flow easily and abundantly in support of actions aimed at genocidal violators.

We must be honest in appreciating the difficulties of our present and future tasks. Nonetheless, those seeking to develop a Global Human Rights Regime capable of protecting against genocide must, in the creative spirit of a more prophetic politics,[24] operate on the reasoned faith that we can—and, indeed, must—succeed in ridding the world of the radical evil of genocide. Theoretically, the mission to overcome genocide is possible. Our challenging creative task is to enhance the probability of that theoretical possibility.

NOTES

1. My response to this question has been stimulated by my exploration of creative breakthroughs in politics. See, especially, Neal Riemer, *Creative Breakthroughs in Politics* (Westport, CT: Praeger, 1996), especially Chapter 7, "Protection Against Genocide: Toward a Global Human Rights Regime." See also my Chapter 12, "The Prophetic Mode and Challenge, Creative Breakthroughs, and the Future of Constitutional Democracy," especially pp. 199–207, in Neal Riemer, ed., *Let Justice Roll: Prophetic Challenges in Religion, Politics, and Society* (Lanham, MD: Rowman & Littlefield, 1996).

2. For a brief introduction to the literature on genocide, see Leo Kuper, *Genocide: Its Political Use in the Twentieth Century* (New Haven: Yale University Press, 1981); Leo Kuper, *The Prevention of Genocide* (New Haven: Yale University Press, 1985); Helen Fein, *Accounting for Genocide* (Chicago: University of Chicago Press, 1984); Helen Fein, *Genocide Watch* (New Haven: Yale University Press, 1992); Helen Fein, *Genocide: A Sociological Perspective* (London: Sage, 1993); Ervin Staub, *The Roots of*

Evil: The Origins of Genocide and other Group Violence (New York: Cambridge University Press, 1992); Israel W. Charney, ed., *Genocide: A Critical Bibliographic Review*, vol. 3 (New Brunswick, NJ: Transaction Publishers, 1994); Irving Louis Horowitz, *Taking Lives: Genocide and State Power*, 4th ed. (New Brunswick, NJ: Transaction Publishers, 1997); Kurt Jonassohn, *Genocide and Gross Human Rights Violations in Comparative Perspective* (New Brunswick, NJ: Transaction Publishers, 1997); Michael N. Dobkowski and Isidor Wallimann, eds., *Genocide in Our Time: An Annotated Bibliography With Analytical Introductions* (Ann Arbor, MI: Pierian Press, 1992); Samuel Totten, William S. Parsons, and Israel W. Charney, eds., *Century of Genocide: Eyewitness Accounts and Critical Views* (New York: Garland, 1997); Ben Whitaker, Special Rapporteur, *1985 UN Report on Genocide* (New York: United Nations, 1985) [E/CN.4/Sub.2/1985/6, July 2, 1985].

For literature on Bosnia and Rwanda, see the following: James Gow, *Triumph of the Lack of Will: International Diplomacy and the Yugoslav War* (New York: Columbia University Press, 1997); Roger Cohen, *Hearts Grown Brutal: Sagas of Sarajevo* (New York: Random House, 1998); Thomas Cushman and Stjepan G. Mestrovic, eds., *This Time We Knew: Western Responses to Genocide in Bosnia* (New York: New York University Press, 1996); Gernard Prunier, *The Rwanda Crisis: History of a Genocide* (New York: Columbia University Press, 1995, 1997); Holly Burkhalter, "The 1994 Rwandan Genocide and U.S. Policy," Testimony, Physicians for Human Rights, Subcommittee on Human Rights and International Operations, May 5, 1998 (http://www.phrususa.org/campaigns/wargenocide.html).

For post-war perspectives on NATO intervention in Kosovo, see Neal Riemer, "Political Scientists and Protection Against Genocide in Kosovo: Critical Reflections on Political Theory and Public Policy," American Political Science Association Annual Meeting, Atlanta, Georgia, September 2, 1999; David Wippman, "NATO Intervention in Kosovo and the Boundaries of International Law," African Society of International and Comparative Law, Harare, Zimbabwe, August 3, 1999; and David Fromkin, *Kosovo Crossing: American Ideals Meet Reality on the Balkan Battlefields* (New York: The Free Press, 1999). See also David Rieff, "A New Age of Liberal Imperialism," *World Policy Journal* 16, No. 2 (Summer 1999), 1–10; Stanley Hoffmann, "Principles in the Balkans, But Not in East Timor?," *New York Times*, September 11, 1999, p. A11; Ronald Steel, "East Timor Isn't Kosovo," *New York Times*, September 12, 1999, p. 19; Richard Holbrooke, "Battles after the War," *New York Times*, September 14, 1999. Postmortems on the wisdom of NATO strategy and tactics and on the challenging tasks of reconciliation and reconstruction have continued after the end of the war in Kosovo and Serbia.

3. On political realism and its varieties, see Douglas Simon's Chapter 2. For background, see also Michael J. Smith, *Realist Thought from Weber to Kissinger* (Baton Rouge: Louisiana State University Press, 1986); and Joel H. Rosenthal, *Righteous Realists: Political Realism, Responsible Power, and American Culture in the Nuclear Age* (Baton Rouge: Louisiana State University Press, 1991).

4. See Neal Riemer, *Creative Breakthroughs in Politics*, Chapter 2, "Roger Williams and Religious Liberty: Harmonizing Truth, Diversity, and Order," Chapter 3, "James Madison and the Extensive Republic: Reconciling Liberty and Large Size," and Chapter 6, "European Union: Beyond War, Economic Malaise, and Political Turmoil via Transnational Integration." Other breakthroughs in progress certainly

would include the breakthrough beyond apartheid in South Africa and would high-light the creative leadership of Frederik W. de Klerk and Nelson Mandela.

5. The full text of the Convention on the Prevention of the Crime of Genocide may be found in Appendix 1.

6. See U.S. Department of State, *Country Reports on Human Rights Practices* (Washington, D.C.: U.S. Government Printing Office, yearly).

7. The problem of ascertaining the meaning of "intent" remains a difficult the-oretical problem; but, practically speaking, most observers of genocide do not have great difficulty determining intent to commit genocide. (The official text uses the world "ethnical," but clearly means "ethnic.")

8. On this point I follow Kuper, *Genocide: Its Political Use in the Twentieth Century*, especially pp. 9–10, and Chapter 8, "Related Atrocities," pp. 138–60. Also see the powerful argument of Beth Van Schaack, "The Crime of Political Genocide: Repairing the Genocide Convention's Blind Spot," *Yale Law Journal* 106, No. 7 (May 1997). She argues that "the *jus cogens* prohibition of genocide, which predates the drafting of the Genocide Convention, provides broader protection than the Con-vention itself" (p. 2272). Hence, political genocide is prohibited under the customary *jus cogens* prohibition, even if political groups are not explicitly included as a group to be protected under the Genocide Convention. And, logically, economic groups would also be protected under the *jus cogens* prohibition against genocide.

9. On the concept of an international regime, see Stephen Krasner, ed., *Inter-national Regimes* (Ithaca, NY: Cornell University Press, 1993).

10. For the weaknesses of the UN Commission on Human Rights, see Jack Don-nelly, *International Human Rights* (Boulder, CO: Westview Press, 1993).

11. On the weaknesses of key actors in connection with genocide in Bosnia, see, for example, James Gow, *Triumph of the Lack of Will: International Diplomacy and the Yugoslav War* (New York: Columbia University Press, 1997), and Richard Hol-brooke, *To End A War* (New York: Random House, 1998); and on Rwanda, see Gerard Prunier, *The Rwanda Crisis: History of a Genocide* (New York: Columbia University Press, 1995, 1997).

12. For fuller exploration of the Permanent International Criminal Court, see David Wippman's Chapter 7. For additional background on the movement to estab-lish a Permanent International Criminal Court, see *The UN Security Council and the International Criminal Court: How Should They Relate? Report of the Twenty-Ninth United Nations Issues Conference* (Muscatine, IA: Stanley Foundation, 1998). See also Lori Fisler Damrosch, "Genocide and Ethnic Conflict," Chapter 10 in David Wippman, ed., *International Law and Ethnic Conflict* (Ithaca, NY: Cornell Univer-sity Press, 1998), pp. 256–279. On the Rome Conference to establish a Permanent International Criminal Tribunal, see Belinda Cooper, "US Courts a Loss of Lead-ership," *Newsweek*, July 29, 1998.

13. See Saul Mendlovitz and John Fousek, Chapter 6; and also their article, "The Prevention and Punishment of the Crime of Genocide," in Charles B. Strozier and Michael Flynn, *Genocide, War, and Human Survival* (Lanham, MD: Rowman & Littlefield, 1996), pp. 137–151.

14. Although I concentrate on the UN, I emphasize that I do not exclude atten-tion to protection against genocide at the level of effective regional organizations. The strengthening of comparable institutions at the regional level is quite in harmony with my argument. NATO's role in Kosovo is an important test case.

15. Although my focus is on genocide (as the most egregious violation of a basic human right to life), the ethical vision that animates a Global Human Rights Regime is also captured in such other UN documents as the UN Universal Declaration of Human Rights (1948); the International Covenant on the Elimination of All Forms of Racial Discrimination (adopted 1965, in force 1969); the International Covenant on Civil and Political Rights (1976); the International Covenant on Economic, Social, and Cultural Rights (in force 1976); the UN Convention against Torture and Other Cruel, Inhuman or Degrading Treatment or Punishment (signed 1984, in force 1987).

16. Democracy is a much used—and abused—term. For ancient Greeks, the term meant rule by the people, or citizens, in their own interest, not necessarily in the interest of justice. Moreover, not all residents (e.g., slaves, or Greek women) in Greek cities were citizens and entitled to a voice in rule. The American Founding Fathers thought of themselves as republicans, and preferred representative, constitutional government and the rule of law, not direct democracy in the Greek sense. And, of course, the American Republic at its founding and through 1865 was characterized by slavery, and women did not receive the right to vote in all states until 1920. More full-scale liberal democracy, characterized by both generous popular rule (via widespread suffrage and representative institutions), and more widespread constitutional protection of basic rights for all, thus did not emerge in the United States until well into the twentieth century; in the United States the poll tax was only made unconstitutional by the Twenty-Fourth Amendment in 1964. The road to mature constitutional democracy, characterized by both genuinely popular rule via elections and representative institutions and the protection of basic rights, has been even more difficult for countries lacking the substantial, if sometimes seriously flawed, constitutional history and culture of a United States. See Helen Fein's warning in Chapter 2 about an easy reliance upon "democracy" as the answer to prevention of genocide.

17. See David P. Forsythe, *Human Rights and Peace: International and National Dimensions* (Lincoln, University of Nebraska Press, 1993); and see also David P. Forsythe, *Human Rights and World Politics*, 2d ed. (Lincoln: University of Nebraska Press, 1989). To anticipate one criticism, let me note that mature constitutional democracies in the modern world have engaged in war, but not with other mature constitutional democracies. Historically, moreover, the track record of *maturing* constitutional democracies (such as the United States) in dealing with Native Americans, blacks, and women has by no means been exemplary. Similar historic points could be made about other maturing constitutional democracies (e.g., the United Kingdom, France, Belgium, Holland) and their relationship to the people of their former colonies. See, also, Spencer R. Weart, *Never At War: Why Democracies Will Not Fight One Another* (New Haven: Yale University Press, 1998). It must also be recognized, as Helen Fein emphasizes in Chapter 2, that some of the most egregious examples of genocide in the post-World War II period (e.g., in Cambodia, the former Yugoslavia, and Rwanda) have occurred within nations.

18. On monitoring, the annual and special reports of key nongovernmental organizations (NGOs) are invaluable. See, especially, the reports of Human Rights Watch and Amnesty International, for example, Human Rights Watch, *Slaughter Among Neighbors: The Political Origins of Communal Violence* (New Haven: Yale University Press, 1995). See, also, U.S. Department of State, *Country Reports on*

Human Rights Practices (Washington, D.C.: U.S. Government Printing Office, yearly.)

19. On economic sanctions, see Chapter 4 by George Lopez in this volume. Lopez's title, "Economic Sanctions and Genocide: Too Little, Too Late, and Sometimes Too Much," highlights the difficulties involved in utilizing sanctions. The harm to innocent civilians is a particularly agonizing problem. Sanctions in Iraq, after the Gulf War, have been particularly controversial. On police and military intervention, see Chapter 5 by Saul Mendlovitz and John Fousek in this volume. See also Thomas G. Weiss, David Cortright, George A. Lopez, and Larry Minear, eds., *Political Gain and Civilian Pain: Humanitarian Impacts of Economic Sanctions* (Lanham, MD: Rowman and Littlefield, 1997).

20. On just humanitarian intervention, see Chapter 6 by Michael Joseph Smith in this volume. For the literature on intervention, see Stanley Hoffmann, with contributions by Robert C. Johansen, James P. Sterba, and Raimo Vayrynen, *The Ethics and Politics of Humanitarian Intervention*. (Notre Dame, IN: University of Notre Dame Press, 1996); Fernando R. Tesón, *Humanitarian Intervention: An Inquiry into Law and Morality* (Dobbs Ferry, NY: Transnational Publishers, 1988); Richard B. Lillich, ed., *Humanitarian Intervention and the United Nations* (Charlottesville, VA: University Press of America, 1973); R. J. Vincent, *Human Rights and International Relations* (Cambridge: Cambridge University Press, 1986); Oliver Ramsbotham and Tom Woodhouse, *Humanitarian Intervention in Contemporary Conflict: A Reconceptualization* (Cambridge, UK: Polity Press, 1996); Thomas G. Weiss and Cindy Collins, *Humanitarian Challenges and Intervention: World Politics and the Dilemmas of Help* (Boulder, CO: Westview Press, 1996); Lori Fisler Damrosch, ed., *Enforcing Restraint: Collective Intervention in Internal Conflicts* (New York: Council on Foreign Relations Press, 1993); Hedley Bull, ed., *Intervention in World Politics* (Oxford: Clarendon Press, 1984); Robert L. Phillips and Duane L. Cady, *Humanitarian Intervention: Just War vs. Pacifism* (Lanham, MD: Rowman & Littlefield, 1996); James Mayall, ed., *The New Interventionism, 1991–1994: United Nations Experience in Cambodia, former Yugoslavia and Somalia* (Cambridge: Cambridge University Press, 1996); Lawrence Freedman, ed., *Military Intervention in European Conflicts* (Oxford: Blackwell, 1994); J. Bryan Hehir, "Expanding Military Intervention: Promise or Peril?, *Social Research* 62, No. 1 (Spring 1995). See also Andrew S. Natsios, *U.S. Foreign Policy and the Four Horsemen of the Apocalypse: Humanitarian Relief in Complex Emergencies* (Westport, CT: Praeger, 1997). And for the problems facing those who would intervene in the former Yugoslavia, see Richard Holbrooke, *To End A War* (New York: Random House, 1998). My view of just humanitarian intervention owes a great deal to just-war theory; and all the difficulties that confront just-war theory also confront just humanitarian intervention.

21. Debate still occurs on the question of appropriate authority. Some would deem NATO an appropriate authority to intervene in the former Yugoslavia. Others argue that other regional authorities might be appropriate authorities in their regions of the world. But what if the UN is impotent, and if regional organizations, such as NATO, are either nonexistent, powerless, or indecisive in other regions of the world where genocide is brewing or has broken out? Still others contend that individual nations might, in certain circumstances, be the appropriate authorities to engage in just humanitarian intervention. Tough questions about appropriate authority remain

to be more adequately addressed. See Stanley Hoffmann et al., *The Ethics and Politics of Humanitarian Intervention.*

22. Needless to say, "prudent appraisal" remains a most difficult, if necessary, responsibility for creative leadership. This same responsibility must also be exercised in assessments of "reasonable chance of success" and "humane and proportionate means." These difficult responsibilities were dramatically underscored in NATO's military intervention in the Kosovo crisis in the spring of 1999.

23. My concern, I emphasize, is not with broad-minded, imaginative, ethically sensitive realists, but with narrow-minded (and, if you will, old-fashioned) realists who are not in tune with emerging realities and who do not seriously address the need to balance the sometimes competing demands of *realpolitik* and ethics.

24. Neal Riemer, *The Future of the Democratic Revolution: Toward a More Prophetic Politics.* New York: Praeger, 1984.

2

The Evolution of the International System and Its Impact On Protection Against Genocide

Douglas W. Simon

INTRODUCTION

When it comes to assessing the ability of the international system to prevent, stop, or punish the crime of genocide, a review of the history of the twentieth century is not encouraging. As we enter the twenty-first century, is it possible to express any optimism about the ability and, more importantly, the willingness of the international community to deal with these terrible acts in a more positive way—either by prevention, forceful intervention, or at least by holding perpetrators accountable?

Most of the analyses of the international community's willingness and ability to deal with genocide are characterized by a depressing tone of frustration, cynicism, and pessimism. The primary reason for these dismal assessments is to be found in the power and persistence of the realist paradigm in international affairs. Put simply, the propensity of nation-states to base their foreign policy decisions on the acquisition of power, protection of sovereignty, and the preservation of national self-interest has consistently prevented meaningful action in the face of egregious violations of human rights, especially in connection with the protection against genocide. Additionally, "realism" has maintained a skeptical distrust about the efficacy of international organizations and international law, two critical instruments in the battle for the protection of human rights.

THESIS

The impact of the realist paradigm on state behavior cannot and should not be minimized. To the contrary, as we enter the twenty-first century, there is ample evidence that for many states, realism remains a formidable guide to foreign policy decision-making. How then can we expect the international system to be any more inclined to deal effectively with genocide than in the past? The answer may lie in a series of propositions which in part find their foundation in the belief that while still powerful, realism's hold on the thinking of policy makers is eroding. As noted by Charles Kegley, the end of the Cold War has led to many serious attacks on realist thought as well as to attempts to rethink and reformulate realism in the form of neorealism. It has also led to a revival of liberal theory in international relations.[1]

For the critics of realism, the theory is not only inherently limited and rigid, it is an increasingly inappropriate guide to state behavior. Given the enormous changes in the international system, realism no longer provides a clear understanding of world politics. Developments such as the greater attention paid to international organizations, the rise of powerful nonstate actors, the negotiation of meaningful strategic nuclear disarmament agreements like the Strategic Arms Reduction Talks (START), the dynamics of the modern global economy, and a renewed interest in international law, seem to fly in the face of realist thought.

Neorealists like Kenneth Waltz reformulate traditional realism, rejecting the notion of power acquisition as a natural condition of humankind.[2] Additionally, neorealists elevate the level of analysis from the state to the system and seek an understanding of international politics through patterns of power distribution and exchange at the global level. Despite these reformulations, critics charge that like its predecessor, classic realism, neorealism remains a too narrow and not very accurate reflection of contemporary reality.

Structural realists like Barry Buzan, Charles Jones, and Richard Little have formulated a more flexible notion of realism, in which actors in the system display high degrees of cooperative as well as competitive behavior.[3] Whereas traditional realists are highly distrustful of international organizations, structural realists consider alliances, coalitions, and other institutions for international cooperation, integral and important parts of the system. Further, interdependence is not incompatible with structural realism.

Neoliberals go even further, making a complete break with the realist tradition and resurrecting the Wilsonian dream of an open, democratic, cooperative, peace-loving world. For these theorists, state behavior is not fixated on the acquisition of power or on its use. The world is becoming more genuinely democratic and thus more protective of human rights. It is headed down a path of economic interdependence. It must rely increasingly on international organizations to deal with transnational problems and on international law to give it order.[4]

Whether, in the long run, the traditional realists, neorealists, structural realists, or neoliberals come to dominate international relations thinking in the future is open for debate. To answer this question is beyond the scope and purpose of the task at hand. Perhaps, as Charles Kegley has suggested, what is needed is some melding of these positions.[5] Regardless, given this theoretical background, the following propositions are advanced.

First, the political and economic structure of the international system profoundly conditions the behavior of states, including their propensity to respect human rights or to engage in such egregious violations of human rights as genocide. Moreover, the system structure also influences the reactions of the international community to genocidal violations.

Second, the realist paradigm remains operable in the international system, but the manner in which it is understood and guides state behavior changes as the system evolves. In other words, our concepts of national power, sovereignty, and national self-interest adapt to new realities in the system.

Third, at this particular juncture in history, the international system is undergoing profound changes based on four significant developments—four important realities—manifesting themselves as we enter into a challenging new century: (1) a fundamental redistribution of power as a result of the end of the Cold War, (2) the intensified globalization of the international economy, (3) the rapid (if uneven and often problematic) spread of genuine democratic systems, and (4) the communications revolution, characterized by the availability, use, and pervasiveness of computer-based communications technology.

These three propositions provide the basis for formulating a central question: *Are recent major changes in the international system causing states and international organizations to begin taking more effective steps to confront the problem of genocide?* Relying on limited evidence and a great deal of reasoned speculation, the answer to this question is "perhaps." A more refined response would be that the international system has an increased "potential" for confronting the horrors of genocide. This guarded assessment certainly does not mean that we are in the midst of a dramatic revolution; that states are suddenly abandoning their traditional notions of sovereignty and self-interest. What is being asserted here is that the system is undergoing a significant evolutionary shift brought on by the end of the Cold War, economic integration, genuine democratization, and technological advancements in communications. These developments are altering the political and economic environment in which states operate, and *may* be causing them, in their own self-interest, to begin confronting the horrors of genocide. These developments *may* also provide a window of opportunity for actors—individuals and groups—who are strong advocates of human rights, to exploit these forces to the maximum in pressuring states and international organizations to deal more aggressively with the scourge of genocide.

A final note of caution. Although each of these developments may hold promise for more progressive behavior, each has a dark side, capable of thwarting the international community's ability and willingness to deal with genocide.

THE END OF THE COLD WAR

For over fifty years, Cold War tensions provided an excuse for international inaction in a number of functional areas, including human rights. The fear of escalation was used to justify nonintervention into conflict situations in which widespread human rights violations were taking place. With the end of the Cold War, the excuse for inaction dissipated. Logic would dictate that the victorious western powers, either alone or in concert with their former adversaries, would feel much freer to take the initiative in dealing with genocidal behavior. Two concerns will be examined in order to assess the impact of the end of the Cold War—humanitarian intervention and the establishment of a Permanent International Criminal Court.

Humanitarian Intervention

Overall, the record of humanitarian intervention into genocidal and potential genocidal situations in the post–Cold War period has been disappointing, but not without hope. Most recently we have witnessed interventions into Kosovo and East Timor. This chapter will examine four earlier operations: northern Iraq in 1991, Somalia in 1992, Bosnia in 1994, and Rwanda, also in 1994.

Northern Iraq, Somalia, and Bosnia

These three situations are treated together for several reasons. First, at some point in each of these cases, a significant international military intervention took place in an effort to deal with the crisis. Second, although each intervention was seriously flawed, the assertion can be made that all three had some limited degree of success. It is not difficult to build a case asserting that these operations were failures—perhaps total failures. But that judgment is far too harsh. It is true that Operation Provide Comfort in northern Iraq suffered from lapses of attention by Western powers coupled with disruption emanating from factional fighting among the Kurds themselves. The Somalian operation, Restore Hope, fell victim to shifting objectives or "mission creep," and was prematurely ended. The international community's response to the horrors of ethnic cleansing in Bosnia was far too late; clearly, if initiated earlier, it would have saved thousands of lives. Despite these realities, it should also be recognized that at some point each of these operations saved countless lives, and violent crises were calmed.

There were other common characteristics as well. Each of these operations, either explicitly or implicitly, had the relief of human suffering as part of its motivation. All three missions were multilateral in nature. The northern Iraq and Somalia operations were authorized by the UN Security Council, something that would have been almost unthinkable during the Cold War. The rather late Bosnian action started out as a UN mission but was eventually taken over by NATO. Finally, as K. Mills has noted, these operations illustrate a growing flexibility in the traditional concept of sovereignty, that it can be challenged and even overridden.[6]

In 1991, on the heels of the defeat of Iraq in Operation Desert Storm, the United States and its allies, France and the United Kingdom, established a no-fly zone and safe havens in order to protect the Kurds of northern Iraq, who were at risk from attack by the still potent forces of Saddam Hussein. Underpinning this action was UN Security Council Resolution 688. The resolution did not call for action specifically on the basis of human rights violations per se, but on the basis of the threat to international peace and security that the violations would cause.[7] Specifically, the resolution called for immediate access into northern Iraq for humanitarian organizations. The resolution carried with it a good deal of controversy. China, for instance, felt that it might well violate Article 2, Section 7 of the Charter, which deals with domestic jurisdiction. Others, like France, felt that massive human rights violations were imminent and that intervention was more than justified.[8] Despite the controversy, the mission was organized and put into the field. Considering that Iraq was once a client state of the Soviet Union, it is hard to imagine Provide Comfort ever being approved during the Cold War.

The Somalian case was, of course, not one of genocide. It is, nevertheless, worth examining. The intervention initially seemed to provide a glimmer of hope that perhaps major powers, in concert with other elements of the international community, were more willing to intervene purely to relieve human suffering.

What had transpired in Somalia was a collapse of government in the country, the vacuum being filled by several warlords. Anarchy prevailed. Food was used as a weapon by various factions, people were malnourished and starving, and the security of international relief workers was threatened. In the spring of 1992, as images of the chaos and human suffering were projected onto America's television screens, the United States finally sought some legitimization from the UN under Security Council Resolution 775 and then played the major role in leading a military force of 24,000 soldiers into Somalia to protect relief workers, in order to feed the people. Whether it was these images that caused sufficient pressure on the White House to intervene is a question addressed later. In May of 1993, the operation was given over to the UN through the UN Operation in Somalia II (UNSOM II). In June, twenty-four Pakistani soldiers serving in the UN force were killed, and the mission was expanded to go after the warlords, particularly General Aidid in the Mogadishu area. In October, eighteen U.S. soldiers were killed in an ambush. Not long after these incidents, participating nations, most importantly the United States, announced their intention to leave the country.

The Somalian operation is significant to the issue of genocide for two reasons. First, while officially labeled by the Security Council as a threat to international peace and security, there is little doubt that in reality, it was a humanitarian intervention. Certainly, for the United States there was no readily observable national self-interest at stake—no oil, natural gas, uranium, copper, or cobalt. Second, and most pertinent to the discussion here, the end of the Cold War facilitated the creation of the Somalian intervention force. During the Cold War years, Somalia and the whole horn of Africa *had been* considered by both the United States and the Soviet Union as strategically important. With its proximity to the Red Sea and the Arabian peninsula, it was a geopolitical battleground. No longer.

To some degree, the light of hope offered by this mission was dimmed, if not extinguished, by the decision of the United States and other participating countries to leave Somalia and prematurely end the operation with the full knowledge that the country would be likely to once again fall into chaos. But important precedents were established by operation Restore Hope, no doubt facilitated by the end of the Cold War.

As defective as the international community's response was to the tragedy in Bosnia, it is safe to say that had a similar conflict broken out in communist Yugoslavia during the Cold War it is doubtful that any international response would have been possible, particularly any led by western powers.

The causes of the crisis that gripped the Balkans in the early 1990s are complex and controversial. A considerable part of one's understanding of these causes depends on one's interpretation and assessment of the impact of history. When the Yugoslav Communist Party disintegrated in June 1990, a fragmentation process was initiated in the Balkans. For years, the Communist Party under Josip Broz Tito had held the disparate provinces of the country together. With Tito's death in 1980, strains within the Communist Party and the Balkan community began to surface. In 1991, Slovenia and Croatia became independent. Croatia and Yugoslavia (which was now Serbia, Montenegro, and Kosovo) quickly became embroiled in a military conflict. As that conflict ebbed and flowed, Bosnia-Herzegovina, with a 44 percent Muslim plurality, began asserting itself by means of a 1992 referendum in favor of independence. The Bosnian Serbs, who constituted 31 percent of the population, did not recognize the referendum. In April 1992, the European Community recognized Bosnia.

Throughout this period, elements within the Bosnian Serb community, backed by Yugoslav president Slobodan Milosevic, began to take increasingly violent action against the ill-equipped Muslim communities throughout Bosnia. Specifically, Radovan Karadzic, head of the Bosnian Serb community, and General Ratko Mladic, who headed the Bosnian military, are enormously to blame for this increased activity. By May of 1992, the violence began to take on genocidal characteristics and was labeled "ethnic cleansing," denoting the process whereby Muslims were forced from their homes; thousands were placed in compounds reminiscent of concentration camps; hundreds, perhaps thousands, of women were raped; and tens of thousands of citizens were murdered. Before the violence was ended in 1995, as many as 200,000 Bosnian Muslims had perished, and the number of refugees had reached nearly three million.

The international community, particularly the European states, utterly failed to take forceful early action to prevent or halt ethnic cleansing. Indeed, as pointed out by Helen Fein, Executive Director of the Institute for the Study of Genocide, there were a number of ways in which major outside actors might have changed the dynamic between ethnic communities in Bosnia and altered the course of history. Germany could have heeded warnings of disaster and not recognized Croatia. The European Community (EC), rather than recognizing the Yugoslav fragmentation process, might have worked with regional leaders to seek more creative solutions to the problem of ethnic divisions. Nongovernmental organizations might have devoted resources to exposing the hate propaganda emanating from the Serbian-controlled radio stations. Finally, as the ethnic cleansing progressed, a timely and forceful intervention by NATO or UN forces might have put a stop to the horrors that were unfolding.[9]

In September 1991, the UN Security Council utilized Chapter VII of the Charter in imposing an arms embargo on the entire region. The UN Protection Force (UNPROFOR) was initially sent into the Krajina region in Croatia to protect refugees and later was sent into Bosnia to assist in the delivery of humanitarian aid. Thomas G. Weiss and Cindy Collins captured what is widely considered an apt description of the operation when they wrote, "UNPROFOR was set into motion half-funded, halfhearted, and with its role and authorized range of behavior unclear."[10] As the tragedy in Bosnia unfolded over the next three years, a number of low points were reached—the fall of the UN safe area of Srebrenica in 1994, the shelling of Sarajevo in 1995, and the capture by the Bosnian Serbs of 325 UN peacekeepers who were then held hostage in strategic locations to deter NATO bombing. Only in the summer of 1995, after Bosnian Serbs artillery killed thirty-seven civilians in a Sarajevo marketplace, did the United States and NATO finally take meaningful action.

On August 30, 1995, Operation Deliberate Force began. It was the beginning of heavy NATO bombing of Serb positions around Sarajevo and was the largest military action ever undertaken by the organization.[11] The bombing was eventually combined with a vigorous diplomatic effort culminating in the negotiations at Wright-Patterson Air Force Base in Ohio, resulting in the Dayton Accords of November 21, 1995. The agreement effectively ended the war. However, although Bosnia is now officially composed of a Muslim-Croat federation and a Bosnian Serb republic, some argue that the Dayton Accords, for all intents and purposes, partitioned Bosnia.

The UN response to the Bosnian crisis can clearly be viewed as a failure and the tardiness of NATO's action a disgrace. But it is also true that eventually NATO under U.S. leadership did act, and through the combined use of military force (Implementation Force or IFOR) and high-pressure diplomacy brought the conflict and ethnic cleansing under some degree of control. However, there is disturbing evidence that, in the post-Dayton era, many of the abuses that constitute ethnic cleansing continue in the Serb-controlled area known as the Republika Srpska (RS), and those responsible for the pre-Dayton cleansing campaigns remain not only at large but in positions of still considerable influence.[12]

The end of the Cold War certainly did not facilitate early action in Bosnia. Indeed, concerns expressed by a former superpower played a role in its delay. The Russian Republic, traditionally sympathetic to Serbia, constantly signaled the West that it would look with great disfavor on any forceful action taken against either Serbia or the Bosnian Serb community. Eventually, however, this situation was overcome, and Russian military forces became part of the IFOR effort. As described by Richard Holbrooke, this was a rather remarkable development:

Not since World War II had Russian, American, and other Western European forces served together under a common command. But President Clinton, Perry [U.S. Secretary of Defense], and Strobe Talbott [National Security Advisor], the President's most influential advisor on Russian policy, believed that if Russia participated in Bosnia, it would be a historic step in the development of cooperation between countries that had been Cold War adversaries only four years earlier.[13]

The Rwanda Tragedy

The end of the Cold War should have made it easier to intervene in Rwanda, as it did in other regions of the world, such as Somalia. However, other factors inhibited the United States, the UN, and other key actors from effective intervention to protect against this particular case of genocide. Only belatedly did some humanitarian assistance reach Rwanda, and then not with uniformly good results.

The response by the international community to the genocide in Rwanda cannot even be classified as a partial or limited success. By just about all measures, it was a total failure. Major powers, which at one time might have been concerned about Soviet and American forces or their surrogates squaring off against each other with a danger of escalation, reacted to the slaughter as if it were not happening. Indeed, one major European power, France, was complicit in the genocide by virtue of its uncritical support of the Hutu-dominated government, whose paramilitary militia, the Akazu, perpetrated the earliest killings of Tutsi.[14]

As for the United States, there was an increased wariness about military intervention. Put simply, crises that seemed to call out for action were piling up at an alarming rate. Since the Gulf War in 1990–1991, the United States had committed forces to northern Iraq, Haiti, Bosnia, and Somalia. There was concern about America once again finding itself cast in the role of world policeman. Additionally, the memories of American soldiers ambushed and killed in the streets of Mogadishu were fresh in the minds of members of Congress as well as the American people. The mood of the country was to slow down the rate of American action and institute some limits. As Milton Leitenberg, Senior Fellow at the Center for International and Security Studies at the University of Maryland, notes, "The major reason for Security Council inaction was the criticism and opposition by the United States. Rwanda became the first application of President Clinton's admonition in an address to the United Nations on September 27, 1993, that the UN must learn 'when to say no.' "[15]

The UN speech was further developed into Presidential Decision Directive 25 (PDD-25), which placed very stringent conditions on the employment of United States forces in multilateral peacekeeping operations. Only belatedly did President Clinton, on a visit to Rwanda, acknowledge the failure to act to stop the Rwanda genocide.

The impact of the end of the Cold War on the willingness of the international community to deal with humanitarian crises, including potential genocide, is limited. Two things are evident, however. First, geopolitical reality has changed. Areas that were once inside the spheres of influence of one superpower or the other are now more open to humanitarian intervention by multilateral forces. This was certainly the case in northern Iraq, Somalia, Bosnia and more recently Kosovo. Second, power realities have also changed, and nowhere is this more evident than in the Security Council of the UN, where, during the Cold War, multilateral interventions were rarely even considered and, if they did reach the floor of the Council, were likely to be vetoed by one superpower or the other. The current reality is that a greatly diminished Russia is in no position to seriously threaten or block United States or collective European actions. To the contrary, the Russians have more often than not sought ways to be part of these actions, as in the case of Bosnia.

The Permanent International Criminal Court (ICC)

One arena in which the end of United States–Soviet hostility seems to have had a positive impact was the movement to establish a permanent International Criminal Court (ICC). The idea of such a court was first put forth in the 1919 Paris Peace Treaty. The Nuremberg and Tokyo Tribunals lent further support to the idea. Finally, the 1948 Genocide Convention called for trials for those who committed crimes against humanity. Although there were no doubt a variety of reasons why the international community was unwilling and/or unable to establish a court, hostility between the major powers during the Cold War certainly ruled out any chance for the establishment of such a body.

The end of the Cold War made an enormous difference. As noted by Jelena Pejic, "The Yugoslavia and Rwanda Tribunals, to be realistic, came into being because the five permanent members of the Security Council managed to agree on their establishment."[16] Moving beyond these two ad hoc courts, final arrangements for the permanent International Criminal Court were finalized in July 1998. To be sure, at various junctures, resistance to the Court was provided by major powers, but an extraordinary coalition of small and mid-sized governments along with a significant number of NGOs were able to prevail.[17]

The problem for the future is not, however, in the existence of the court. Two disturbing issues loom. The first is the reluctance of the United States to support an independent court. United States opposition to an independent and strong court was painfully evident at the founding conference in Rome in mid-1998. One hundred twenty countries supported the establishment of the international court, but the United States did not even show up at the signing ceremony. As Belinda Cooper, senior fellow at the World Policy Institute of the New School for Social Research, notes:

Influenced by a Pentagon with an unreasonable fear of seeing its soldiers hauled before the tribunal and a senator—Jesse Helms (R-N.C.)—with an irrational bias against international bodies, the United States tried to limit the court's powers. In the process, it betrayed its own legacy of leadership in the prosecution of war crimes at Nuremberg and at the current tribunals on Rwanda and the former Yugoslavia.[18]

Cooper goes on to point out that the United States is now pressuring some of its friends who originally supported the court—Germany, Canada, and Britain—to reject the proposed treaty establishing the judicial body.[19] If the United States succeeds in this effort, it is hard to see how the court will function effectively.

The second problem threatening the effectiveness of the new Permanent International Criminal Court comes from the reluctance to go after the perpetrators of genocide and place them on trial. It is true that in 1997, Jean Kambanda, former Rwandan prime minister, was arrested in Nairobi, Kenya and placed on trial for genocide, specifically for his role in the slaughter of more than 500,000 Rwandans in 1994. On May 1, 1998, he pled guilty before a UN tribunal and was sentenced to life imprisonment. Although this may be a positive step, the problem remains severe. This has become painfully clear in the case of the International Criminal Tribunal for the Former Yugoslavia. The NATO force in Bosnia (IFOR) has remained paralyzed by its failure to seek out and bring to justice the worst perpetrators of ethnic cleansing, Radovan Karadzic and General Mladic.[20] The Pentagon, still smarting over the disastrous attempt to track down the Somalian warlord, General Aidid, has never been particularly enamored with the idea of going after high-profile war criminals in Bosnia. To be sure, over a two-year period, the United States spent millions of dollars, trained commandoes, gathered intelligence, and developed elaborate plans for a mission to seize Karadzic and Mladic. Despite these efforts, Washington decided to leave these plans on the shelf to gather dust, believing the risk to American soldiers was just too great and fearing that such action would trigger a violent Serbian response.[21]

Despite these problems, the end of the Cold war was probably a major factor in enabling the treaty establishing the Permanent International Criminal Court to be opened for ratification. This is a significant achievement for the advancement of human rights and should not be minimized.

GLOBALIZATION OF THE INTERNATIONAL COMMUNITY

A second development in the international system is the globalization of the world's economy—in other words, the significant increase in international economic activities such as trade, investment, banking, and travel. This increasingly intense economic activity leads to states becoming more interdependent. The concept of "national" economy becomes less and less relevant and the term "overseas" remains a geographic but not an economic term.

The issue of the impact of globalization on human rights is extremely controversial and filled with irony. From early in this century through the 1970s, large multinational corporations were looked on by many as the embodiment of evil. By exploiting workers and supporting corrupt authoritarian regimes, they were certainly considered no friend to human rights. Globalization in the 1990s has brought with it enormous multinational corporate activity, particularly in the developing world. With more and more economies instituting free-market systems, multinational investment has been by and large welcomed rather than reviled.

As the economic system becomes more interdependent, violent conflict and instability incur ever higher economic and political costs, not only for individual states and corporations, but for the system itself.[22] If this is true, then states as a matter of choice should be less inclined to engage in violent conflict. Moreover, in order to protect its interests, the international community should be more inclined to intervene collectively to prevent or halt violent conflict, including massive violations of human rights and, specifically, genocide.

Theoretically, human rights violations should also be costly for private businesses. At a 1996 conference on globalization and trade held in Toronto, Thomas d'Aquino, President and Chief Executive of the Business Council on National Issues (BCNI), made the following observation, which implied the symbiotic relationship between human rights and good business:

Whether at the World Trade Organization, or at the OECD, or at the United Nations, an irrefutable case can be made that a universal acceptance of the rule of law, the outlawing of corrupt practices, respect for workers' rights, high health and safety standards, sensitivity to the environment, support for education and the protection and nurturing of children—are not only justifiable against the criteria of morality and justice. The simple truth is that these are good for business and most business people recognize this.[23]

Mr. David Culver, former CEO of Alcan Aluminum, was even more explicit: "Legitimate business today is a very human activity. You cannot get anything done except through people. And people who are not extended the types of human rights we want them to have are frankly not very useful in business."[24] Balanced against this rather progressive position is a still powerful traditional perspective, which basically asserts that business is the business of business, not human rights. Multinational corporations tend to invest on the basis of self-interest, namely increased profit, and not on the basis of the human rights record of the country in which they invest. Perhaps it is too early to make a firm assessment of globalization's impact on the definition of self-interest and whether or not human rights will become a more important factor in the calculation.

A concurrent phenomenon, encouraged by globalization, has been the greater utilization of multilateral machinery, particularly the formation of regional trading blocs like the European Union and the North American Free Trade Agreement (NAFTA) as well as global institutions like the International Monetary Fund, the World Bank, and the World Trade Organization. The implications of these developments could be profound for putting in place more effective machinery for dealing with genocide. Why? Because the vesting of more power in international organizations, be they regional or global, indicates a willingness and a recognition of the necessity for states to share costs and risks. This development could make the task of preventive intervention or halting of genocide more palatable to individual states. Several examples of this movement have already been alluded to— the approval of a number of "humanitarian" interventions by the UN Security Council and by NATO as well as the establishment of a permanent International Criminal Court. We have also witnessed a new and vigorous interest in human rights in regional organizations. For example, the European Union explicitly ties human rights performance with its agreements on aid and trade benefits.[25] The Organization of American States (OAS) amended its charter in 1996 to support constitutional democracy and to criticize governments that come to power by coup d'etat.[26] The Southern

Africa Development Community (SADC) took a very strong stand in favor of an independent International Criminal Court.[27] Finally, it should be noted that a number of regional organizations—the Council of Europe, the Organization of American States (OAS), the Organization of African Unity (OAU), and the Organization on Security and Cooperation in Europe—have all drafted and adopted a significant number of human rights conventions and charters.

Despite the activities mentioned above, there is precious little evidence today that the international community has taken timely and strong collective action on human rights as a direct result of globalization. Certainly the international community's reactions to the Rwanda tragedy, and particularly the European reaction to Bosnia, give us little reason to believe that globalization makes much difference. Of course these two cases must be tempered by the knowledge that Bosnia, and particularly Rwanda, were not critical actors in the economic globalization process. Neither is a member of any of the more powerful regional trade organizations that have either been founded or strengthened in recent years.

Although economic globalization may not offer immediate hope of an imminent breakthrough with regard to the enhancement of protection against genocide, it does auger well for the long-term protection of human rights, particularly as more and more countries are pulled within the orbit of the global economy.

THE SPREAD OF CONSTITUTIONAL DEMOCRACY

The end of the Cold War has witnessed the spread of constitutional democracy around the world, from the Russian Republic to the former centrally planned economies in Africa to the formerly military junta-ruled republics of Latin America. The growth in democracy has been stunning. In 1974, roughly 27.5 percent of the world's governments were democratic. By 1990 that number had grown to 46.1 percent and as of 1995, there were 117 democracies out of 191 countries, or 61.3 percent.[28]

Theoretically, this should bode well in the battle against genocidal behavior. Genuine constitutional democracies by their very nature are more protective of human rights than authoritarian systems. It is worth noting that virtually every case of twentieth-century genocide occurred within authoritarian political systems or systems with strong authoritarian tendencies. It is not, therefore, unreasonable to assert that the more nations adopt genuinely democratic political systems and a culture of respect for human rights, the lower the probability of genocide.

The spread of genuine democracy may also enhance the willingness of states to support both governments and private institutions in taking action to prevent, halt, and punish genocide. Further, there is a role to be played by well-established democratic states in promoting democracy *as a means to head off major human rights violations, including genocide.* Steven Burg, Associate Professor at Brandeis University, has asserted as much: "Democratic states of the Euro-Atlantic community, working individually, in concert, and especially through such multilateral institutions as the CSCE [Conference on Security and Cooperation in Europe] and the U.N. Security Council, must shift the bases of international recognition and legitimation of state entities away from ethnicity (nationalism) and toward democracy and human rights."[29]

The spread of democracy should be viewed as a positive development in the war against genocide. But it does have its dark side. A great deal depends on how one defines democracy. To what degree does a democracy merely go through the motions of elections? Are there major power centers of government, such as the military, which are not accountable to elected officials? Does the democracy have anything akin to the American Bill of Rights, guaranteeing basic individual freedoms and rights? Does the political system provide any rights and protection for minorities? These are conceptual problems of considerable importance.

There are also practical problems. For instance, many of the fledgling democracies are built on fragile economies. As economic expectations are dashed and frustration grows on the part of both the public and government, are these democratic systems susceptible to reversion to authoritarian practices? Indeed, Fareed Zakaria has contended that a number of newer regimes have regressed, and we are seeing a growth in what he calls "illiberal democracies," where authoritarian policies are beginning to eat away fundamental democratic principles.[30] Larry Diamond, a senior fellow at the Hoover Institution, notes:

The trends of increasing (or persisting) disorder, human rights violations, legislative and judicial inefficacy, corruption, and military impunity and prerogative have been evident in other third-wave democracies around the world—not only major countries like Turkey and Pakistan but smaller ones such as Zambia and most of the electoral regimes of the former Soviet Union. Indeed, in the former Soviet Union, Africa, parts of Asia, and the Middle East, elections themselves are increasingly hollow and uncompetitive, a thin disguise for the authoritarian hegemony of despots and ruling parties.[31]

Some scholars have asserted that immature democracies in particular may actually facilitate human rights violations.[32] For instance, the pluralistic nature of democracy may play into the hands of diverse ethnic groups, causing divisiveness, fragmentation, and perhaps violence.

Obviously, human rights stand the best chance of protection in mature constitutional democracies, and it is painfully clear that not all so-called "democracies," particularly the more recent versions, fall into that category. Yet, for advancement of human rights, including protection against genocide, democracy with all its faults is generally preferable to ruthless authoritarian systems of government. The contemporary movement of nations toward mature—or more mature—constitutional democracy is a development that needs to be encouraged and carefully monitored. It is a slow and frustrating process and does not always respond to the more immediate need to confront genocide. In the long run, however, the global democratic movement offers a fruitful prospect in the mission to protect against genocide.

THE COMMUNICATIONS REVOLUTION

Of all the changes in the international system, the communications revolution may be the most profound. In her recent book, Cairin Cross of the *Economist* went so far as to assert:

The death of distance as a determinant of the cost of communications will probably be the single most important economic force shaping society in the first half of the next century. It will alter, in ways that only are dimly imaginable, decisions about where people live and work; concepts of national borders; patterns of international trade. Its effects will be as pervasive as those of the discovery of electricity.[33]

There are currently 150 million computers in use today; more than 90 percent are personal computers. Their number is growing by as many as eighteen to twenty million annually and, as a recently revamped Moore's Law asserts, computer power and capacity now double every nine months.[34] In addition to satellite, cellular, and FAX communications systems, the development of the Internet has been a revolution unto itself. In 1995, roughly 40 million people had access to the net. In the year 2000 that number is expected to reach 700 million.

The communications revolution, resting on a rapid, pervasive computer technology, may be critical to the war against genocide in at least four ways. First, the use of computers has made it easier to track responsibility for gross violations of human rights. Second, it may make it increasingly difficult for states to keep their internal behavior—horrendous behavior such as mass killings and genocide—hidden. Third, it may provide the means for the establishment of an effective genocide early warning system. Fourth, it may accelerate the integration process between nations as well as between nations and nongovernmental organizations concerned with human rights.

Tracking Responsibility

The cyber revolution has greatly enhanced the collection, processing, and dissemination of data on human rights violations. One impressive example is the work of the Canadian-U.S. Human Rights Information and Documen tation Network (CUSHRID Net),[35] a consortium of human rights organizations, legal aid groups, educational centers, government agencies, and individuals, linked electronically and involved in human rights information and documentation efforts. The American Association for the Advancement of Science (AAAS) acts as the secretariat for CUSHRID and has been very active in developing expertise in forensic science, statistical gathering, analysis, and information management in the human rights area.[36]

Publicity and Policy

A great deal has been written, particularly in the popular press, about the relationship between the increasingly pervasive and aggressive news media and its impact on post–Cold War foreign policy. That there historically has always been some relationship between the press and policy is nothing new. William Randolph Hearst's "yellow journalism" was pivotal in forcing America into the Spanish-American War. Certainly America's Vietnam experience gave us another glimpse of the power of the electronic media. But it is in the post–Cold War period, with advances in satellite communications, cable television, and 24-hour news broadcasts, combined with the fierce competition for ratings, that the scope and availability of real-time news has been dramatically altered. What we found in cases like Bosnia, Haiti, northern Iraq, Somalia, and more recently Kosovo and East Timor, was that images of death and suffering, particularly of innocents, can be very powerful and intrusive visitors into our living rooms. What is not clear, however, is whether powerful reporting and images are in and of themselves potent enough to drive prudent policy, specifically decisions to engage in wise humanitarian intervention. There is need for caution before concluding that the modern news media is the decisive factor affecting such foreign policy decisions as humanitarian intervention. Such caution is underscored in Warren Strobel's's enormously useful and sophisticated study of this phenomenon, *Late-Breaking Foreign Policy: The News Media's Influence on Peace Operations.*[37] On the most notable recent case, Somalia, Strobel, contrary to conventional wisdom, argues, "It is clear that the effect of the images broadcast on CNN, ABC, NBC, and CBS is far less—and much different— than is widely assumed. The pictures of the dead and dying, the refugees, and the hopelessness in Somalia did not push the United States into that country in the summer and fall of 1992."[38]

Rather, what powerful images can do is "reinforce other policy considerations that point to the launching of a peace operation for humanitarian purposes."[39] For instance, in the most celebrated example of the "CNN effect," Somalia, there were a variety of forces pressuring President Bush to act—sympathetic members of Washington's bureaucracy, certain members of Congress, and international relief groups. The difficult question remains: Even if the media was only one of several forces, was it at all decisive in the decision-making process?

Thomas G. Weiss and Cindy Collins also raise questions about the impact of the media on foreign policy decision-making. They contend that recent media influence has taken a quantitative jump—more coverage and real time—but not a qualitative leap.[40] Referring to the increase in news coverage, they go on to point out:

This explains the coining of the term CNN effect, but this term hardly explains adequately the causal links between information and opinion, on the one hand, and decisions and actions, on the other. . . . [n]either the public nor policymakers necessarily have a better command of the state of affairs in war zones now than they did a decade ago. Even though the connections between the media and political and humanitarian action in civil wars are thus recurrent, the chemistry of interactions between public exposure and international engagement requires more serious analytical review than it has received to date.[41]

Decision-makers themselves have recognized the power of the media to influence, if not determine, policy. In discussing the Somalian case, Warren Strobel notes that several key advisors to President Bush—Brent Scowcroft, Lawrence Eagleburger, and Herman Cohen—all questioned whether the United States would have acted in the absence of powerful imagery.[42]

The debate over the power of the press to influence human rights policy will no doubt continue. But there is no denying that with the use of more sophisticated technology, the world's press has dramatically increased its ability to penetrate the walls of sovereignty, to provide the world a vivid picture of the dark side of human behavior. We know that it plays a role in decision-making. How much of a role is yet to be more precisely determined, but clearly the potential to impact policy is enormous.

A Genocide Early Warning System

In recent years, there has been considerable research on the risks of ethnic conflict and on early warning of genocide, and a number of proposals have been made. Perhaps the best known is the Minorities At Risk Project, directed by Ted Robert Gurr at the Center for International Development and Conflict Management (CIDCM) at the University of Maryland.[43] This project has compiled and is analyzing information from 1990 to 1995, on 270 communal groups, with particular attention to their status and conflicts. A significant number of Internet sites, such as the International Work Group for Indigenous Affairs[44] and Survival International,[45] have been created to deal with the protection of indigenous peoples. Other sites, such as International Alert[46] and Human Rights Internet Urgent Page,[47] have been established for the early identification of volatile areas where the potential for human rights violations is high. Certainly, the technology is available for the construction of an early warning system specifically devoted to identifying and alerting the world to situations where genocide is in its early stages.

The question is whether such a "new" system need be created at all. The evidence that emerges from recent cases of genocidal behavior is that early warning is not *the* problem. The industrial countries of the world have invested billions of dollars in elaborate global intelligence systems. The world's great news media, both electronic and print, have enormous assets in virtually every region of the globe, making them fully capable of early warning of human rights disasters.

Indeed, in the cases of Bosnia and Rwanda, early warning was more than adequate. The case of Rwanda is particularly disturbing. As early as 1990, four years before the genocide began, there were numerous reports of civil violence against the Tutsi community. Two reports, one by the International Commission of Inquiry and the other by the UN Commission on Human Rights, determined that the violence had all the earmarks of genocide.[48]

Even more disturbing, just months before the genocide began, reports began to reach diplomatic circles that should have prompted action. As reported by John Eriksson in the *Journal of Humanitarian Assistance*:

In the months immediately preceding the genocide, many additional signs indicated that the implementation of the Arusha Accords was faltering and that massive violence was being planned. The air was full of extremist rhetoric on radio, in public rallies and at official cocktail parties. There were assassinations and organized violence. Detailed intelligence reports were passed to New York and the Belgian military authorities by the unofficial UNAMIR intelligence unit documenting the military training of militias, hidden arms caches, and plans for violent action. Unequivocal warnings reached the UN Secretariat in January regarding a planned coup, an assault on the UN forces to drive them out, provocations to resume the civil war, and even detailed plans for carrying out genocidal killings in the capital.[49]

Put simply, although governments and international organizations may plead ignorance of genocide after the fact, protesting that they somehow did not have adequate warning or did not realize how serious the situation was, the evidence in recent years clearly shows otherwise. There *is* an early warning system in place. For whatever reasons, powerful actors in the international system often choose to ignore the warnings that are provided them.

Global Integration and the Crucial Role of NGOs

One area in which the growth of global communications may have been an asset is in the increased cooperation between NGOs working in the human rights area. A new era seems to be dawning in which NGOs, working with each other and with mid-sized and developing states, increasingly set the international human rights agenda despite resistance from some major powers.[50] This was most evident in the campaigns to ban antipersonnel land mines and to establish a permanent International Criminal Court (ICC).[51] It is clear that NGOs—drawing upon rapid global communications—have been playing, and will continue to play, a vital role in the battle against genocide and other egregious violations of human rights.

CONCLUSION

As the international system undergoes massive change, is it any more willing or equipped to deal with the horrors of genocide? The answer to this question has been a highly cautious "yes." But even this assessment relies more on the "potential" that the evolving international system offers, and, regrettably, less on overwhelming hard evidence.

The end of the Cold War has eliminated one of the primary stumbling blocks to effective collective action in the name of human rights: the paralysis induced by the constant check and counter-check of superpower rivalry. Additionally, there are geographical regions of the world no longer within the spheres of influence of the superpowers that are now more accessible to collective action to reverse human rights violations, including genocide. Although cooperation between the former superpower adversaries both within and outside the UN has been considerable, we must face the reality that since the end of the Cold War, the record of the international community in four major cases of widespread human rights violations, including genocidal behavior—northern Iraq, Somalia, Bosnia, and Rwanda—has ranged from marginal success to outright failure.

Similarly, the collapse of communism probably facilitated the founding of the permanent International Criminal Court. But, to the distress of many, the remaining superpower, the United States, is proving to be the greatest impediment to the establishment of a genuinely independent and powerful court in which the perpetrators of genocide could be held accountable.

Economic globalization is a reality now upon us. Its promising potential to make an impact on human rights and effective antigenocide policy cannot be definitively established. On the one hand, logic would dictate that states that are increasingly interdependent and banding together in more formidable regional and global organizations would have a strong interest in collectively countering violent actions that threaten their economic interests. On the other hand, we see all too many examples of economic interests between states forcing human rights into the background. Put simply, our positive assessment of this phenomenon remains highly suggestive but still speculative.

There seems little doubt that for a variety of reasons, the post–Cold War spread of constitutional democracy is to the advantage of human rights. However, it is a movement that needs constant encouragement and nurturing. Further, the mere establishment of a democracy in name and form does not mean that a regime will manifest the characteristics of a mature constitutional democracy, with protection of individual rights and rule of law. Nevertheless, given the historically authoritarian nature of the perpetrators of genocide, the global enlargement of constitutional democracy must be seen as a positive development.

The enhanced ability of individuals to almost instantaneously communicate on a global basis and to be informed of world events in real time is perhaps the most profound development of the last decade and may prove to be the most significant development for the approaching century. Because of heightened communications, decision-makers, NGOs, and the public are better informed about massive human rights violations, certainly have better early warning about impending genocidal situations, and have an enhanced ability to communicate and coordinate antigenocidal activities and policies. Nevertheless, the definitive answer to the question of what effect these increased capabilities may have remains open.

In sum, profound changes in the international system, particularly since the end of the Cold War, provide considerable potential for more meaningful action to counter genocidal behavior. Whether the primary actors in the system—namely, states and their leaders as well as international organizations—take advantage of the changing climate to deal with genocide is a question that only the future can answer. Although logic tells us that it is in the interest of the state system to prevent or halt this kind of costly behavior, logic, unfortunately, has not always been the hallmark of international relations. However, the more flexible structural-realist and neoliberal interpretations of international relations recognize that the future does not always slavishly repeat the past; that prudent adaptation to new realities may, in fact, open the door to more effective protection against genocide in the future.

NOTES

1. Charles W. Kegley, Jr., "The Neoliberal Challenge to Realist Theories of World Politics: An Introduction," in Charles W. Kegley, *Controversies in International Relations Theory: Realism and the Neoliberal Challenge* (New York: St. Martin's Press, 1995), pp. 1–24.

2. Kenneth Waltz, *Theory of International Politics* (Reading, MA: Addison-Wesley Publishing, 1979). Also, Kenneth Waltz, "Realist Thought and Neorealist Theory," *Journal of International Affairs* 44 (Spring/Summer 1990): 21–37.

3. Barry Buzan, Charles Jones, and Richard Little, *The Logic of Anarchy: Neorealism to Structural Realism* (New York: Columbia University Press, 1993).

4. Francis Fukuyama, "The Beginning of Foreign Policy," *The New Republic*,

No. 207 (August 17 and 24, 1992): 24–32; Charles Kegley, "The Neoidealist Moment in International Studies? Realist Myths and the New International Realities," *International Studies Quarterly* 37 (June 1993): 131–146; Stanley Kober, "Idealpolitik," *Foreign Policy*, No. 79 (Summer 1990): 3–24.

5. Kegley, "The Neoliberal Challenge to Realist Theories of World Politics," p. 17.

6. K. Mills, "Sovereignty Eclipsed?: The Legitimacy of Humanitarian Access and Intervention," *Journal of Humanitarian Assistance* (http://www=jha.sps.coam.ac.uk/a/a012.htm), reposted on July 4, 1997.

7. Ibid., p. 10.

8. Ibid.

9. Helen Fein, "Patrons, Prevention and Punishment of Genocide: Observations on Bosnia and Rwanda," in Helen Fein, ed., "The Prevention of Genocide: Rwanda and Yugoslavia Reconsidered," a Working Paper of the Institute for the Study of Genocide, 1994.

10. Thomas G. Weiss and Cindy Collins, *Humanitarian Challenges and Intervention: World Politics and the Dilemmas of Help* (Boulder, CO: Westview Press, 1996), p. 83.

11. The most up-to-date, detailed, and fascinating account of the decision-making process resulting in the 1995 bombing campaign as well as the subsequent Dayton negotiations is to be found in Richard Holbrooke, *To End a War* (New York: Random House, 1998).

12. "Bosnia-Hercegovina: The Continuing Influence of Bosnia's Warlords," *Human Rights Watch* 8, No. 7 (D) (December 1996); and "Bosnia-Hercegovina—"A Dark and Closed Place—Past and Present Abuses in Foca," *Human Rights Watch* (DI005) (June 1998).

13. Holbrooke, *To End a War*, p. 203.

14. Fein, "Patrons, Prevention and Punishment of Genocide," p. 8.

15. Milton Leitenberg, "U.S. and U.N. Actions Escalate Genocide and Increase Costs in Rwanda," in Helen Fein, ed., "The Prevention of Genocide: Rwanda and Yugoslavia Reconsidered," a Working Paper of the Institute for the Study of Genocide, 1994.

16. Jelena Pejic, "What Is an International Criminal Court?," *Human Rights* 23, No. 4 (Fall 1996); American Bar Association (http://www.abanet.org/irr/hr/icc.html).

17. Human Rights Watch World Report 1998 (http://www.hrw.org/research/world).

18. Belinda Cooper, "U.S. Courts a Loss of Leadership," *Newsday*, July 29, 1998, A37.

19. Ibid.

20. Human Rights Watch World Report 1998 (http://www.hrw.org/research/world).

21. Tim Weiner, "U.S. Cancels Plans for Raid on Bosnia to Capture 2 Serbs," the *New York Times*, July 26, 1998, p. 1.

22. One study on the cost of large-scale state-sponsored killing, genocide, and domocide has recently been carried out by Gerald Scully of the University of Texas. While noting that authoritarian states are more likely than democracies to engage in this kind of behavior, Scully's most important finding is that the cost of genocidal

behavior is very high as measured by lost wealth. While perhaps a bit oversimplistic, Scully contends that the richer the country, the lower the propensity to engage in mass killing. See Gerald W. Scully, "Murder by the State," National Center for Policy Analysis, September 1997 (http://www.public-policy.org/ncpa/studies). Helen Fein, among others, has noted the heavy cost of postgenocidal activities (peacekeeping, refugee support, tribunals, etc.) as compared to prevention. See Fein's Chapter 3 in this volume.

23. Thomas d'Aquino, Comments Made at the Conference on Globalization, Trade and Human Rights: The Canadian Perspective, February 22, 1996, Toronto, Canada, Summary Report, p. 4.

24. David Culver, Comments Made at the Conference on Globalization, Trade and Human Rights: The Canadian Perspective, February 22, 1996, Toronto, Canada, Summary Report, p. 2.

25. *Human Rights Watch World Report 1998*, p. 12 (http://www.hrw.org/research/world).

26. Ibid., pp. 19–20.

27. Ibid., p. 20.

28. Freedom House, *Freedom in the World: The Annual Survey of Political Rights and Civil Liberties, 1990–91, 1991–92, 1992–93, 1993–94, 1994–95* (New York: Freedom House, 1996).

29. Steven L. Burg, "Ethnic Nationalism, Breakdown, and Genocide in Yugoslavia," in Helen Fein, ed., "The Prevention of Genocide: Rwanda and Yugoslavia Reconsidered," a Working Paper of the Institute for the Study of Genocide, 1994, pp. 14–15. Also see Steven L. Burg, *War or Peace? Nationalism, Democracy and American Foreign Policy in Post Communist Europe* (New York: New York University Press, 1996).

30. Fareed Zakaria, "The Rise of Illiberal Democracy," *Foreign Affairs* (November/December 1997): 22–43.

31. Larry Diamond, "Is the Third Wave Over?" *Journal of Democracy* 7, No. 3 (1996): 7.

32. Fein, "The Three P's of Genocide Prevention," pp. 8–9.

33. Cairin Cross, *The Death of Distance* (Boston: Harvard Business School Press, 1997), p. 1.

34. Moore's Law is named for the founder of INTEL and originally asserted that computing power and capacity double every eighteen months. In 1998, authorities at INTEL announced that the Law had been revised with the time required for the doubling of computing power cut in half.

35. http://shr.aaas.org/cushrid/who.htm.

36. http://shr.aaas.org/program/about.htm#AAASHRAN.

37. Warren P. Strobel, *Late-Breaking Foreign Policy: The News Media's Influence on Peace Operations* (Washington, D.C.: United States Institute of Peace Press, 1997).

38. Ibid., p. 141.

39. Ibid., p. 142.

40. Thomas G. Weiss and Cindy Collins, *Humanitarian Challenges and Intervention: World Politics and the Dilemmas of Help* (Boulder, CO: Westview Press, 1996), p. 166.

41. Ibid.

42. Strobel, *Late-Breaking Foreign Policy*, p. 141.

43. Also see Ted R. Gurr and Barbara Harff, *Early Warning of Communal Conflict and Genocide: Linking Empirical Research to International Responses* (Tokyo: UN University Press, 1996). Ted Gurr has worked on risk assessments of ethnic conflict. Barbara Harff has done empirical work on risk assessments and early warning of genocide. Barbara Harff's model has achieved 80% accuracy in postdicting past cases of geno/politicide and is being used by the U.S. Administration to prepare lists of high-risk contemporary cases. For an extraordinarily valuable and thorough listing and description of research in the area of international Early Warning, see Susan Schmeidl, Selected Efforts./Research in the Area of Early Warning (http://www.yorku.ca/research/crs/prevent/eweffort.htm).

44. http://pip.dknet.dk/dk~pap1917/iaffair.htm.

45. http://www.survival.org.uk/about3.htm.

46. http://www.international-alert.org/simple/home.htm.

47. http://www.hri.ca/index.htm.

48. John Eriksson, "The International Response to Conflict and Genocide: Lessons from the Rwanda Experience," Steering Committee of the Joint Evaluation of Emergency Assistance to Rwanda, *Journal of Humanitarian Assistance* (March 1996): 2.

49. Ibid., p. 3.

50. *Human Rights Watch World Report 1998* (http://www.hrw.org/research/world report).

51. For additional analysis of the growing influence of NGOs, see P. J. Simmons, "Learning to Live with NGOs," *Foreign Policy* (Fall 1998): 82–96.

3

The Three P's of Genocide Prevention: With Application to a Genocide Foretold—Rwanda

Helen Fein

INTRODUCTION

Neal Riemer has asked, "Can we develop a far-sighted, coherent, and effective policy of prudent prevention of genocide?" I shall make a case that this depends on positive answers to three questions: (1) Is it our problem? (2) Is it not only prudent but in our interest to do so? and (3) Is it really possible to detect genocide? And can one demonstrate how to employ a paradigm to organize intelligence on the ground to anticipate genocide? In this essay, I will show that there are positive answers to all three questions. I will also show the high cost of tolerating genocide (especially as compared to prevention) both in terms of geopolitical strategy and economic rationality.

First, there is the preliminary question: "Who are we?" By "we," the "international community" (usually an oxymoron) is often implied. Rather than assuming such an entity, let us look at how we as citizens of the United States cope with threats as a community, nation, and state. Let us also assume that the obligations we accept for ourselves apply to other states with similar responsibilities. However, other states' responsibilities in particular situations may be greater or lesser than ours, depending on their access to the situation in question, their resources, their interest, and their influence.

No one doubts that when we set out to do so, we can (and have) developed warning systems or indicators for earthquakes, fire, floods, hunger, pollution and weather trends (i.e., global warming). In the case of man-made disasters, we have developed codes, devices, and regimens for prevention and containment of such threats: building codes, dikes, food banks, pollution standards. Few planners in developed countries deny that there is a responsibility to prevent and contain such threats and to cooperate with other states to do so, although there is disagreement on methods and priorities. Nor do the most conservative parties deny humanitarian responsibility for relief of hunger and humanitarian disasters today.

Genocide is a prime target for prevention because it is a man-made, not a natural, disaster. It can be forecast because we know the warning signs; and it could be stopped—if it were not prevented—if we learned to recognize it promptly, discriminating it from warfare. Genocide is a calculated and rational crime of state (or pretenders to the state) and their calculus of costs and benefit can be altered. Their first question is "will we get away with it?"

Until now, the answer has been yes, most of the time. A few cases of genocide have led to interstate wars or upsets by an invading army with state losses of land or regime control (in Rwanda 1994, Cambodia 1979, Uganda 1979, and Pakistan 1971) but not before there was a terrible toll in victims. As Leo Kuper said over a decade ago, "The sovereign territorial state claims, as an integral part of its sovereignty, the right to commit genocide, or engage in genocidal massacres, against peoples under its rule, and . . . the United Nations, for all practical purposes, defends this right."[1] In 1998, the UN did not so much defend the right—it acknowledged war crimes and crimes against humanity and set up tribunals for judgment in the cases of the former Yugoslavia and Rwanda—but it scarcely recognizes genocide and gross violations of human rights in process. Such crimes are distanced by framing them with a neutral label that avoids perception of the criminal causes of such events: refugee or humanitarian crises, complex humanitarian emergencies; or civil wars and internal or ethnic conflict, implying there are two equally culpable parties. This serves to obscure both cause and perpetrator; thus, there is no crime, such as genocide, requiring international attention.

IS IT OUR PROBLEM?

But states argue (usually out of hearing) that it is not their problem, despite the fact that they are signatories of the UN Genocide Convention. Often, states distinguish their national interest from international obligations, putting short-range or narrow economic interests above their own long-term interests. To argue my case that the prevention of genocide is in our national interest because of its effect, when undeterred, on international security and economy, let us take the narrowest assumption. That is, as U.S. citizens—even if we take a simple view of our own interests as a community, a nation, and a state as the most minimal consensus—it can be shown that genocide, expanding and undeterred, is an impediment to our international goals and to our vision of ourselves in the world. This vision, or ideal of

what kind of world we stand for, is itself an element of our collective identity—an ideal or bond among us, reiterating what kind of people we are,
and a vision that may stir other peoples to identify with us.

Further, the prevention of genocide affects goals for international and
regional security. It is an imperative for the prevention of further war, destabilization and regional crises, and massive refugee flows. Besides generating wars, genocide and gross violations of human rights often trigger the
exodus of great numbers of refugees, sometimes called "people bombing."
When they succeed in getting rid of an unwanted group—massacres are the
quickest means to propel flight—*genocidaires* (a French term I will continue
using as it has no English equivalent) externalize the cost of maintaining
the unwanted on neighboring states and the world community. Refugees
often create environmental degradation and public health and food emergencies in the states to which they flee. In addition, the states they flee (often
poor to begin) may degenerate developmentally as state resources, infrastructure, and the economy are destroyed—land eroding and food declining
if crops are not planted.

Studies show that the overwhelming majority of the world's refugees are
created by states committing genocide and gross violations of human rights.[2]
If we were to reframe the worldwide refugee problem as we frame programs
of domestic assistance, we would label it a crisis of forced homelessness and
dependency: 13.6 million refugees and 16.2 to 18.7 million internally displaced at last count.[3]

Further, refugees sometimes impose costs on their host country of social
destabilization, competing in the labor market, raising prices, and raising
natives' perception of their relative deprivation. The role of refugee has also
been exploited by armed forces who have committed genocide and other
crimes. In some instances (i.e., Cambodia and Rwanda), international humanitarian relief has been used by criminal organizations such as the Khmer
Rouge and the *Interhamwe*. Such refugees are not always innocent victims
but may have been perpetrators or become warriors to regain their moth-
erland, committing crimes against others.

IS IT PRUDENT TO PREVENT GENOCIDE?

Although there is widespread support for humanitarian assistance for victims of war and genocide, it is often assumed that we cannot afford to
intervene because the cost of intervention is too high. But prevention in
genocide, as in public health, is cheaper than response to an outbreak or
epidemic. The cost of a short-term UN peace-enforcement action in Rwanda
has been estimated at $100 million, whereas international assistance to
Rwanda from April 1994 to December 1995 was over $2 billion—a 20:1
ratio for the cost of assistance to that of prevention.[4] The cost to the United
States alone in Rwanda from April to November 1994 was eight times the

estimated cost of its assessment for a peace-keeping force (which it rejected because of costs) in April 1994.[5] A comprehensive recent analysis, which assumed the need for a more long-term intervention in Rwanda beginning in March 1994, estimated that the maximal cost would have been $1.3 billion over three years compared with the actual direct costs to the international community and states for Rwanda of $4.5 billion from April 1994 through 1996 for humanitarian relief, economic and military costs, without including costs to NGOs and the cost of the International Criminal Tribunal for Rwanda—$332.55 million for 1996 alone.[6] If the cost of the Tribunal is added to other direct costs, making the total expenditures $4.9 billion, the ratio of the cost of prevention to that of assistance and related costs is 1:3.8. So we are talking about cost ratios of 4 to 1 to 20 to 1 in favor of prevention, depending on the assumptions of force level and longevity and the completeness of expenditure aggregation. Brown and Rosecrance note that their estimate of the cost of a preventive force is an overestimate and conclude that "At the very least, preventive action in Rwanda could have saved $3.2 billion" and observe that the postgenocide expenditures have "done nothing to solve the problems that caused it [the genocide] or prevent another outbreak of violence. Thus, the question is not only how much could have been saved, but how much might still have to be paid in the future."[7] The United States alone has spent $1.23 billion for humanitarian assistance to the Great Lakes countries and the International Criminal Tribunal for Rwanda since 1994.[8] And the meter is still ticking.

These figures do not take into account the economic costs to perpetrators and victims. Rwanda, which had climbed between 1976 and 1990 from the seventh to the nineteenth place from the bottom among least-developed countries, descended to become the second poorest country on earth in 1997.[9]

IS DEMOCRACY THE ANSWER?

One question is outstanding: How do we anticipate potential genocides, and when should we intervene? Is democracy the answer, as some argue? Nondemocratic regimes are much more likely to engage in external wars and to practice genocide, but genocide almost always occurs during internal wars—and sometimes precipitates wars with neighbors.[10] The democratic peace thesis has been qualified by comparative research[11] and does not extend to internal war. Further, I found that in 1987, about one third to one half of the states with the worst violations of life-integrity directed at ethnic groups were democracies—depending on whose index and criteria were used.[12] Although this does not imply that half of democracies were gross violators (further discussed later), it makes us aware that democracies, including democracies in existence for fifty years, can and do tolerate pogroms and race riots—genocidal massacres—and gross human rights violations.

Developing mature democracies is an oxymoron; we need to remember that the United States protected slavery for seventy-five years after the formation of the union and did not mandate protection of the franchise for all until a full one hundred years after the abolition of slavery (the Civil Rights Act of 1965). The gap between what democracy promises and how democracies act can be better understood by deconstructing democracy as a goal, a set of institutional norms, and a process. At best, the international community can instigate processes that may lead to transformative steps toward democracy. Institutional norms of liberal democracy assume inclusion of all as equals regardless of gender, ethnicity, and race. They guarantee (a) free elections for representation, (b) civil liberties, and (c) rule of law. But the Achilles' heel of democratization is often the lack of agreement on who is to be included; who are "we, the people"?—a problem intensified in divided or plural societies.[13]

Regimes in divided societies in transition to democracy (e.g., Rwanda and Bosnia) are prone to the rise of ethnic entrepreneurs from groups whose domination appears threatened by power-sharing arrangements; democratization can enhance their power and fuel human rights violations.[14] Democratization in the former Yugoslavia reinforced processes that led to schism and genocide and in Rwanda led to polarizing processes among the Hutu elite, who precipitated genocide.[15] In other societies, when authoritarian regimes falter and there is a popular, democratic, nonviolent revolt, the military, security personnel, and criminal gangs may divert crowds representing the mainstream with antiminority violence, such as in Indonesia in 1998, where Chinese women were systematically raped and Chinese property burned. Division of states during decolonization and the breakdown of empires and multinational states often instigates groups to get resources and land by "ethnic cleansing" and expulsion. Democratic states with Westminster-type systems may also provoke ethnic polarization and exclusion, leading to rebellion and state massacres in retaliation, as in Sri Lanka.[16]

States in the middle—partly free states with some democratic forms—were in 1987 actually more prone than unfree states to practice gross violations of life-integrity.[17] This seems to be best explained by the fact that some freedom enables deprived classes and groups to challenge elites, provoking threatened elites to retaliate violently in order to repress opposition. Yet states that had protected some civil liberties were less apt to be violators than states that protected some political rights without protecting civil liberties. This suggests that institutionalizing civil liberties and the rule of law would be a better strategy for the protection of human rights in new democracies than merely imposing elections.

To prevent genocide and advance human rights and democracy, we need to focus both on security to protect lives and transformative steps toward an inclusive regime. However, the present international emphasis is almost exclusively on multiparty elections which the international community uses to legitimate governments, even when these are neither free nor fair, as in Cambodia in 1998,[18] or when free elections serve to legitimate ethnic cleansing by electing ethnic nationalist parties that prevent the return of refugees to their homes, as in Bosnia in 1998.

Security involves guaranteeing the inviolability of life and personal property by reform of police, army, and justice systems, and implementing the rule of law while annulling the culture of impunity. Transformative steps might include eliminating ethnic registration cards and distinctive regional signs labelling people, instituting trials or truth commissions to sanction past offenders, protecting civil liberties as far as possible while remaining consistent with security (civil liberties may need to be restricted to prevent the dissemination of hate propaganda, denial of past genocide, and incitement to violence), fostering local cooperation across ethnic lines with the incentive of foreign aid, integrating schools (where necessary and practicable), and instituting political parties in such a way as to open up alternatives other than group domination before elections.

If parties are based on ethnic groups, elections themselves may further polarize these groups and provide incentives to use illegitimate means to repress the opposition. There are, however, structural models to prevent this.[19] In some situations, where it is unlikely that two groups will accept representation in one polity, the international community should push for separation through nonviolent means, such as mediation.

HOW CAN WE ANTICIPATE AND DETER GENOCIDE?

To anticipate and deter genocide, we need to focus directly on protecting both individuals and groups against gross violations of life-integrity by using intelligence analysis, historical interpretation, monitoring, and warning systems. Past research shows us which states are most likely to be violators and which groups are most likely to be "minorities at risk,"[20] assuming that genocide is triggered by group conflict (which is true in most but not all cases). Anticipation demands a more specific analysis of conditions, contexts, and processes that are most likely to lead to genocide, taking into account that there is no single model of genocide. For example, neither the Holocaust nor another genocide is typical of all genocides. Some persons question whether "genocide" is more than rhetoric or a value judgment. Although scholars have distinguished several types of genocide—ideological, retributive, developmental, and despotic[21]—some underlying observable characteristics are the same. These are specified in my paradigm for detecting and tracing genocide:

1. There was a sustained attack or continuity of attacks by the perpetrator to physically destroy group members.

2. The perpetrator was a collective or organized actor or commander of organized actors.

3. Victims were selected because they were members of a collectivity.

4. The victims were defenseless or were killed regardless of whether they surrendered or resisted.

5. The destruction of group members was undertaken with intent to kill, and murder was sanctioned by the perpetrator.[22]

The first criteria includes indirect means of destroying a group (criminalized in the UN Genocide Convention in Article 2 b & c), including "genocide by attrition"—imposed starvation, poisoning of air and water, and consequent disease and death[23]—and systematic rape and sexual violence.

FORECASTING AND PREVENTION OF GENOCIDE: THE CASE OF RWANDA

Before 1994, several studies enabled us to forecast (using different methods) what kind of regimes, conflicts and processes may precipitate genocide. I shall illustrate this with the case of Rwanda.

When we look at the most prevalent condition preceding genocide, however, we find that ethnic stratification—systems in which one group is excluded from power and participation because of their ethnoclass—is most likely to promote group rebellion, which, in turn, provokes genocidal response from the dominant ethnoclass. Rwanda exemplifies a variation of this process.

What would early warning and response be? Although we can trace the historical processes back for thirty years, I shall show that we could discern the processes and steps leading to the genocide in the four years preceding it (mid-term detection) and the next-to-final stage of preparation in the year preceding it, in which the process might be braked abruptly. Such a time sequence—preceding political generation, present regime/crisis, and pre-genocidal preparation—seems to work in my mental experiments in surveying other genocides. For prudent prevention, intervening in the middle stage would be optimal.

I shall show how this might have worked in Rwanda, drawing on both my inductively and historically based theory and that of Barbara Harff, who derives findings from an empirical cross-tabulation of post-1945 genocides.[24] Comparing warning signs derived from theories presented at a conference in 1993, I showed much consensus between us (see Figures 3.1 and 3.2). Both Harff and I largely agree on underlying conditions (Figure 3.2); the exclusion of the Other (group to be victimized) from the universe of obligation of the dominant group,[25] a challenge to the solidarity and legitimacy underlying the polity, a crisis or opportunity related to the victim,

Figure 3.1
Processes Leading Toward Genocide/Politicide

(potential checks/interventions in this table written in *bold italics*)

g¹ (Past Generations)	g² (Present Generations)	Precipating Events
Abrupt breakdown Change in regime or decline in state	**STATE:** Nondemocratic weak state Transfer of power/ breakdown	**WAR with other states or within state**
		STATE CONSOLIDATION OF FORCES OF VIOLENCE
Despotism	**ENFORCEMENT OF CIVIL LIBERTIES: absent or discriminatory GROSS VIOLATIONS OF HUMAN RIGHTS** *HRNGO monitoring Withhold aid Strengthen civil society*	**ESCALATION GROSS VIOLATION OF HUMAN RIGHTS**
History of genocide, pograms, or communal violence	**ETHNIC HIERARCHY:** Political exclusion, discrimination, and severe inequality *Advise depolarizing structures International disinvestment Sanctions*	**ETHNIC/CLASS MOBILIZATION** **REBELLION OR POLITICAL CHALLENGE** (fear of elite losing control)
Isolation of indigenous peoples from dominant group related to urban/ rural split and undeveloped land	**POLITICAL ECONOMY:** Conflict over land use triggered by economic development in regions inhabited by indigenous peoples *Require human rights and environmental impact reports Withhold aid Lobby multinationals Develop competing uses to protect indigenous peoples*	

Figure 3.1. (continued)

Explicit or implicit racism	VICTIM PERCEIVED AS, OR IS, CHALLENGER	JUSTIFICATION OF ANNIHILATION OF VICTIM
	Assist nonviolent challengers through international aid/local NGOs *Increase visibility*	
	IDEOLOGY: Growth of hate movements Exclusive nationalist, racist, Marxist-Leninist, or fascist parties rising *Monitor local press reports of refugees, NGOs, etc.* *Denial of recognition* *Strengthen domestic opposition* *Diplomatic warnings*	CONQUEST OF STATE
	EXTERNAL CONTROL: Protected by international or regional hegemonic state (versus checked by such state) *Bans on military sales and transfers* *International/regional sanctions* *Third-party warnings to patron states*	IMMUNITY NO CHECKS BY PATRONS OR ALLIES

and the lack of external checks on the power of the perpetrator, as manifested by either encouragement and toleration by patrons and allies of the perpetrator's use of violence or by empty threats against the perpetrator.

Gurr and Harff have gone on to explore "instigators"—immediate warning signs.[26] Harff and Gurr, Fein, and Kuper also view ethnic stratification and the struggle for power in plural societies as a breeding ground for genocide.[27]

Modern Times—The Past Generation: 1960–1990 (Figure 3.1, Column 1)

Looking at the precedents of genocide as a historical process in Rwanda (Figure 3.1), we observe that the past generation experienced the reversal

Figure 3.2
Comparison of Fein and Harff Explanations of Genocide/Politicide (1994)

Fein Theory	Harff Model	Agree?
I. Necessary Preconditions		
No check on power	State reliance on coercion vs. democratic experience	Yes
Solidarity/legitimacy, conflict/challenge based on ethnoclass exclusion	Intergroup stratification	Yes
Moral exclusion leading to justification of annihilation; definition of group "outside of the universe of obligation of the perpetrator"	Intervening condition: "Commitment to an ideology that excludes categories of people . . . from the universe of obligation"	Yes
	Degree of stability in the multipolar system	Lack of agreement
Past experience of genocide rewarded	Lack of consistent collective . . . responses to ethnic strife and/or humanitarian crises	Yes
II. Intervening Conditions		
	Fragmentation of the governing elite	Lack of agreement
State consolidation of forces of violence	Indicated by lack of restraints on state security agencies	Yes
Ideology	Ideology	Yes
	Charismatic leadership	Lack of agreement
	Economic hardship that results in increased differential treatment	Lack of agreement
III. Precipitating or Accelerating Events		
Crisis or opportunity	Political upheaval (background condition)	Yes
1. War		
2. Development in regions of indigenous peoples	Victims in the way of development	Yes

Figure 3.2 (continued)

Patrons' tolerance (no checks by patrons or allies)	Empty threats of external involvement	Yes
	Increase in external support for targeted groups	Disagree
Ethnic/class mobilization and rebellion or political challenge	Occurence of clashes between regime supporters and targeted groups	Yes
Political exclusion and discrimination	New discriminatory or restrictive policies	Yes
Escalation of gross violations of human rights/ life-integrity violations	Rapid increase in frequency and severity of life-integrity violations	Yes

of political fortunes of Hutu and Tutsi—viewed as ethnoclasses with differing access to power (although the economic status of ordinary Hutu and Tutsi did not differ much,[28]—in the few years before decolonization). The ranking and status of both groups, which previously had many overlapping bonds (e.g., clientage, loyalty to the king), was fixed by the Belgian colonizers, who had co-opted the Tutsis (about 14 percent of the population) as administrators and soldiers and prevented individual mobility between groups by imposing identity as an administrative classification with identity cards. The Belgian colonizers, who had established the myth of Tutsi racial superiority, switched sides in the years before decolonization and began to support the Hutus as an emerging political force. The new Hutu leaders developed a "Rwandese ideology" based on race, and colonial authorities began replacing Tutsi chiefs with Hutu chiefs. "These immediately organized the persecution of the Tutsi on the hills they now controlled, which started a mass exodus of refugees abroad, which eventually took some 130,000 Rwandese Tutsi to the Belgian Congo, Burundi, Tanganyika and Uganda by late 1963."[29] Genocidal massacres of the Tutsi—at first spontaneous and later government-organized, in response to incidents of Tutsi violence—propelled their flight. A report of the UN (which had previously called for group reconciliation) in 1961 concluded that "the developments of these last eighteen months have brought about the racial dictatorship of the one party. . . . An oppressive system has been replaced by another one. . . . It is quite possible that some day we will witness violent reactions on the part of the Tutsi."[30] Tutsis were subject to quotas in public employment and schools and virtually excluded from the government and the army. The invasion by some Tutsi exiles in 1963 not only provoked government slaughter of an estimated 10,000 Tutsis but the execution of all surviving Tutsi politicians in Rwanda.[31]

The mirror image of this may be seen in Burundi, the other state created from the Belgian Congo, in which the dominant Tutsi elite committed assasinations and genocide against Hutus in 1965 and 1972, after attacks by Hutu rebels.[32]

Early-Warning Time: 1990–July 1993 (Figure 3.1, Column 2)

Rwanda was ruled by military dictatorships between 1962 and 1991 and became a one-party state under President (former General) Habyarimana in 1973. The World Bank and other aid donors, who contributed 70 percent of public investment between 1982–1987, believed Rwanda to be a model developing country and overlooked the evidence of institutionalized inequality and racism.[33] However, the economic and social stability of Rwanda declined gravely beginning in 1985 and continued through the 1990s because of a drop in international commodity prices. The situation was aggravated by a decline in food production, increased reliance on foreign loans, and an increase in military spending.[34] This led to greater competition among elites for the foreign aid needed to maintain the style of life to which they had been accustomed, as well as to general hopelessness about the future.[35]

The political crisis in Rwanda began with the 1990 invasion by the Rwandan Patriotic Front (RPF), led by Tutsi exiles and their children trained in Uganda. Although these Rwandans had been very active in the National Resistance Army (NRA) of Uganda, which led to the victory of President Museveni in 1986, internal pressures against the Rwandans in Uganda led them to call for the "Right of Return" at a World Congress of Rwandese refugees in 1988. France, Belgium, and Zaire sent troops to aid the government of Rwanda. The French viewed the RPF invasion as part of the worldwide "Anglo-Saxon" or anglophone conspiracy against francophones.[36] "This is how Paris found itself backing an ailing dictatorship in a tiny distant country producing only bananas and a declining coffee crop without even asking for political reform as a price for its support. This blind commitment was to have catastrophic consequences because, as the situation radicalised, the Rwandese leadership kept believing that *no matter what it did*, French support would always be forthcoming."[37]

Responding to domestic critics, President Habyarimana promised democratic multiparty elections in 1991 in Rwanda and an end to ethnic identity cards. This led to the formation of several parties including an openly racist Hutu party: the Coalition for the Defense of the Republic (CDR). Human rights organizations and a very partisan-free press also emerged.

Both the war and the economic crisis (fed by increased government spending, which produced inflation and currency depreciation) instigated opposition parties to agree to meet with the RPF, leading to the Arusha negotiations. The Arusha Accords, concluded in August 1993, authorized the return of Tutsi refugees and sharing of power with them in a transitional government prior to elections. The refugees, now 500,000, would add one to every 13.6 Rwandans in the most densely populated country in Africa. This was a portent of more intense competition for resources and power in the future—a key to foreign aid, franchises, and government preferences.

Warning signs during this period of crisis and political transition include an escalating series of gross violations of human rights. Between 1990 and 1993, government officials organized anti-Tutsi massacres on at least six occasions in response to the RPF victories, false allegations of a local Tutsi rising and plans for massacre, and the Arusha agreement. Each incident took the lives of 30 to 300 persons.[38] In a press conference in Brussels in October 1992, Professor Reyntjens revealed the existence of a "Xero Network," or death squad, of soldiers and militiamen on the Latin American model that included the prime movers, relatives, and agents of the Habyarimana regime.[39]

In 1993, Hutu parties and factions began organizing massacres. The *Interhamwe* (literally "those who work together"), the youth movement of the government party, *Mouvement Revolutionnaire National pour le Developpement et la Democratie* (MRND[D]), organized massacres in March and August of 1993. Leaders of the *Interhamwe* later organized the 1994 genocide. The RPF also killed eight civil servants and nine of their relatives in Ruhengeri in February 1993. "It seems that the victims were shot simply in reprisal for the recent massacres."[40]

The violence stopped when a monitoring mission, the International Commission on Human Rights, came to Rwanda on January 7, 1993 to investigate. It was renewed when the Commission left later that month, attesting to the control of the *bourgmestres* (local officials) of the communes, who openly decreed when to stop violence and when to start it.[41] Thus, there was a repertoire of collective violence authorized by the government, sometimes termed "collective work obligations." Although the Commission used the term "genocide" to describe the situation between 1990 and 1992, it later withdrew the term. However, the term was repeated in a report by the UN Commission on Human Rights a few months later.

Yet some moderate Hutu or opposition parties in Rwanda were initially willing to work with the RPF, whose own training was in the Ugandan movement and government of President Museveni. Although Museveni professed antitribal values, the actuality of his politics led the RPF to believe that they could co-opt other groups without giving up domination by a Tutsi core.[42] Distrust of the other groups, rumors, and myths on all sides reinforced the volatility of the political situation.

What potential checks were there during this period? The French were not only the biggest donors, but their army was in charge of counterinsurgency in Rwanda. Arms suppliers could have cut off sales and military aid, and allies—principally France—could have made support contingent upon speedy implementation of the Arusha Accords, suppression of internal forces using and threatening violence, and prosecution of government officials and private citizens fomenting ethnic violence. Donor countries played a large role in Rwanda, as foreign aid constituted 22 percent of the government's budget in 1991.[43]

Donors viewed Rwanda as a prime example of successful administration of development assistance.[44] The United States did not stress and France did not include human rights conditionality in their aid policies, and the donors who did—Belgium, Canada, and Switzerland—had less influence. The donors did not apply human rights conditionality for two reasons. Rwanda was known for its effective local administration (which also organized genocidal massacres) and its ability to absorb money. But the more fundamental reason was the donors' emphasis on democratization. "Project feasibility helps to explain the continued inflow from two traditional donors, France and Belgium. . . . Support for democratization and the related peace process implied continuous economic and diplomatic engagement in Rwanda. From this perspective, the threat of ultimately imposing sanctions by withdrawing aid—as western human rights organizations called for in 1992–93—was counterproductive. Donors thus became hostage to their own policies."[45]

There were some differences among donors. France was committed to President Habyarimana because of its francophone foreign policy and continued to aid the government even after the genocide started. The United States and Germany suspended their aid programs in 1994, and most of European Union aid was put on hold at that time.

Another positive step foreign donors could have taken to make genocide less possible was not implemented. This was the replacement of the Rwandan ethnic identity cards with new cards with no mention of ethnicity. Identification is a critical step in tracking potential victims.[46] In fact, the Rwandan cards were used as screening devices in the genocide of 1994, for neither name nor visage are reliable markers of identity in Rwanda. Two United States Agency for International Development (USAID) consultants, Alison Des Forges and Catherine Newbury, recommended in 1991 that USAID support the compilation of new cards and neutral birth records in the communes, but this was not done.[47]

Crisis-Warning Time: August 1993–April 1994 (Figure 3.1, Column 3)

The concessions the government made in Arusha incited the President's former supporters, the *akazi*, to organize extralegal action against him by organizing an extremist media and distributing arms to paramilitary forces.

The Arusha agreements provided for a Broad-Based Transitional Government (BBTG), with portfolios precisely allocated to contending parties within Rwanda and the RPF. Had a BBTG ever been implemented, it probably would have been paralyzed. In addition, the parties now controlling the distribution of incoming foreign exchange and state corporations might have lost control. Many key people within Rwanda might become losers.

After the accord was concluded, the RPF observed a truce and the UN agreed to send in a military monitoring force for peacekeeping, the UN Assistance Mission to Rwanda (UNAMIR), which arrived in October 1993. The army of Rwanda and the RPF were to be integrated into a force of 20,000, which would result in the unemployment of many former soldiers, who would be without a source for their agreed compensation.[48] But the President stalled, and the Agreements, which were supposed to be implemented in February with the installation of the BBTG, were never enforced.

According to Prunier, "the notion of a 'big clean-up,' a 'final solution to the ethnic problem,' had begun to circulate in late 1992."[49] The extremists' calculation of success was reinforced by the anti-Tutsi pogroms conducted by Hutus and the army massacres of Hutus in Burundi, together killing 50,000 ("roughly 60% Tutsi and 40% Hutu") after Burundi's army overthrew the first elected President—a Hutu—in October 1993 with no international intervention.[50] "To the fear of losing one's privileges (rational level) they [radical Hutu groups] added the fear of losing one's life (visceral level) and the fear of losing control of one's world (mythical level)."[51] The moderates lost confidence or were assassinated, and extremists consolidated their hold.

In July 1993, the CDR seized the opportunity to indoctrinate a wider public with its goals and opened a radical racist radio station (government licensed), Radio Television Libre des Mille Collines (RTLMC), which later broadcast injunctions to kill. RTLMC had an inestimable impact as a mobilizing tool and organizational instrument, conveying general and specific orders.

One step the international community could have taken in 1993 would have been to press the Rwandan government to de-license RTLMC, the hate radio, and/or suppress it directly. Broadcasting intervention (used later in Bosnia) is a cheap way to prevent the dissemination of messages to kill and is consonant with the Genocide Convention, which criminalizes "direct and public incitement to commit genocide" (Art. 3), as well as the International Covenant on Civil and Political Rights, which states that "any advocacy of national, racial, or religious hatred that constitutes incitement to discrimination, hostility or violence should be prohibited by law."[52] However, jamming was rejected by the United States.[53]

Warnings Ignored

There were several warnings and many signs of a conspiracy to commit genocide. General Romeo Dallaire, the UNAMIR commander, had received warnings beginning in December 1993. He cabled UN headquarters on January 11, 1994 to report that a key informant had told him plans were being made to massacre 800,000 Tutsi—the whole group—and thousands of Hutus who might oppose the genocidal plot. The planners were compiling lists, training the *interhamwe* to kill, and storing arms.[54] Their plan was to incite a civil war and massacre the Belgian troops, the core element of the UNAMIR force, provoking them to withdraw. Dallaire asked permission to raid weapons caches and help the informant, a former member of the Rwandan President's security staff, escape with his family from Rwanda. The fax reached the then Under-Secretary-General for Peacekeeping Operations, Kofi Annan, who refused, saying that the "operation contemplated" was not within the peacekeeping mandate, and that Dallaire should inform the Rwandan President and the Ambassadors to Rwanda from Belgium, France, and the United States. In 1997, Kofi Annan refused to let Dallaire testify before a Belgian Senate investigatory commission, saying that he did not believe waiving the diplomatic immunity of past and present UN officials was "in the interest of the Organization."[55]

Belgian diplomats and intelligence, the diplomatic corps in Kigali, a Catholic bishop, and others noted what was going on.[56] Des Forges notes that in January 1994, "an analyst of the US Central Intelligence Agency knew enough to predict that as many as half a million persons might die in case of renewed conflict," but his prediction was not credited and was buried in agency files.[57] RTLMC broadcast hate propaganda with incitements to kill Tutsis. *Interhamwe* militias organized mob demonstrations in Kigali, killing dozens of people; some moderate politicians were also slain, and even diplomats received death threats.

In early April, both the European Union and the Rwandan President's African colleagues pressed President Habyarimana to implement the Arusha Accords. Returning from a meeting of African heads of state at Dar Es Salaam on April 6, President Habyarimana responded positively to a request for a lift from his neighbor, the President of Burundi. The plane was shot down by missiles in Kigali airport, killing all aboard, which served as a trigger for the genocide to follow. The men who downed the plane have never been definitively identified; all kinds of plotters have been alleged—French, Belgians, white mercenaries, the RPF, and the *genocidaires* themselves.[58]

The scenario developed as General Dallaire's informant had described in January: the Belgian troops were targetted (ten murdered), withdrawn by Belgium, disarming UNAMIR, and the UNAMIR troops stayed in their barracks (except for taking out the Europeans) before they were withdrawn by the UN. The UNAMIR force, sent in to help carry out the Arusha Accords, was underfunded and undermanned by the UN out of concern for economy. However, General Dallaire has stated that had he been equipped with a well-armed force of 5,000 members committed to a peace-enforcement mission (under Article 7 of the UN Charter), the massacres could have been stopped.[59]

Des Forges observes that there was nothing inevitable about the way the genocide unrolled; it depended on co-opting the local authorities to mobilize people to do the dirty work of killing. "The genocide was not a killing machine that rolled inexorably forward but rather a campaign to which participants were recruited over time by the use of threat and incentives."[60]

The UN Security Council (UNSC) and the Secretary-General failed to respond. Not only did the UNSC fail to respond, it never challenged the legitimacy of the representative of Rwanda on the UNSC at the time, and key members avoided calling the genocide a genocide, preferring neutral frameworks that implied no responsibility: tribal killings, ethnic conflict, chaos, a failed state.

Both France and the United States as UNSC members can be faulted. "Rwanda became the first application of President Clinton's admonition in an address to the United Nations on September 27, 1993, that the UN must learn 'when to say no.' "[61] Responding to its perceived defeat in Somalia (the causes of which were never properly analyzed), the U.S. President in May 1994 decreed Presidential Decision Directive 25 (PPD-25), which decrees sixteen stringent conditions that the United States would consider before sanctioning and engaging in any intervention. The administration reinforced its defense by refusing to recognize the events in Rwanda as genocide, telling officials to talk of "acts of genocide" if they must use the g-word.[62]

The French intervention in June and the RPF victory (some believe the intervention was to allow the *genocidaires* to escape) precluded further international dithering over what was to be done, provoked on April 29 by the UN Secretary-General, who had had a change of heart and confessed his failure.

Consequences and Aftermath of Genocide in Rwanda

The immediate consequences of the genocide were that about 500,000 Tutsi were killed, 10,000 to 30,000 Hutus (also targetted by the *genocidaires*) were killed, and a substantial number of Tutsi women were raped, tortured and sexually mutilated. These events led to high personal and social trauma stemming from the deaths, degradation, and destruction of families, and the disadvantages of being women in a patriarchal culture.[63]

The RPF was found to have committed massacres during the genocide and war, perhaps killing 25,000 to 45,000, and afterward, apparently provoked by vengeance against suspected killers of Tutsis, collective reprisals against Hutus. These massacres may have been tolerated (if not calculated) for social control through terror.[64]

The subsequent flight of over 1,500,000 Hutu to refugee camps in Zaire and Tanzania included many perpetrators (who were to use the other Hutus as hostages). These camps, in turn, were run by the *genocidaires*. When the UN High Commissioner of Refugees requested assistance to disarm the refugees and exclude armed men from the camps, he did not get it. The growth, expense, and political implications of such refugees are well known. In Zaire, the *genocidaires* activated conflicts against peoples of Tutsi origin, destabilizing the country. The security implications for Rwanda and the intermittent massacres perpetrated by forces of the *genocidaires* at the border were among the factors that led the army of Rwanda to help Laurent Kabila overthrow the government of Mobutu and perpetrate genocidal massacres against those refugees who had been driven east, away from Rwandan borders. The UN, now led by Secretary-General Kofi Annan, first withdrew one team of investigators, complying with Kabila's demands, and finally withdrew its last team, in response to obstruction: the Security Council took no action after being given evidence that both the government of the Congo and of Rwanda were responsible.[65]

The government of Rwanda is confronted with a continuing external security problem—raids by remnants of the *interhamwe* from across the western border and massacres of Rwandans—and internal security and human rights problems. The latter results first from keeping over 100,000 persons, most not charged, under detention because of their alleged role in the genocide, and second, from the impossibility of giving them a fair trial, given the lack of resources of the Rwandan judicial system and the impossibility of releasing them. Ethnic mistrust and fear has been reinforced by memories of the genocide, border raids, assassination of witnesses in trials, the return of Tutsi and Hutu refugees from neighboring countries, false charges of genocide stemming from competition for land, and the unrepresentative character of the government, termed an "ethnocracy" by some.

Thus, this rare case of victory by representatives of the victim group demonstrates what a pyrrhic victory this is. The memory of genocide is used as political capital by the RPF-dominated government, which denies the massacres and gross violations of human rights that have taken place since that time. Conversely, Hutus often deny or justify the genocide and focus on their grievances, "using the RPF human rights violations as a kind of moral ransom money to redeem the horrors of April–June 1994."[66] This threatens both the stability and legitimacy of the government and reinforces the possibility of chronic civil war (as in Burundi) and renewed genocide.

The regional consequences still continue to evolve. It appears now that the government of Rwanda has turned against the rule of Laurent Kabila in Zaire for failing to guarantee security on Rwanda's western border and is supporting a rebel force, while Kabila's regime is alleged to have rounded up Tutsis in the capital. The dynamic of ethnic genocide and repression, rebellion, reprisals and transnational intervention continues.

CONCLUSION: THE POTENTIAL FOR AND
IMPEDIMENTS TO PREVENTION

My analysis has shown that preventing genocide is our problem, that it is in the interest of the United States to curb it, and that it is prudent to do so, given the human, geopolitical, and economic consequences of tolerating genocide without intervention. This analysis has also shown that genocide cannot only be detected in process but can be anticipated.

This was demonstrated by examining the development and consequences of genocide in Rwanda (April 1994), a genocide that was both forseen and flagged. Not only were there many signs of impending genocide, but a warning was given to the UN in January 1994 based on insider information. The UN, however, did not heed the recommendations of its UNAMIR commander, General Dallaire, to intervene preemptively. This genocide has fueled a continuing latent internal conflict in Rwanda and a regional crisis in the Great Lakes, as both ethnic conflicts and interventions have become transnational: civil war and rebellion in Congo; genocidal massacres in 1997 in Zaire/Congo; massacres in Rwanda and Burundi by antigovernment groups drawn from the disaffected Hutus, and army massacres in response; grave violations of human rights in all countries; low legitimacy and high distrust among citizens of all countries; and massive flows of refugees (1994–1998) with resettlement of older refugee cohorts, leading to economic rivalry that is sometimes masked by false accusation.

There is general suspicion and distrust in Rwanda.[67] At this point, talk of reconciliation and conflict resolution by outsiders has become simply a sign of western palliatives and an inability to understand what it is like for former victims and perpetrators to co-exist in a postgenocidal society.

For the bystanders in the world community, the moral, political, and economic costs have been great. Humanitarian aid (and costs of the International Tribunal) for Rwanda have exceeded the cost of an intervention by estimates of 4:1 to 20:1 (depending on assumptions about the force level and longevity of an intervention). For the United States, which has spent $1.23 billion in the Great Lakes since 1994, and probably $877.2 million of that amount for Rwanda and its refugees alone, expenditures have been three to eight times what it would have spent for an intervention. Rather than asking, "Can we afford to prevent genocide?," the question should be, "Can we afford not to prevent genocide?" Further, what would prevention imply?

To be effective, a U.S. early warning-early response program to deter genocide must be consistent with a more general human rights policy, focussing on enforcement of sanctions against violators of life-integrity: torture, calculated executions or "disappearances," massacres, and imposition of life-threatening conditions on a group. Consistency is necessary for two reasons: (1) genocide is usually preceded by other life-integrity violations;

and (2) we cannot predict the degree of escalation—whether the perpetrators will proceed from calculated execution to genocidal massacres to genocide. My research has shown that life-integrity violations are highly related; perpetrators of group massacre are also perpetrators of "disappearances," extrajudicial executions, and torture.[68] States both escalate and de-escalate on the scale of the violations, but gross violators seldom give up these practices unless there is a substantive change in regime.

Further, U.S. law since 1961 requires that we not give economic assistance to gross violators of human rights (unless it helps needy people) nor military assistance unless U.S. security interests are affected. These loopholes have been widely exploited. But if it were shown that such practices make genocide more likely and endanger both international and regional security, the evasion of these laws might be more difficult.

Holly Burkhalter (Physicians for Human Rights) proposed (in testimony before the House of Representatives Subcommittee on Human Rights and International Relations on May 5, 1998) a series of steps the United States could take immediately "to develop a 'Genocide Prevention and Response' policy initiative": the President should declare that prevention and suppression of genocide is a vital U.S. interest, should replace Presidential Decision Directive 25 (re: U.S. guidelines for participation and support of multilateral peacekeeping) with another directive that supports UN-sanctioned military operations, and should appoint a senior official to direct intelligence gathering and analysis for the purpose of protecting vulnerable communities. Further, the United States should stop the flow of weapons and military aid to the perpetrators, respond quickly to early warnings of genocide in the making, condemn actions that foment ethnic hatred, use nonhumanitarian foreign aid to pressure governments, deny visas to and seize assets of genocide-provoking individuals, stop the broadcasting of incitements to kill and injure minorities directly and indirectly—jamming the airwaves if necessary—before genocide occurs. She proposed other steps to stop genocide in progress and showed the application of these to Rwanda. This is a good beginning for consideration of what is needed institutionally and tactically to prevent genocide in the future. But to authorize this requires sustained commitment on the highest level. At present, we see intermittent commitment and sustained focus on impediments.

One impediment to a proactive policy is frequently raised: the ghost of American defeat and withdrawal in Somalia and Vietnam. These signify the fear of failure, national shame, and embarrassment. But neither of these interventions has been analyzed to evaluate (1) whether the proposed intervention and these earlier situations are good analogies, and (2) the cause of earlier perceived failures—the decision to intervene or the goals, strategy, and tactics of intervention (including the lack of coordination with other allies).[69]

We are continually misled by false metaphors. But Vietnam was not Munich, Bosnia was not Vietnam, and Rwanda was not Somalia. First, on an analytic level, we are misled by lumping together diverse situations which may legitimately call for different responses. The responsibility under international law to prevent genocide is clear, but it is not clear that it would be deemed right, permissible, or wise to intervene or aid intervenors in the case of civil war and failed states. Interventions to prevent genocide or liberate people who are victims of gross violations of human rights and humanitarian disasters (such as slavery and starvation) are often considered legitimate humanitarian interventions, but interventions to change the form of government are not considered legitimate under international law.[70]

The argument for early warning and early response based on cost and interests may be countered by another assumption: there is an economy based on money and an economy based on blood. U.S. citizens, it is said, will not bear the costs of losing "their boys" in foreign lands that do not threaten the United States. The fact that ours is a volunteer army does not seem to enter into the reasoning of such critics. They say that our soldiers do not enlist in order to be killed. If the fear of domestic reaction is a potent political argument against such interventions by democracies (not only in the United States), an international rapid reaction force based on volunteers who know the risk could answer this objection.

Yet, many consider this an impossible innovation because of the entrenched political hostility to international institutions in the United States; institutions—including the International Criminal Court proposed in July 1998—said to undermine American sovereignty. However, recent analyses of public opinion and elite opinion show that the American public accepts global responsibilities and does not want to go it alone.[71] These authors conclude:

A significant gap exists between the US foreign policy community's perceptions of public attitudes and the results of polls that ask Americans what role the US should play in the world. . . . The majority of Americans supports a foreign policy of broad global engagement, provided that the US is not playing the role of dominant world leader (or "world policeman") and is contributing its "fair share" to multilateral efforts to resolve international problems. . . . Contrary to policy practitioners' view that the public wants US foreign policy tied to a narrow concept of US national interests, a strong majority of Americans supports a foreign policy that takes into account global and humanitarian concerns.[72]

Two thirds to nine out of ten Americans polled believed that it would be better to address problems requiring military force through the UN rather than have the United States act on its own, and 69 to 79 percent agreed that the United States should work with the UN "to maintain peace, protect human rights and promote economic development"—the differences in percentages reflect whether the question is put negatively or positively.[73]

Questions regarding genocide were also raised. Sixty-five percent of Americans polled in 1994 said that the UN, including the United States, should always or in most cases intervene with whatever force is necessary to stop acts of genocide; 80 percent said they would favor intervention in Bosnia or Rwanda if a UN commission determined that genocide was occurring. "This moral conviction was strong in focus groups. 'I think any reason for deciding whether someone lives or dies because of culture or race . . . or religion is wrong' said a Kalamazoo man in spring 1995. 'If Bosnia was an issue of . . . territory, then maybe you should just let them fight it out. But . . . genocide is wrong and when that is occurring, something needs to be done to stop it.' "[74]

Further, the Americans polled favored more robust peacekeeping and were not deterred by fear of some deaths. Contrary to elite and media perceptions, the majority of Americans favored increased involvement in Somalia after the firefight in 1995 rather than withdrawal.[75]

This implies that a strong and articulate U.S. President could rally Americans to back a policy preventing genocide that would require international cooperation, including (but not limited to) intervention. Such a rationale must go beyond the earlier ideological splits over intervention versus nonintervention that reflected ideological divisions between 1945 and 1990. Just as the conflicts that tear countries apart today cannot be explained by Cold War ideology, the means of their resolution cannot be evaluated by Cold War standards.

Besides pragmatism (needed to calculate the efficacy of proposed strategies), we need a practical idealism on the part of leaders that takes into account the fact that the majority of United States citizens do want to prevent genocide. Plans for changed American response and visions of a changed UN response (first proposed by Kuper 1985) require (1) that the United States abandon PDD 25 (which restricts American authorization and participation in multilateral peacekeeping) and (2) an investigation of why the United States did not respond in Rwanda in 1994.[76]

In order to pursue a proactive policy to prevent genocide, we need not only institutional change but direct communication with the American people. We need a political leadership ready to talk in Akron, Boston, Chicago, and San Diego about our responsibilities to prevent genocide, rather than just in Kigali. Recent war crimes and crimes against humanity (which may include genocide) in Kosovo and East Timor in 1999 indicate that this will be a persisting problem unless we pursue a policy of prevention.

NOTES

1. Leo Kuper, *Genocide: Its Political Use in the Twentieth Century* (New Haven, CT: Yale University Press, 1981), p. 161.

2. Helen Fein, ed., *The Prevention of Genocide: Rwanda and Yugoslavia Reconsidered* (New York: Institute for the Study of Genocide, November 1994), p. 13.

3. United States Committee on Refugees, *1998 World Refugee Survey* (Washington, D.C.: USCR, 1998), pp. 4–6.

4. John Eriksson, *The International Response to Conflict and Genocide: Lessons from the Rwanda Experience, Synthesis Report.* (Copenhagen: Joint Evaluation of Emergency Assistance to Rwanda, 1996), p. 34.

5. Milton Leitenberg, "US and UN Actions Escalate Genocide and Increase Costs in Rwanda," in *The Prevention of Genocide: Rwanda and Yugoslavia Reconsidered*, ed. Helen Fein, pp. 41–42.

6. Michael Brown and Richard Rosecrance, eds., *The Cost of Conflict: Prevention and Cure in the Global Arena*, Report to the Carnegie Commission on Preventing Deadly Conflict (Washington, D.C.: Carnegie Commission, 1998), p. 77.

7. Ibid., pp. 80–81.

8. U.S. State Department, *Memoranda and Conversations with Simon Whittemore*, Coordinator for Great Lakes Affairs, Bureau of Population, Refugees and Migration, and Tom Warrick, War Crimes Investigation Unit (Washington, D.C.: Government Printing Office, August 1998).

9. Gerard Prunier, *The Rwanda Crisis: History of a Genocide* (New York: Columbia University Press, 1995), p. 78; United States Committee on Refugees, *Life after Death: Suspicion and Reintegration in Post-Genocide Rwanda* (Washington, D.C.: USCR, February 1998), p. 6.

10. Helen Fein, "Accounting for Genocide after 1945: Theories and Some Findings," *Journal of Group Rights* (1993): 79–106.

11. Miriam Fendius Elman, *Paths to Peace: Is Democracy the Answer?* CSIA Studies in International Security (Cambridge, MA: MIT Press, 1997).

12. Helen Fein, *Lives at Risk: A Study of Life Integrity Violations in 50 States in 1987, Based on the Amnesty International 1988 Report* (New York: Institute for the Study of Genocide, 1990).

13. Larry Diamond and Marc F. Plattner, eds., *Nationalism, Ethnic Conflict, and Democracy* (Baltimore: Johns Hopkins Press, 1994), pp. xiii–xxii.

14. Steven L. Burg, "Ethnic Nationalism, Breakdown, and Genocide in Yugoslavia," in Helen Fein, ed., *The Prevention of Genocide: Rwanda and Yugoslavia Reconsidered* (New York: Institute for the Study of Genocide, 1994); Helen Fein, *The Prevention of Genocide, op. cit.*; Joint Evaluation of Emergency Assistance to Rwanda, *The International Response to Conflict and Genocide: Lessons from the Rwanda Experience*, 5 vols. (Copenhagen: Steering Committee of the Joint Evaluation of Emergency Assistance to Rwanda, 1996), pp. 2, 76.

15. Arthur J. Klinghoffer, "Democratization and Genocide: A Rwandan Case Study," paper presented at the Human Symposium on Democratization and Human Rights, Binghamton University, State University of New York, September 1998.

16. Donald Horowitz, *Ethnic Groups in Conflict* (Berkeley: University of California Press, 1985); Helen Fein, "Accounting for Genocide after 1945."

17. Helen Fein, "More Murder in the Middle: Life-Integrity Violations and Democracy in the World, 1987," *Human Rights Quarterly* 17, No. 1 (February 1995); 170–191.

18. Tina Rosenberg, "Hun Sen Stages an Election," *New York Times Magazine*, August 30, 1998, pp. 20–29.

19. Horowitz, *Ethnic Groups in Conflict*.

20. Ted R. Gurr et al., *Minorities at Risk: A Global View of Ethnopolitical Conflict* (Washington, D.C.: United States Institute for Peace Press, 1993). See also website: bsos.umd.edu/cid/mar for current data.

21. Helen Fein, *Genocide: A Sociological Perspective* (London: Sage, 1993), pp. 28–31.

22. Ibid., pp. 25–26.

23. Elaborated in Helen Fein, "Genocide by Attrition, 1939–1993—The Warsaw Ghetto, Cambodia, and Sudan: Links between Human Rights, Health, and Mass Death," *Health and Human Rights* 2, No. 2 (1997); 10–45.

24. Helen Fein, "Tools and Alarms: Uses of Models for Explanation and Anticipation," *Journal of Ethno-Development* (July 1994); 31–35; Barbara Harff, "A Theoretical Model of Genocides and Politicides," *Journal of Ethno-Development* 4, No. 4 (July 1994); 31–35.

25. Helen Fein, *Accounting for Genocide: National Responses and Jewish Victimization During the Holocaust* (New York: Free Press, 1979), Chapter 1.

26. Ted R. Gurr and Barbara Harff, *Early Warning of Communal Conflicts and Humanitarian Crises* (New York: United Nations University Press, 1995).

27. Barbara Harff and Ted R. Gurr, "Victims of the State: Genocides, Politicides and Group Repression since 1945," *International Review of Victimology* (1989), 23–24; Fein, *The Prevention of Genocide*, "Accounting for Genocide After 1945," *Genocide: A Sociological Perspective*; Helen Fein, "Scenarios of Genocide: Models of Genocide and Critical Responses," in *The Book of the International Conference on Holocaust and Genocide: Towards Understanding, Intervention, and Prevention of Genocide*, vol. 2, eds. I. Charny and S. Davidson (Boulder, CO: Westview Press, 1984), pp. 3–31; Kuper, *Genocide: Its Political Use in the Twentieth Century*, and Leo Kuper, *The Pity of It All* (Minneapolis: University of Minnesota Press, 1977).

28. Prunier, *The Rwanda Crisis: History of a Genocide*, p. 50.

29. Ibid., p. 51.

30. Ibid., p. 53.

31. Ibid., p. 56.

32. Kuper, *Genocide: Its Political Use in the Twentieth Century*, pp. 62–63.

33. Peter Uvin, *Aiding Violence: The Development Enterprise in Rwanda* (West Hartford, CT: Kumarian Press, 1998), pp. 40–46.

34. Ibid., pp. 52–57.

35. Prunier, *The Rwanda Crisis: History of a Genocide*, p. 84.

36. Ibid., pp. 104–107.

37. Ibid., p. 107.

38. Ibid., pp. 136–137, 162.

39. Ibid., p. 168.

40. Ibid., p. 175.

41. Ibid., p. 173.

42. Ibid., pp. 151–159.

43. Ibid., p. 79.

44. Joint Evaluation of Emergency Assistance to Rwanda, *International Response to Conflict and Genocide*, Vol. 2, p. 37; Uvin, *Aiding Violence: The Development Enterprise in Rwanda*.

45. Joint Evaluation of Emergency Assistance to Rwanda, *International Response to Conflict and Genocide*, Vol. 2, p. 32.

46. Raoul Hilberg, *The Destruction of the European Jews* (Chicago: Quadrangle Press, 1963); Fein, *Accounting for Genocide*.

47. Alison Des Forges, quoted in Fein, *The Prevention of Genocide*, p. 26.

48. Prunier, *The Rwandan Crisis: History of a Genocide*, p. 193.

49. Ibid., p. 200.

50. Ibid., p. 199.

51. Ibid., p. 200.

52. Jamie Metzl, "Information Intervention," *Foreign Affairs* 76, No. 6 (November–December 1997), 15–21.

53. Alison Des Forges, *The Killing Campaign: The 1994 Genocide in Rwanda* (New York: Human Rights Watch, 1998), p. 20.

54. Charles Truehart, "UN Alerted to Plans for Rwanda Bloodbath," *Washington Post*, September 25, 1997; *New York Times*, January 28, 1998 [McKinley]; Philip Gourevitch, "The Genocide Fax," *New Yorker*, May 11, 1998, pp. 42–45.

55. Gourevitch, "The Genocide Fax," pp. 43–44.

56. Des Forges, *The Killing Campaign*, p. 22; Joint Evaluation of Emergency Assistance to Rwanda, *International Response to Conflict and Genocide*, Vol. 2, p. 38.

57. Ibid., pp. 15–16.

58. Prunier, *The Rwanda Crisis: History of a Genocide*, pp. 213–229.

59. *New York Times*, January 28, 1998 [McKinley]; Carnegie Commission on Preventing Deadly Conflict, *Preventing Deadly Conflict*, Final Report (New York: Carnegie Corporation, 1997), p. 6.

60. Des Forges, *The Killing Campaign*, p. 5.

61. Milton Leitenberg, "US and UN Actions Escalate Genocide and Increase Costs in Rwanda," in Helen Fein, ed., *The Prevention of Genocide*, p. 37.

62. *New York Times*, June 10, 1994.

63. Prunier, *The Rwanda Crisis: History of a Genocide*, pp. 261–265; Human Rights Watch/Africa, *Shattered Lives: Sexual Violence during the Rwandan Genocide and Its Aftermath* (New York: Human Rights Watch, 1996); and Alison Des Forges, *"Leave None to Tell the Story": Genocide in Rwanda* (New York/Paris: Human Rights Watch/International Federation of Human Rights, 1999), pp. 15–16.

64. Gerard Prunier, *The Rwanda Crisis: History of a Genocide*, with a new chapter. (London: Hurst & Co., 1997), pp. 359–362; Des Forges, *The Killing Campaign: The 1994 Genocide in Rwanda*, p. 22; Des Forges, *"Leave None to Tell the Story,"* pp. 16, 702–722.

65. *New York Times*, July 29, 1998 [Crossette], April 16, 1998 [Crossette], July 11, 1997, July 2, 1997 [Crossette], June 8, 1997, June 1, 1997 [McNeil], May 28, 1997 [Crossette], May 27, 1997 [McNeil], May 15, 1997 [McNeil].

66. Prunier, *The Rwanda Crisis: History of a Genocide*, with a new chapter, p. 372.

67. United States Committee on Refugees, *Life After Death: Suspicion and Reintegration in Post-Genocide Rwanda* (Washington, D.C.: USCR, February 1998).

68. Helen Fein, "More Murder in the Middle," pp. 174–175, 186.

69. Tom J. Farer, "Intervention in Unnatural Humanitarian Emergencies: Lessons for the First Phase," *Human Rights Quarterly* 18, No. 1 (February 1996): 1–22.

70. Michael Walzer, *Just and Unjust Wars: A Moral Argument with Historical Illustrations* (New York: Basic Books, 1977); Richard B. Lillich, *Humanitarian In-*

tervention and the United Nations (Charlottesville: University of Virginia Press, 1973).

71. Steven Kull, I. M. Destler, and Clay Ramsay, *The Foreign Policy Gap: How Policymakers Misread the Public* (College Park: Center for International and Security Studies at the University of Maryland, October 1997).

72. Ibid., p. iii.

73. Ibid., pp. 27, 36.

74. Ibid., pp. 78–79.

75. Ibid., pp. 80–81, 91–93.

76. Holly Burkhalter, "US Failure in Rwanda—And How to Prevent Future Genocides," *Institute for the Study of Genocide Newsletter*, No. 21 (Summer/Fall 1998).

4

Economic Sanctions and Genocide: Too Little, Too Late, and Sometimes Too Much

George A. Lopez

INTRODUCTION

Economic sanctions have become a common feature of multilateral, regional, and big-power foreign policy in the 1990s.[1] After invoking their sanctions power in only two cases during the UN's first forty-five years (Rhodesia, 1966; South Africa, 1977), the UN Security Council has imposed sanctions, both comprehensive and partial, eleven times during this decade. The cases include sanctions against Iraq (UN, 1990), the former Yugoslavia (UN and Organization for Security and Cooperation in Europe [OSCE], 1991), Libya (UN, 1992, 1993), Somalia (UN and Organization of African Unity [OAU] 1992), Liberia (UN, 1992), Haiti (Organization of American States [OAS], 1991; UN, 1993), Union for the Total Independence of Angola (UNITA) faction in Angola (UN, 1993), Rwanda (UN, 1994), the Khmer Rouge (UN, 1995), Burundi (OAU, 1996), Sierra Leone (UN and OAU, 1997). Parallel to these actions, unilateral sanction, often imposed by the United States, were imposed more than three dozen times.[2]

In many of the Security Council cases, the rationale for sanctions has been the need to respond to the occurrence of massive abuse of human rights or the potential for such abuse during brutal internal wars. Although the language of Security Council resolutions does not use the term "genocide" itself, it is fair to state that in at least two instances—that of Rwanda and the former Yugoslavia (and later, by extension, the Bosnian Serbs)—and with an eye toward such occurrences in the recent past (sanctions against the Khmer Rouge), the council has consciously used sanctions to reduce the means by which a national group can pursue genocide. A related course of action designed to thwart mass killing was pursued by the OAU's economic sanctions and border closing of Burundi in July, 1996.[3] Although these comprise a very small set of cases from which to judge, it is not an implausible claim that an international consensus exists about economic sanctions as a legitimate and effective instrument for deterring the potential for genocide, for limiting genocide as it unfolds, and for punishing a genocidal set of actors after the fact of the crime.

Yet an examination of the outcome of multilateral sanctions may lead to a somewhat different conclusion: that sanctions, not unlike other measures of international diplomacy or coercion, do little to deter genocide when it is in the offing and are ineffective at halting it when it is occurring. In this chapter I first present whatever plausible notions may exist for considering some particular types of sanctions as a deterrent to genocide. Next, I briefly scrutinize the cases of Rwanda and the former Yugoslavia, where sanctions were imposed as a means of condemning genocide or near-genocidal conditions. I then address the concern of some analysts and activists that sanctions against Iraq by the mid-1990s actually caused genocide. Finally, I raise the most current topic of investigation and inspiration to sanctions specialists, that of targeted "smart" sanctions as a near-future device for stifling genocidal elites.

CAN SANCTIONS EFFECTIVELY PROTECT POPULATIONS AGAINST GENOCIDE?

To consider how sanctions might be an effective policy for protecting a population from genocide or for enhancing human rights in a nation on the brink of genocide, we must examine, albeit briefly, (1) what we know about the ways in which persons who may be targets of genocide and their human rights come to be protected and improved in any society, and (2) what we know about the effectiveness of sanctions generally.

Regarding the first point, because there are a number of different types of rights-abusive and genocide-prone regimes that might be targeted for sanctions, "improvement" can take on very different meanings. For example, in nations where brutal treatment of citizens by their government has sparked international concern, rights improvement clearly means ending the terror of the state against its own people. In such cases, sanctions may play a role by (1) denying repressive leaders the resources (often arms) they need to continue their repressive policies, or by (2) changing the internal paradigm of repressive leaders, so that they perceive sanctions as creating both declining gains and increasing (and now unacceptable) costs for their rights-abusive behavior. This is what appears to have led to the reasonable claim that in the cases of Rhodesia and South Africa, the pressure of sanctions played a major role in the devolution of power-holding to black majority rule.[4]

In nations where a general system of oppression or repression reigns, it is clear that changes in the basic structural conditions of the political and economic orders that serve to protect groups at risk are required to enhance and protect human beings and their rights. Among necessary conditions are: police and military institutions that are guided by civilian oversight and, like the civilian government itself, are disciplined by the rule of law; a functioning constitution; an independent and functional judiciary system; and the existence of a degree of social peace characterized by the absence of large-scale crime or political violence. Further, it is generally the case that political and civil rights are more protected in societies with thriving economies, whereas rights are more restricted in situations of economic crisis.

Such structural conditions develop very gradually, and are the result of more slowly evolving "democratizing" and "rights-protective" processes. Because they are slow to develop, especially in societies with a history of repression, they are less likely to emerge as the short-term result of external factors, such as a sanctions policy. On the positive side, however, sanctions can have, albeit indirectly, a major impact on the emergence of these trends, either by depriving the repressive regime of resources used to stifle such development, or by enhancing the prospect that the rights-conscious and democratic-minded groups will have a greater voice in the society. Sanctions may therefore help create an equalization of power between a government and an opposition that would result (in some situations) in the enhancement and protection of human rights. Sanctions—in their purpose and design—are meant to counteract some of the proximate conditions needed for genocide to emerge.

Although sanctions are frequently called upon to achieve purposes such as advancing human rights or stifling mass murder, many analysts doubt their effectiveness. The available evidence confirms that sanctions by themselves are seldom able to achieve either substantive political changes or the replacement of the leadership in a targeted regime. According to the major empirical study in the field, conducted by the Institute for International Economics (IIE), "sanctions are seldom effective in impairing the military potential of an important power, or in bringing about major changes in the policy of the target country."[5] If the goal is rolling back military aggression, impairing the military capability of an adversary, or forcing a change in the leadership of a regime, sanctions alone are unlikely to be effective. These realities led the United States General Accounting Office to conclude that "the primary goal of sanctions is usually the most difficult to achieve."[6]

Yet these conventional assumptions may be too pessimistic. Sanctions may be ineffective at times, not because of the inherent limitations in the instrument but because of flaws in implementation and enforcement. In Haiti, for example, sanctions alone did not succeed in restoring President Jean Bertrand Aristide, but this was due in large part to the flawed nature of the Governors Island Agreement (which lifted sanctions before Aristide's actual return) and the inept and inconsistent implementation of sanctions. Claudette Werleigh, former minister of the Aristide government, has argued that sanctions against Haiti could have been much more effective if they had been properly enforced.[7]

The case of South Africa is particularly controversial. Most analyses published before 1992, including the IIE study, judged the sanctions against apartheid as ineffective. At the time such assessments seemed reasonable, since more than two decades of economic pressure and diplomatic isolation had failed to dislodge the apartheid system. Nonetheless, financial pressures on the Pretoria government eventually had a significant impact on economic and political dynamics within South Africa, and contributed to the sweeping political transformation that brought Nelson Mandela and the African National Congress to power in 1994. From this perspective, sanctions against the apartheid regime could be judged a partial success, albeit an indirect and slow one. Compared to the human costs and rights abuse of civil war as a means of ending apartheid, sanctions were a major success.

Yet evidence can also give a more negative direction to our assessment. As was the case in the former Yugoslavia, and also in Iraq, sanctions may also play a major role in the further deterioration of the human rights situation in a target nation, thus creating a favorable climate for genocide. In rights-abusive nations, the leaders of the target government may, in fact, increase their repression of opponents and others as a "justifiable action" in light of the economic hardship caused by sanctions. In addition, the impact of sanctions on the economic and social infrastructure of a target nation can cause a serious decline in the "second order" rights of the people of that country. Those most abused in this situation are likely to be the most vulnerable: women, children, and those heavily dependent on the societal "safety net" that is often provided by international agencies.

The conventional assumption about sanctions is that economic hardship is directly proportional to political change. The greater the economic pain caused by sanctions, the higher the probability of political compliance. This conventional view is mostly based on the assumption that the population in the target state will redirect the pain of sanctions onto political leaders and force a change in policy. But this mechanism requires that (1) some level of democratic or popular influence of the citizenry on the elites operates in the society, and that (2) time is on the side of the sanctioners, as historically sanctions require nearly three years to achieve their objectives. Analysts are quick to point out, however, that the greatest economic impact of sanctions occurs in the first year, after which effectiveness declines as target states adapt to new conditions.[8] And finally, as I will discuss in the last section of this chapter, one of the most important empirical findings about the effect-iveness of sanctions concerns the use of financial restrictions. According to the IIE report, financial sanctions have a higher political success rate (41 percent) than do the more widely imposed general trade sanctions (25 per-cent).[9]

At times, economic sanctions may actually strengthen a targeted regime by generating a "rally-around-the-flag" effect. Rather than causing political disintegration, sanctions may evoke nationalist sentiments and generate au-tarky in the target country. In some cases, sanctions may enrich and enhance the power of elites who respond to sanctions by organizing and profiting from smuggling and illicit trade activities. In Haiti, critics charged that mil-itary and business elites close to the military regime of Raoul Cedras con-trolled the black market trading of oil and other vital commodities. In former Yugoslavia, hard-line militia groups used their control of check points and transportation routes to enrich themselves and consolidate po-litical power. In this later case, the means of control necessary to undertake genocide are reinforced, however inadvertently, by sanctions. And the reality of sanctions is used by the elite as a nationalist rallying cry, permitting a leader to further augment whatever ideological or nationalist underpinning the momentum to genocide may already have.

In contrast, the principle intention of imposing sanctions against a rights-violating regime is the generation of an "internal opposition effect." In this situation, sanctions have the effect of empowering internal political forces, thus rendering them more effective in their opposition to a regime's objec-tionable policies.[10] As the U.S. General Accounting Office has observed, "if the targeted country has a domestic opposition to the policies of the gov-ernment in power, sanctions can strengthen this opposition and improve the likelihood of a positive political response to the sanctions."[11] In the case of South Africa, the opposition African National Congress actively encouraged stronger international sanctions and gained moral and political support from the solidarity thus expressed by the world community. In South Africa, ex-ternal sanctions combined with the internal resistance campaign of the United Democratic Front to create political turmoil and economic uncer-tainty, which prompted foreign investors to deny long-term credit in the mid-1980s. This led sectors of the white business community to lobby for changes in the apartheid system and to urge dialogue with Nelson Man-dela.[12]

Although a "blood bath" had been predicted by many as the only way in which majority black rule would come to South Africa, sanctions played an essential role in leading those who ruled under the apartheid system to a set of choices that prevented this. Sanctions also served as a proactive strategy that blacks could support as an alternative to such direct violence as a means of changing the regime. In this sense, it is not inaccurate to claim that sanctions were an effective means of preventing such massive violence, which would have bordered on, if it did not actually become, a genocide of blacks, of whites, or of each, in South Africa. Unfortunately, circumstances—the pace of events and the inability of sanctions on their own, or in conjunction with other policies, to prevent genocide, or stifle it as it unfolded—were different in the cases of Rwanda and the former Yugoslavia.

The Rwandan Case

The series of events that led to the genocide in Rwanda was not without its warning signs. Those who knew the region well, and who would have seen in the plane crash killing President Juvenal Habyarimana the beginning of a major series of events, may not have been surprised by *what* occurred—that is, the political murdering of Tutsis (and moderate Hutus) by Hutus—but the scale of the slaughter, *how* it unfolded, and its rapidity were certainly shocking.[13]

A UN "concern" about tensions in Rwanda had developed in the form of the creation of the UN Assistance Mission for Rwanda (UNAMIR), which was created by Security Council Resolution 872, passed in 1993. This resolution was to give the UN a presence in the region and was meant to serve as a support of and cease-fire monitoring mechanism for the Arusha Accords, signed by the nations of the region that year. Perhaps now, in full hindsight, one might wonder why the Security Council did not attempt to further bolster the peace process through an arms embargo against all major factional and state actors when it created UNAMIR. Such an action might have stifled a bit of the violence, or might have made government forces less bold.

Yet the harsh truth may be that so much propaganda had already been broadcast throughout Rwanda that fueled the genocidal urge, and so much of the killing was "up-close" in the form of machete murders or killings by machine gun or rifle over the short span of April to June 1994, that no international mechanism such as sanctions would be an effective response to such mass killing. Acting under the "threat to peace" rubric provided by Chapter VII of the UN Charter, the Security Council actions regarding the Rwandan crisis commenced with the adoption of Resolution 918 on May 17, 1994. In this resolution, the council imposed a mandatory embargo on the supply or sale to Rwanda of arms and all related material, including military vehicles, equipment, and spare parts, as well as a ban on weapons and ammunition, and the supply of police and paramilitary equipment and spare parts. The council considered both UNAMIR, a relatively weak presence on the scene for stifling genocide, and especially Resolution 918 as actions responding to the genocide in its own terms, and also as supportive of the diplomatic, political, and humanitarian efforts existing in the region under the auspices of the OAU and the special regional facilitator of Tanzania.

In early 1995, the Council recognized that the free flow of arms in this genocide, which had already claimed more than 750,000 ethnic Tutsi and 50,000 moderate Hutus, had to be halted. Thus, through Resolution 997, it "called upon" the neighboring states of Rwanda to make special efforts in this regard. Later that same year, in Resolution 1005, the Council approved the importation and use of explosives and related devices for the sole purpose of supporting humanitarian demining efforts underway in Rwanda. But by this time, the incredible damage of genocide had already been done. Worse yet, many acknowledged that the arms embargo was generally unenforceable when various factions in front-line, border states had so much to gain economically and politically by violating it.

The Rwandan genocide illustrates the ineffectiveness of instruments like economic sanctions when the policy goal is to end mass murder in a short period of time. Economic sanctions can clearly deprive a regime of the tools of genocide, most especially weapons that may be used in such undertakings. But for this outcome, sanctions must be imposed during the time period when emotions, propaganda, and mobilization—but not killing—are running high. Such sanctions must also be subject to intense monitoring. That sanctions should also be bolstered by other forms of pressures and incentives aimed at genocide prevention is a necessity as well. By March of 1994, however, all the elements for genocide were in place in Rwanda. The small size and diffuse character of the regional peacekeeping mandate of UNAMIR meant that neither that mission nor UN sanctions were going to alter the course of the gruesome events that would unfold in the next three months.

Sanctions and the Yugoslav War

The genocide of Bosnian Muslims during the Yugoslav war through the Serbian policy of ethnic cleansing proved an embarrassment to UN peacekeeping functions, as in varying ways the UN force was either unable or unwilling to halt what obviously were direct Serbian attacks on reasonably defenseless Bosnians. If UN protective forces on the ground during the war were meant to be a first-line order of defense of innocent civilians, then sanctions were meant to be a second-order strategy, whereby the parties assumed to be perpetrating the atrocities—first the Serbs of Yugoslavia-Montenegro and then the Bosnian Serbs—would be deprived of arms for continuing the killing and economic resources that would support the general war effort.[14]

With Security Council Resolution 713 of September, 1991, which imposed an arms embargo on the entire region, the UN began its extensive involvement in the conflicts in the former Yugoslavia.[15] The Council confirmed its intention that the embargo apply to all parts of the former Yugoslavia in Resolution 727, passed in January, 1992, the same month in which the European Community (EC) recognized Slovenia and Croatia as independent states. The conditions for lifting the arms embargo were more than ambiguous, with the embargo not formally lifted until November 22, 1995, when the Security Council passed Resolution 1021 in response to the Dayton Accords peace agreement signed by the warring factions.

Although intended to prevent or at least limit the fighting in the region, the arms embargo, in fact, effectively helped set the balance of military power in favor of the Serbs, and to some extent the Croats, who were both better armed than the Bosnian Muslims. Due to the nature of the former Yugoslav federation, individual republics did not maintain active military forces, or even police. Serbia controlled the army of the former Yugoslavia (JNA) although many of the troops came from Bosnia. Both Croatia and Bosnia, but especially the latter, were short of arms, training, and seasoned soldiers.

Precipitated by an attack that killed up to 22 people waiting in a bread line in Sarajevo, the UN Security Council imposed comprehensive international sanctions against the Federal Republic of Yugoslavia in May, 1992. The UN's involvement followed the EC and US withdrawal of economic and financial aid to the region in May and June of 1991, in an attempt to prevent the disintegration of the former Yugoslavia. The EC had also imposed trade sanctions against the entire region after fighting broke out in Slovenia and Croatia in July, 1991. With the UN's action in May, the EC lifted its trade embargo on all of the republics *except* the Federal Republic of Yugoslavia (FRY).

On May 15, 1992, the Security Council passed Resolution 752, a unanimous request that the FRY end its military interference, withdraw the JNA, and disband and disarm the irregular forces operating in Bosnia-Herzegovina. This resolution provided the foundation for all subsequent sanctions resolutions. Two weeks later, in Resolution 757, passed on May 30, 1992, the Council imposed comprehensive sanctions against the FRY, including a boycott on all exports and imports of goods and services from FRY, the interdiction of air traffic and related services, a ban on all financial transactions, the reduction of staff at diplomatic missions, a ban on FRY's representation at sport and cultural events, the suspension of scientific and technical cooperation and cultural exchanges, and a provision that no legal claims could result from the consequences of implementing sanctions. In this resolution, the Security Council did not prohibit the transshipment of goods through the FRY, mainly in deference to the economic strain this would put on neighboring economies, especially Bulgaria and Rumania.

Partly because of numerous violations of sanctions through these porous borders, the sanctions reportedly were having little effect six months later. Thus, on November 16, 1992, the Security Council passed Resolution 787, tightening the sanctions by prohibiting transshipment of certain strategic items, such as crude oil and petroleum products, iron, steel, chemicals, and energy-related products through the FRY unless specifically authorized by the Security Council. On April 17, 1993, almost one year after their imposition, Resolution 820 confirmed, partly restructured, and tightened the earlier sanctions. Specifically, they strengthened the sanctions' monitoring and control mechanisms through the Sanctions Monitoring System (SAMS) and permitted Bosnia and Croatia to move goods on and to their respective territories. These sanctions were thus aimed directly at the Bosnian Serbs and at Belgrade, as the council considered these parties the aggressors in a war of ethnic cleansing in Bosnia during which other measures of international opinion or invoking international law had failed to halt the large-scale killing.

After many months of pressure from the council, in August 1994, President Milosevic finally agreed to enforce an embargo on the Bosnian Serbs after they again rejected a United States-backed peace plan. By this time, Serbs occupied almost 70 percent of Bosnia as well as a large section of Croatia. The full sanctions package against the FRY had been in place for almost a year and a half and had firmly taken hold. The FRY economy had nearly collapsed in late 1993, and although stabilizing somewhat since internal economic reforms in January 1994, its gains were tentative. Milosevic had seemingly had a "change of heart" and had begun to work with the international community to establish peace in the region. But as was already suspected, he and the Bosnian Serb leader Radovan Karadzic had been able to take 70 percent of the territory within Bosnia-Herzegovina, and had displaced over 250,000 Muslims, with tens of thousands more killed in the war and ethnic cleansing operations.

In September 1994, when Security Council Resolution 942 extended the UN sanctions to Bosnian-Serb territory in eastern Bosnia bordering Serbia, Milosevic, who was now anxious for peace, permitted UN observers to monitor the border and verify his compliance with the blockade. Because of the debilitating impact of the sanctions on the Serb economy, most international observers credit the sanctions with bringing about these changes in Milosevic's policies. However, a number of questions still remain about the actual impact of the sanctions in light of the pre-existing conditions in the country and its continuing economic policies.

Clearly, at the very least, the sanctions accelerated and intensified the economic and social crises within the FRY and increased the costs to the Belgrade government of its unqualified support for the Bosnian-Serb's war effort. But sanctions were simply not very effective in changing the character or volume of the killing "on the ground" in Bosnia, particularly by the Bosnian Serbs, who came rather unwillingly both to the peace table and to affirm its results in the Dayton Accords. Unlike the case of Rwanda, where the genocide occurred so quickly that any international action, especially multilateral sanctions, seemed doomed from the start, sanctions in the FRY were imposed and refined in response to the changing conditions of the war and coexisted with the deployment of the UN peacekeeping mission troops called the UN Protection Force (UNPROFOR). But like that force, sanctions involved too little coercion and always seemed to lag behind the horrors that were being perpetrated against civilians in this brutal war.

Iraq's Ordeal: Can Sanctions Be Genocidal?

As if it were not a sufficient concern that sanctions fail to prevent or curtail genocide, the open-ended and continually devastating nature of the comprehensive economic sanctions imposed on Iraq in August of 1990 in Security Council Resolution 661 (and then reconstituted and amplified in the Gulf War ceasefire Resolution 687) have been claimed by a number of activists and analysts alike to be so harsh that they comprise a genocide against the Iraqi people.[16] In attempting to end Iraqi aggression against Kuwait, and then as a means of controlling the Iraqi development of weapons of mass destruction, the economic sanctions imposed by the UN were not intended to produce such loss of life and debilitation of the quality of life on Iraqi society or to generate, even as a rhetorical claim, the possibility of genocide. Can sanctions have such an effect?

Because of concern about the humanitarian consequences of sanctions in Iraq, no humanitarian situation in the world has been more intensely studied in recent years than the crisis in Iraq resulting from the Gulf War and more than eight years of UN sanctions. By 1990 more than a dozen major studies had been conducted on the impact of the war and sanctions, including reports from the UN Secretariat, UNICEF, the World Health Organization, the UN Food and Agriculture Organization (FAO), the Harvard study team, the Center for Economic and Social Rights in New York, and Greenpeace. A December 1995 report in *The Lancet*, the journal of the British Medical Association, drawing from a study of the food and nutritional situation by FAO, claimed that sanctions against Baghdad had been responsible for the deaths of 567,000 Iraqi children since the end of the Gulf War.[17] Release of the FAO study and *The Lancet* report generated considerable publicity. A *New York Times* article in December 1995 flatly declared, "Iraq Sanctions Kill Children."[18] A feature segment on the widely viewed CBS television program "60 Minutes" also depicted sanctions as a murderous assault on children.[19] Critics have called the UN sanctions a "massive violation of human rights" and have described the situation in catastrophic terms: "More Iraqi children have died as a result of sanctions than the combined total of two atomic bombs on Japan and the recent scourge of ethnic cleansing in former Yugoslavia."[20] This is the type of data that generates claims of genocide.[21]

That the people of Iraq have suffered grievously since the Gulf War is undeniable, but the scale of the crisis is uncertain, as is the assertion that sanctions have been the primary cause of Iraq's ordeal. Even more doubtful is the charge that responsibility for the humanitarian suffering lies exclusively or primarily with Western governments and the UN Security Council. The eight-year war that Iraq fought with Iran imposed a heavy burden on Iraq, leaving more than 100,000 soldiers dead, a foreign debt of nearly $100 billion, foreign currencies depleted, and widespread labor force and economic disruptions. These effects were compounded by the Gulf War, especially by the allied air bombardment. More than 90,000 tons of explosives rained down on Iraq during the Gulf War, much of it targeted on the country's economic infrastructure. Allied air commanders went to great lengths to avoid the bombing of civilian neighborhoods, striking instead industrial and communications facilities that were deemed essential to Iraq's military capability. The bombing destroyed industrial complexes, oil refineries, sewage pumping stations, telecommunications facilities, roads, railroads, and dozens of bridges. Eighteen of Iraq's twenty power-generating plants were destroyed or incapacitated in the first days of the war, reducing electricity generation to just 4 percent of prewar levels.[22] In total, the bombing campaign caused an estimated $232 billion worth of damage to Iraq's economy.[23]

Ironically, although allied commanders sought to avoid civilian casualties in the air war, the destruction of Iraq's electrical generating capacity and industrial infrastructure may have had an impact equivalent to that of bombing residential neighborhoods. The crippling of Iraq's electrical and water supply systems had a devastating effect on the country's population and created conditions that led to disease, suffering, and death *after* the war. A report issued immediately after the war by UN Undersecretary General Martti Ahtisaari described "near apocalyptic destruction" in Iraq. The report asserted that Iraq had been "relegated to a preindustrial age" in which "most means of modern life support have been destroyed or rendered tenuous."[24] Reports from UNICEF and FAO in June and July 1991 warned of rising malnutrition and disease rates, especially among children.[25] Thus, it is not out of the realm of possibility to suggest that massive attacks on civilians, which is at least the equivalent of mass murder, began indirectly during the Gulf War but had a fuller impact in the form of disease and death long after the bombs were silent.

Unquestionably, this situation has left such a fragile social, medical, physical, and economic infrastructure that the comprehensive and tightly enforced UN sanctions have compounded and intensified these diverse hardships resulting from the war. The cumulative impacts of sanctions and the war have been simply overwhelming. Health and mortality statistics from Iraq during this decade have been shocking. Typhoid incidence jumped from eleven per 100,000 in 1990 to 142 per 100,000 in 1994.[26] Cholera, scarcely detected in the 1980s, jumped to near epidemic levels after the Gulf War. Malnourishment among children has risen sharply as well. The percentage of underweight children under five rose from 7 percent in 1991 to 29 percent in 1995. Rates of stunting and wasting among children jumped

230 percent and 400 percent, respectively, during the same period.[27] Most disastrous of all has been the reported increase in the rate of infant and under-five-years mortality. There has been much debate about the accurate number of child deaths and how to assess such deaths accurately. Those who often refer to sanctions as constituting a genocide against the Iraqi people cite child deaths under five years of age from 1990 to 1998 at about the 600,000 mark, with the total population deaths attributable to sanctions being more than 1 million. This author agrees with lower estimates that would place the former figure at about 230,000.[28]

These are truly horrifying figures, reflecting an unspeakable human tragedy. They show beyond doubt that the Gulf War and continuing sanctions have had a devastating impact on the Iraqi people. Whether these results constitute genocide in any traditional sense may be a matter of judgment, but they are certainly not what sanctions were intended to produce as conceived of by past and current UN officials.

THE FUTURE OF SANCTIONS IN DEALING WITH GENOCIDE

Without question, sanctions have been too little and too late in dealing with genocide and near-genocidal occurrences in recent international affairs. It also is the case that rapid injection of military forces to prevent genocide has seldom been an effective option. What, then, will the international community seek in a mechanism like sanctions when faced with such situations? Or, what adaptations in what now comprises economic sanctions policy might be developed to contribute more to the global capacity to prevent or stifle genocide? Among the improvements and alternatives attracting the widest attention within the UN community has been the concept of "smart sanctions."

As discussed by both UN practitioners and sanctions scholars, smart sanctions include *targeted financial measures*, including asset freezes, more comprehensive approaches to *arms embargoes*, and *restrictive international travel and participation bans*. Although arms embargoes are often the first sanctions imposed during a genocidal crisis, the case evidence suggests that little effort has been made to monitor or enforce these measures, and inadequate attention has been devoted to improving their design and implementation. Even less attention has been devoted to travel bans and the denial of participation in international activities, despite the fact that such sanctions have been imposed with increasing frequency in recent years.

Although smart sanctions are not a magic bullet for dealing with violators of general international law, this array of sanctions, when strategically combined, may prove to be a more effective tool than general trade sanctions, especially because of their rapid impact on decisional elites. With just a glance at their own central bank computers, leaders will find that the international reaction to their massive extermination of a foe has been the blocking of all state and personal bank accounts. Since the UN community is experiencing "sanctions fatigue" from dealing with the terrible human costs associated with sanctions in Iraq and the seemingly ineffective use of sanctions in Rwanda and elsewhere, smart sanctions may soon be the only politically viable economic measure the Council invokes.

FINANCIAL SANCTIONS

The centerpiece of any serious targeted sanctions effort lies in the imposition of elite-targeted, financial sanctions. In March 1998, and again at the 1999 meetings at Interlaken, Switzerland, progress was made on formulating the contours of policies that would control the flow of assets and link international institutions in enforcing such controls.

Analysts and practitioners agree that much of the work that needs to be undertaken to bring financial sanctions to reality is of a technical, legal, and administrative kind, with more work to be done to clarify the language, technical, and (in some cases) legal distinctions that exist among various types of financial options. For example, more precision about and differences regarding such terms and processes as blocking assets and freezing assets is needed, as is more clarity regarding the diverse legal standing of these actions in different nations.

Some newer trends of the last decade, notably the increased speed of money made possible by both increased currency convertibility in the post-1989 era and the computerization of international banking technology, may pose particular difficulties for full implementation of targeted financial sanctions. Moreover, the presence of an international money-laundering industry and the related existence of various "safe havens," such as the Cayman Islands, may make it easier to hide money than to find it.

Despite such concerns and cautions, asset control and constraint may be a powerful financial sanction not yet fully utilized. But a substantial agenda of what yet needs to be further investigated exists. The most pressing concern is that the diplomatic and scholarly communities need a shared lexicon, both of the distinctive options that exist for financial sanctions and of what the Security Council might, in fact, choose to impose. In too many nations at this moment, the differences between such terms as "blocking," and "freezing"; "monetary" and "financial"; "assets" and "holdings," to name a few, have very different economic, banking, and legal meanings. So too, from a policy and international law perspective does the difference between targeting public funds and the private accounts of individuals.

Thus, in light of the major differences that exist in national legal control of banks, governments need to develop legislation that synchronizes control and action policies, in order to make any Security Council action effective. Further, it is widely acknowledged that the success of financial sanctions is tied to the speed and discretion with which they can be applied. That such sanctions can now only be imposed after open, and sometimes lengthy, political debate becomes self-defeating. How this fundamental dilemma can be overcome is unclear, but the problem is not insurmountable.

The benefit of such financial tools *vis-à-vis* the genocidal state is that such constraints may deprive leaders of the resources that provide their arms or that guarantee their ability to reward supporters. In particular, many analysts hope that targeting elite assets would cut deeply into the ability of such elites to purchase arms.

ARMS EMBARGOES

Arms embargoes have been rather prominent in sanctions episodes of the past decade, most obviously in cases where the parties are engaged in violent conflict. Arms embargoes are considered by most states to be an important mechanism for accomplishing the dual goals of reducing the real (or potential) level of violence involved in a dispute, and refraining from contributing to the harm embargoes cause civilians. The UN's seriousness with regard to fulfilling this mandate is manifest in a number of ways, but none may be more apparent than the imposition of arms sanctions by the Security Council, in three instances in the 1990s, against subnational entities (UNITA, Khmer Rouge, Bosnian Serbs) in order to halt the progress of civil war and genocidal violence. Certainly in the latter case it failed miserably.

Despite the Council's positive contribution of general support for arms embargoes, sanctions on the international exchange of weapons, ammunition, arms replacement parts, technical advisors, and even of soldiers themselves, continue to pose unique challenges to the UN system. Among the most prominent difficulties encountered in imposing effective arms embargoes are that they require a very high level of national cooperation in transparency, public identification of national violators, and ongoing monitoring. In addition, because of the great economic benefits that accrue to trading states from international arms sales, arms exporters and their resident businesses often consider themselves uncompensated third parties (in an Article 51 sense) who are very negatively affected by Council arms sanctions. Under these conditions, incentives to support the embargoes through self-restraint and other policies are nonexistent.

At least two important actions might be undertaken to strengthen the effectiveness of arms embargoes. Each of these requires additional research and more detailed consideration of implementation strategies by member states of the UN Security Council. First, arms embargoes must be adopted with more tightly crafted specifications regarding the items banned, monitoring compliance of states, interdiction authority, and the specific consequences that ensue if a member state violates the embargo. Secondly, the specific criteria for the removal of an arms embargo must be articulated in the resolution that imposes it. Certain earlier bans on arms were insensitive to real changes in the behavior of targeted groups over time. This has compounded the problem of lack of compliance, as exporters see little resolve to bring closure on events and UN actions even when conditions in a locale have changed.

TRAVEL AND INTERNATIONAL PARTICIPATION BANS

Historically, the Security Council has imposed two types of travel bans: restriction in air travel to and from a targeted state, and restrictions on the travel of targeted individuals. With the latter, individuals may not be "elites" in any economic or political decision-making sense but may be national representatives to international athletic competitions or belong to cultural/entertainment groups. Denial of freedom to participate in international meetings or events brings much of the second travel ban into being.

Certainly such bans by themselves are not expected to provide quick compliance with UN demands. But more than any other form of smart sanctions, these constraining devices have been underinvestigated and their coercive potential has not been fully maximized. In particular, nations such as South Africa, which have suffered under such bans in the past—especially the international sports and cultural restraints—have noted the sense of psychological isolation, the denial of legitimacy, and damaged national pride that accompany such bans. Such realities can take their toll. Travel bans, especially, can move quickly from being matters of inconvenience to matters effecting the economic and diplomatic business of a nation. And in situations of genocide, they can be clear and direct *personal* condemnations of individuals on the basis of their actions.

Although easier to enforce than arms embargoes, travel and participation bans are not without controversy. Among other areas for future research and policy formulation, model Security Council resolutions must fully and appropriately sketch what a travel ban means in operational form for airlines and other forms of transportation. Moreover, a research agenda should also rank highly the need for increased monitoring of travel bans and, often, the need for special sanctions assistance missions, which often comprise are customs officers from member countries.

THE FUTURE AGENDA

Financial mechanisms, arms embargoes, and travel and participation bans are each underutilized as components of a targeted sanctions policy, and may be undervalued due to a lack of full understanding of their efficacy, especially when employed in tandem. More than general trade sanctions, these tools will increase the likelihood that the UN can sting genocidal leaders quickly and *may* force them to dramatically reconsider, if not actually change, their policies.

Although a general air of optimism about smart sanctions prevails among UN members, three issues are now posed—comprising the near-term research and design agenda—that must be addressed if thinking about targeted or smart sanctions is to progress to viable Security Council action in thwarting those bent on genocide. First, nations must recognize that smart sanctions will succeed only if they are part of a strategic design of negotiation and diplomacy with the targeted state. As has often been the case with trade embargoes, when sanctions become *the* policy, they seldom produce the desired results. Secondly, no targeted sanctions approach can succeed without a firm commitment to monitoring, both in the "control of borders" enforcement sense, and in terms of assessing the humanitarian impact of such measures. Finally, UN and member-state technical means of implementation and enforcement are even more critical in these areas than they have been in trade sanctions. But wide variation in institutional capabilities, practices, and preferences means that increased cooperation among members regarding these variations is a must if smart sanctions are to be imposed.

The UN system generally, and the Security Council in particular, face a number of challenges in dealing with members that verge on becoming genocidal states. As these entities often are classified as such because of violent internal conflicts, focused, targeted sanctions have a certain appeal as a means of withdrawing resources from elites bent on genocide. But general trade-based sanctions have produced more state fatigue among Security Council members than they have produced desired results in the target state. And some sanctions cases, as in Council sanctions against Iraq, have been mired in controversy and tragedy because of their adverse impact on the innocent—an impact that some would even label genocide. For these reasons, the time is now ripe for developing a smarter, more targeted sanctions policy than now exists.

NOTES

1. Although he is not a coauthor of this particular chapter, many of the insights in this essay derive from my work with David Cortright over the past eight years. Thus his contribution here is gratefully noted.

2. For a discussion of the rationale behind the increase in use of United Nations sanctions, see George A. Lopez and David Cortright, "The Sanctions Era: An Alternative to Military Intervention," *The Fletcher Forum on World Affairs* 19, No. 2 (Summer/Fall 1995): 65–86. For insights into unilateral sanctions and U.S. sanctions policy in particular, see Richard Haass, *Economic Sanctions and American Diplomacy* (New York: Council on Foreign Relations, 1998).

3. For a discussion of the Burundi case, see Eric Hoskins and Samantha Nutt, "The Humanitarian Impact of Economic Sanctions on Burundi," The Thomas J.

Watson Institute for International Studies, Occasional Paper #29, Brown University, 1997.

4. For a more far-reaching discussion of the role of sanctions in enhancing human rights, see George A. Lopez and David Cortright, "Economic Sanctions and Human Rights: Part of the Solution or Part of the Problem?" *The International Journal of Human Rights* 1, No. 2 (May 1997): 1–25.

5. Gary C. Hufbauer, Jeffery J. Schott, and Kimberly Ann Elliott, *Economic Sanctions Reconsidered: History and Current Policy*, 2d ed. (Washington, DC: Institute for International Economics, 1990).

6. U.S. General Accounting Office. "Economic Sanctions: Effectiveness as Tools of Foreign Policy," report prepared for the Chairman, Committee on Foreign Relations, U.S. Senate, 102nd Cong., 2d sess., 1992, p. 11.

7. See Claudette Antoine Werleigh, "The Use of Sanctions in Haiti: Assessing the Economic Realities," in David Cortwright and George A. Lopez, eds., *Economic Sanctions: Panacea or Peacebuilding in a Post-Cold War World?* (Boulder, CO: Westview Press, 1995), pp. 161–172.

8. Miroslav Nincic and Peter Wallensteen, eds., *Dilemmas of Economic Coercion: Sanctions and World Politics* (New York: Praeger, 1983), p. 109.

9. Hufbauer et al., *Economic Sanctions Reconsidered*, 63ff.

10. Ivan Eland, "Economic Sanctions as Tools," in *Economic Sanctions: Panacea or Peacebuilding in a Post-Cold War World?*, pp. 32–33.

11. U.S. General Accounting Office, "International Trade: Issues Regarding Imposition of an Oil Embargo Against Nigeria," report prepared for the Chairman, Subcommittee on Africa, Committee on Foreign Affairs, U.S. House of Representatives, 103rd Cong., 2d. sess., November 1994, GAO/GGD-95-24, p. 12.

12. See Jennifer Davis, "Sanctions and Apartheid: The Economic Challenge to Discrimination," in *Economic Sanctions: Panacea or Peacebuilding in a Post-Cold War World?*, 173–186.

13. Scott R. Feil. "Preventing Genocide, How the Early Use of Force Might Have Succeeded in Rwanda," Report to the Carnegie Commission on Preventing Deadly Conflict (New York: Carnegie Corporation, 1998).

14. For two accounts of the impact and effectiveness of the UN sanctions on the former Yugoslavia, see Susan L. Woodward, "The Use of Sanctions in Former Yugoslavia: Misunderstanding Political Realities," Economic Sanctions: Panacea or Peacebuilding in a Post-Cold War World?, pp. 141–152; and Julia Devin and Jaleh Dashti-Gibson, "Sanctions in the Former Yugoslavia: Convoluted Goals and Complicated Consequences," in Thomas Weiss et al., eds., *Political Gain and Civilian Pain* (Lanham, MD: Rowman & Littlefield, 1997), pp. 149–198.

15. For a detailed treatment of the various sanctions imposed against the Yugoslav parties, and especially their humanitarian and economic impact, see Julia Devin and Jaleh Dashti-Gibson, "Sanctions in the Former Yugoslavia: Convoluted Goals and Complicated Consequences," in *Political Gain and Civilian Pain*, pp. 149–188.

16. The primary activist group involved in challenging the sanctions against Iraq with these concerns and claims has been the Voices from the Wilderness campaign, whose members also engaged in acts of civil disobedience in protest of U.S. maintenance of restrictions of certain medical goods. These acts primarily entailed "violating" the sanctions by entering Iraq to deliver such goods without an embargo exemption as issued by the U.S. Treasury Department.

17. Sarah Zaidi and Mary C. Smith-Fazi, "Health of Baghdad's Children," *The Lancet* 346, No. 8988 (December 2, 1995): 1485. See also the editorial in the same issue, "Health Effects of Sanctions on Iraq," p. 1439.

18. See Barbara Crossette, "Iraq Sanctions Kill Children, UN Reports," *New York Times*, December 1, 1995, p. A6.

19. CBS Television, "60 Minutes," May 12, 1996.

20. Center for Economic and Social Rights, *UN Sanctioned Suffering: A Human Rights Assessment of United Nations Sanctions on Iraq* (New York: Center for Economic and Social Rights, May 1996), p. 1.

21. For an extensive discussion of the humanitarian impact of sanctions in Iraq and the various controversies surrounding the data that assess this, see Eric Hoskins, "The Humanitarian Impacts of Economic Sanctions and War in Iraq," in Weiss et al., *Political Pain and Civilian Pain*, pp. 91–148; David Cortright and George A. Lopez, "Sanctions and Contending Views of Justice: The Problematic Case of Iraq," *Journal of International Affairs* 52, No. 2 (Spring 1999): 33–53; and David Cortright and George A. Lopez, "Trouble in the Gulf: Pain and Promise," *The Bulletin of the Atomic Scientists* 54, No. 3 (May/June 1998): 39–43.

22. Harvard Study Team, "The Effect of the Gulf Crisis on the Children of Iraq," *New England Journal of Medicine* 325, No. 13 (1991): 977–980.

23. Abbas Alnasrawi, "Does Iraq Have an Economic Future?" *Middle East Executive Reports*, 19, No. 3 (March 1996): 8–18.

24. United Nations, *Report to the Secretary General on Humanitarian Needs in Kuwait and Iraq in the Immediate Post-Crisis Environment by a Mission to the Area Led by Mr. Martti Ahtisaari, Undersecretary General for Administration and Management, Dated 20 March 1991* (New York, 1991).

25. Hoskins, "Humanitarian Impact," in *Political Gain*, p. 30.

26. Ibid., Fig. 5.

27. Food and Agriculture Organization (FAO), *Evaluation of Food and Nutrition Situation, Iraq* (Rome: FAO, October 3, 1997), p. 1.

28. This data controversy is addressed in George A. Lopez and David Cortright, "Trouble in the Gulf: Pain and Promise," *The Bulletin of the Atomic Scientists* 54, No. 3 (May/June 1998): 39–43; and George A. Lopez "The Sanctions Dilemma: Hype Doesn't Help," *Commonweal*, September 11, 1998, pp. 10–12.

5

Can an International Criminal Court Prevent and Punish Genocide?

David Wippman

INTRODUCTION

For more than seventy years, states have worked fitfully towards the creation of a permanent international criminal court. Efforts to create a court in the immediate aftermath of World War II foundered on Cold War disagreements, but the movement gained new life with the collapse of the Soviet Union and the outbreak of large-scale intercommunal violence in the former Yugoslavia and Rwanda. The effort moved closer to fruition in the summer of 1998 when more than 160 states and numerous nongovernmental organizations gathered in Rome to conclude a treaty creating the first permanent international criminal court (ICC) ever.

From the beginning, the drive to create such a court rested in substantial part on the need to prevent and punish the crime of genocide. In the aftermath of World War II, states joined together to transform the motto "never again" into a binding international legal obligation. The result was the 1948 Convention on the Prevention and Punishment of the Crime of Genocide.[1] The Genocide Convention declared that genocide was a crime under international law, and the parties to the Convention undertook, individually and collectively, to "prevent and punish" that crime in the future.

Now as then, the twin goals of prevention and punishment seem unassailable. But the extent to which international courts and conventions can contribute to these two goals in a still decentralized international legal system remains open to question. Although the Genocide Convention was adopted over 50 years ago, the first international criminal tribunals since

Nuremberg were not established until the 1990s, and their first verdict in a genocide case was rendered only in 1998. As the two existing international criminal tribunals (one for Rwanda, the other for former Yugoslavia) work through their dockets, more genocide verdicts in individual cases can be expected. But the numbers are certain to remain small. Moreover, the mandate of each tribunal is limited to a particular place and time, and their impact is therefore necessarily circumscribed.

Advocates of a permanent international criminal court hoped to build on the two existing ad hoc tribunals and to surmount some of their limitations. In the months leading up to the Rome conference, expectations ran high in many quarters. Proponents of the new court routinely described the Rome negotiations as an "historic opportunity to put an end to the impunity granted to those who perpetrate the heinous crimes of genocide, war crimes, and crimes against humanity."[2] The accompanying assumption was that ending impunity would deter the commission of such crimes in the first place.

Such claims may be overstated. Even the best treaty that might fairly have been anticipated to emerge from the Rome negotiations could not, in the reasonably foreseeable future, have accomplished what court boosters hoped to achieve. International courts and prosecutors can contribute to deterring genocide and related crimes and to punishing those who commit them. But ending impunity and eliminating such crimes ultimately requires nothing less than the reshaping of political cultures across the globe, so that politicians cannot see political gain in the turning of one ethnic or religious group against another, and individuals cannot be induced to heed calls for violence against others who differ in race, religion, or nationality.

Of course, if an international court can help even slightly to lessen the frequency or extent of genocidal conflicts, that in itself would be a worthy objective. But the obstacles to even this modest goal should not be underestimated.

First, there are technical problems inherent in the conception and definition of genocide as a crime. By design, the Genocide Convention does not apply to all cases of mass killings, and the specific intent required to establish genocide is often surprisingly difficult to prove.

Second, and more important, the enforcement and compliance issues associated with international law generally are particularly acute in the contexts in which contemporary genocidal violence tends to occur. When the government responsible for genocide remains in power, national prosecutions rarely occur, and international tribunals find it extremely difficult to exact meaningful cooperation in the arrest and prosecution of culpable individuals. On occasion, third states may be able to place enough pressure on a recalcitrant government to force modest cooperation, but only rarely will third states have sufficient incentive to bear the diplomatic and other costs entailed in exerting such pressures, and even then, third state efforts will likely be modest and sporadic. Prospects for meaningful prosecutions are plainly enhanced when the government that is responsible for genocide in a particular case is overthrown, but in such cases, other problems are likely to arise. The newly established government may have its own reasons for resisting a significant role for an international tribunal, or the tribunal may lack the resources or intergovernmental support it needs to do an effective job.

Third, even when an international tribunal is operational and reasonably effective, as is the International Criminal Tribunal for the former Yugoslavia (ICTY), its capacity to deter further offenses, and its ability to prosecute those responsible for offenses that have already occurred, is limited. Although the ICTY began its work while the war in Bosnia was still ongoing, it is hard to demonstrate whether and to what extent its existence worked to deter further crimes, which continued with depressing frequency until NATO forced the parties to accept a negotiated settlement. Similarly, it is uncertain whether and to what extent the tribunal's expressed intention to prosecute those guilty of international criminal offenses committed during the conflict in Kosovo served or will serve to deter further such crimes. In practice, an uncertain risk of future prosecution is simply one factor in the political and personal calculus that surrounds a decision to participate in genocide, crimes against humanity, or war crimes. For these reasons, even the best treaty that might have emerged from the Rome negotiations would not likely have had as much of an impact on the incidence of genocide as advocates have suggested, though it could have reinforced applicable norms and created an institution better suited to the prosecution of genocide and related crimes than any existing international institution.

Unfortunately, the treaty that emerged from Rome was not the best of treaties. The treaty reflects a political compromise crafted to garner the maximum number of votes. From one standpoint, this strategy was successful; the treaty text was adopted by a vote of 120–7, with 21 abstentions. But the cost was heavy. As a concession to governments concerned with state sovereignty issues, the treaty's jurisdictional provisions permit future Pol Pots and Saddam Husseins, leaders willing to commit genocide against their own people, to escape the Court's scrutiny simply by not joining the treaty, so long as those leaders remain in power and confine their atrocities to their own territory.[3] Thus, in the absence of a Security Council referral, there can be no ICC prosecution of some of the world's worst offenders.

At the same time, the treaty's drafters failed to satisfy some of the key concerns of the United States, which has refused to sign the treaty. Whatever one thinks of the positions adopted by the United States during the Rome negotiations, the failure to obtain U.S. support for the Court is a greater blow to the Court's prospects than many realize. Rhetoric aside, the United States has provided the lion's share of the political, financial, diplomatic, and even military support for the two existing international criminal tribunals.[4] It remains to be seen whether other states, individually or collectively, will fill the gap created by the refusal of the United States to join the treaty.

It would be a mistake to conclude that the International Criminal Court envisioned in the Rome treaty cannot contribute significantly to the prevention and punishment of genocide, crimes against humanity, and war crimes. But the work necessary to enable the proposed Court to play that role has only just begun.

CREATING AN INTERNATIONAL CRIMINAL COURT

The creation of the first modern international criminal tribunals, established at Nuremberg and Tokyo after World War II, is commonly celebrated as a defining moment in international law. The Nuremberg tribunal in particular established two fundamental, and in some respects revolutionary, principles: first, that individuals owe a duty to the international community that supersedes any competing obligation to state or group; and second, that those who commit genocide, war crimes, and crimes against humanity can be held individually accountable for their crimes, whether or not they were acting in the service of their governments. In the aftermath of World War II, the UN moved to solidify the still somewhat tenuous legal and institutional bases for international criminal prosecutions. In 1948, the General Assembly promulgated the Genocide Convention, which declared genocide an international crime and envisioned its prosecution in some future international penal tribunal as well as in national courts.[5] In addition, the General Assembly asked the International Law Commission (ILC) "to study the desirability and possibility of establishing an international judicial organ for the trial of persons charged with genocide or other crimes over which jurisdiction will be conferred upon that organ by international conventions."[6] The ILC also began work on a Draft Code of Offenses Against the Peace and Security of Mankind, which was intended to serve as the equivalent of a domestic criminal statute that an international penal tribunal might apply.

On the recommendation of the ILC, the General Assembly in 1950 established a Committee on International Criminal Jurisdiction and directed it to prepare a draft statute for an international criminal court.[7] The Committee submitted an initial draft in 1951, which was revised by a second Committee in 1953. The attempt to create a Court then entered the legal equivalent of suspended animation. Efforts to complete the Draft Code of Crimes, once thought vital to the work of a permanent international criminal court, ran aground on the rock of aggression. States could not agree on a definition, and even though the General Assembly finally adopted a definition in 1947, the controversy effectively derailed efforts to create a court.[8] Thereafter, the forward momentum generated by revulsion at the Holocaust began to dissipate, and Cold War tensions blocked any further progress for more than thirty-five years.

In 1989, as the Cold War came to a close, interest in a permanent international criminal court revived. Trinidad and Tobago, heading up a group of sixteen Caribbean and Latin American states seeking a mechanism to address their own difficulties in prosecuting narcotics traffickers, resuscitated the issue in the General Assembly.[9] At their request, the General Assembly instructed the ILC to resume its work on an international criminal court.

The ILC's efforts acquired greater urgency with the outbreak of war and "ethnic cleansing" in the former Yugoslavia. In 1993, the UN Security Council voted to establish an ad hoc international criminal tribunal to prosecute genocide, crimes against humanity and war crimes arising out of that conflict.[10] That tribunal provided a helpful model for, and a strong impetus to, the continuing work of the ILC. Most important, the creation of the Yugoslavia tribunal demonstrated that the legal and political obstacles long standing in the way of an international penal tribunal could be satisfactorily overcome.[11] In 1994, the ILC submitted a draft statute for a permanent court to the General Assembly, and recommended that an international conference be convened to adopt the statute by treaty.[12] The General Assembly established an Ad Hoc Committee on the Establishment of an International Criminal Court to consider the ILC's draft statute, and then a Preparatory Committee to incorporate comments from states and other interested parties into a consolidated draft text. The Preparatory Committee completed a consolidated draft text in April 1998, paving the way for a UN Diplomatic Conference of Plenipotentiaries on the Establishment of an International Criminal Court, held in Rome from June 15 to July 17, 1998. At the end of a frenetic five weeks, and following vigorous debate, the Rome conference adopted a statute for an international criminal court in a celebratory atmosphere.

The Need for an International Criminal Court

By the commencement of the Rome conference, there was a fairly broad consensus among states, NGOs, and academics on the need for a permanent international criminal court. By 1998, the two existing international criminal tribunals had demonstrated both the feasibility of contemporary international criminal prosecutions and the limits of ad hoc tribunals created for particular situations. Prior to the creation of the Yugoslavia tribunal, many commentators doubted the efficacy of an international tribunal that lacked the obvious situational advantages enjoyed by the Nuremberg and Tokyo tribunals. Both the latter tribunals were established in the wake of the defeat and occupation of enemy states, and had the luxury of access to the evidence and suspects under the control of the occupying powers, the states most interested in pursuing prosecutions for war crimes and crimes against humanity. By contrast, the warring parties responsible for genocide and other crimes in the course of the conflict in Bosnia did not suffer complete military defeat and occupation by forces committed to prosecuting the principal offenders. Although NATO forces deployed to Bosnia in support of the Dayton accord occasionally arrested indicted suspects, their presence is hardly comparable to the occupation of Germany and Japan at the close of World War II. Accordingly, it has been apparent from the outset that the Yugoslavia tribunal would have to rely to a large extent on the cooperation of a number of states and nonstate entities with varying degrees of interest in criminal prosecutions.

Nonetheless, the ICTY has had considerable success in indicting and trying individuals accused of committing war crimes and other atrocities in the former Yugoslavia. Of course, many of the most senior officials sought by the tribunal remain at large, including Slobodan Milosevic, Radovan Karadzic, and Ratko Mladic. But the risk of prosecution has at least forced Karadzic and Mladic to surrender most of the political power they wielded in Bosnia, and each lives under the fear of eventual arrest and surrender to the tribunal.[13] Moreover, although the total number of individuals actually indicted by the ICTY remains small in relation to the number of individuals who participated in the commission of atrocities, public prosecution of even a representative sampling can reinforce the applicable international norms, advance the rule of law, and perhaps even help promote reconciliation in the affected states.

The International Criminal Tribunal for Rwanda (ICTR) has had a more difficult life, even though the forces principally responsible for atrocities in that country were routed on the battlefield. Among other problems, the tribunal's own internal administrative difficulties have seriously impeded its work. Nonetheless, the ICTR has made considerable progress in recent months, and in September 1998, with the conviction of Jean Paul Akayesu, a prominent former Rwandan government official, the ICTR became the first international tribunal ever to render a verdict in a genocide case.

Thus, the operation of the two existing tribunals demonstrated the feasibility of contemporary international criminal prosecutions, even for crimes committed in predominantly internal conflicts. At the same time, the establishment and day-to-day operations of the two tribunals highlighted the problems of ad hoc criminal courts. Creating, staffing, and funding an international criminal court is a complex and difficult endeavor. In each case, the Security Council had to reach consensus on the need for a Court, agree on its mandate, find judges, prosecutors, investigators and staff with suitable experience, locate or construct appropriate facilities, reach agreements with host states, and confront numerous other obstacles. The process is lengthy, difficult, and expensive.

A permanent international criminal court could obviate many of these problems. As a standing body, it would not be necessary to recreate the human and material infrastructure necessary for international criminal trials every time different conflicts come under scrutiny. The Court would be available to handle cases involving genocide and related crimes whether referred to it by the Security Council or in accordance with alternate referral procedures set out in the treaty establishing the Court.

Theoretically, a permanent court could also be set up in a way that eliminates or at least substantially reduces the problem of selectivity many see as inherent in the establishment of ad hoc tribunals. Although it is easy to offer political explanations for establishing tribunals for Rwanda and Yugoslavia, but not, for example, for Sudan or Afghanistan, it is hard to conceive of legal or philosophical justifications. In practice, however, selectivity turns out to be difficult to avoid, and, for reasons discussed below, was not avoided in the Rome treaty.

Nonetheless, most if not all of the 160 states gathered in Rome believed the institutional continuity and the symbolism of a permanent court justified the work and expense required to establish it. In addition, a standing court may obviate the problem of "tribunal fatigue."[14] The cost of ad hoc tribunals, both financial and political, makes it problematic to resort continually to the Security Council to seek the creation of new tribunals for each conflict warranting the prosecution of genocide and other crimes. It is easier to refer situations to a standing tribunal than to create a new one from scratch.

Perhaps the strongest argument in favor of a permanent international criminal court is that it may help deter the commission of future atrocities. The unfortunate historical fact is that most perpetrators of genocide and other heinous crimes have gone unpunished. The military tribunals established in the aftermath of World War II prosecuted only a small fraction of those responsible for genocidal acts, and many of the worst offenders were never brought to justice. Similarly, only a tiny fraction of those responsible for crimes against humanity and war crimes in Bosnia and Rwanda will likely ever be indicted by an international tribunal, and fewer still will be brought to trial. As unfortunate as this relative impunity is, the situation in other cases has been even worse. In Cambodia, for example, Pol Pot and the Khmer Rouge wiped out as many as two million people, but so far there have been no criminal prosecutions for genocide or related offenses.[15] Regrettably, impunity in contemporary (and past) conflicts is not the exception, but the rule. Hundreds of thousands of noncombatants have been murdered under the most horrifying circumstances in recent conflicts, from Afghanistan to Chechnya to the Sudan, but prosecutions are rare. One reason for the dearth of prosecutions is that in the absence of any international penal tribunal with jurisdiction over such crimes, the only alternative is to rely on national courts. Unfortunately, such courts are often under the control or influence of the governments or military forces responsible for precisely the kinds of offenses that should be prosecuted.

The establishment of an ad hoc international criminal tribunal may remedy this problem in part. Although there is little empirical evidence to show that international criminal prosecutions deter further atrocities, anecdotal evidence suggests such prosecutions have at least some deterrent effect. But by the time it becomes sufficiently apparent that a tribunal is needed, and the political consensus necessary for the Security Council to act is generated, many of the atrocities one might hope to deter through the threat of prosecution may already have taken place. Sadly, this has been the case in both Rwanda and former Yugoslavia.[16] Moreover, the delays attendant on the creation of an ad hoc tribunal may allow suspects time to go into hiding, and may lead to the disappearance of witnesses and the deterioration or destruction of physical evidence. Advocates of a permanent international criminal court have long contended that such a court may help deter genocidal and other atrocities before a conflict even begins, in addition to facilitating the prosecution of offenders after a genocidal conflict starts. As Hans Corell, United Nations Under Secretary-General for Legal Affairs optimistically observed, "from now on, all potential warlords must know that, depending on how a conflict develops, there might be established an international tribunal before which those will be brought who violate the laws of war and humanitarian law."[17]

VISIONS OF A PERMANENT INTERNATIONAL CRIMINAL COURT

The concept of an international criminal court evolved dramatically in the years leading up to the adoption of the Rome treaty. In 1992, a Working Group of the International Law Commission suggested that the Court should be a part-time "flexible and supplementary facility" that would give states parties an alternative to trying offenders in national courts or extraditing them to another state.[18] Over the next two years, the Working Group prepared and refined a draft statute that expanded the powers of the Court but retained a focus on creating an institution that would try cases when national court jurisdiction might be unavailable or ineffective. For the court to exercise jurisdiction over crimes against humanity or war crimes, the draft statute required either a referral by the Security Council or the joint consent of the state on the territory of which the crime was committed and the state with custody over the accused. The statute contained a more liberal jurisdictional provision for genocide. Under the ILC's proposal, the Court could exercise its "inherent jurisdiction" on the basis of a referral by any state party that was also a party to the Genocide Convention, on the theory that the Convention expressly contemplates referral of genocide cases to an international penal tribunal.

As the negotiations in Rome began, sharp differences emerged among delegations concerning the scope of the Court's jurisdiction and the "trigger mechanism" for the exercise of that jurisdiction (i.e., the means by which crimes within the Court's jurisdiction would be referred to it for prosecution). Most participating NGOs, which were represented in force in Rome and which played a leading role in the negotiations (some NGO representatives even appeared on and effectively led the delegations from certain smaller states), wanted to maximize the scope of the Court's jurisdiction and minimize the obstacles to invocation of that jurisdiction. In particular, most NGOs favored automatic jurisdiction over the "core crimes" of genocide, crimes against humanity, and war crimes, so that all treaty parties would be subject to the Court's jurisdiction over those crimes without any need for further state consent. Similarly, NGOs supported "universal jurisdiction" over the core crimes, to permit the Court to prosecute such crimes no matter where they might have been committed. Nongovernmental organizations strongly opposed any provision that would require either UN Security Council approval for prosecutions or the consent of particular states, such as the state of nationality of the accused. Further, NGOs vigorously supported an independent, self-initiating prosecutor able to commence prosecutions on his or her own authority (including on the basis of information supplied by NGOs), without having to rely on referrals by individual states or by the Security Council.

A broad group of predominantly western states, including Canada and most of western Europe, supported most of the NGO positions, though with varying degrees of qualification. This so-called "Like-Minded Group" formed the core of international political support for what proponents viewed as a strong treaty.

The views of the nonaligned states are harder to characterize, and varied widely depending on the specific issue under discussion. Many nonaligned states had reason to be concerned about a Court with an inherent jurisdiction broad enough to encompass the investigation and prosecution of crimes that occur within a state's own territory in the course of an internal conflict. A significant number, led by India, wanted to include the threat or use of nuclear weapons as a war crime. Many Arab states wanted the definition of war crimes to include language concerning the treatment of populations in occupied territory that would permit them to characterize Israeli settlement policies and other actions in the occupied territories as criminal. Although some of the positions advocated by nonaligned states were anathema to the like-minded governments (and to NGOs), the differences were ultimately resolved through some fairly direct bargaining, which resulted in a statute both groupings could support.

In one of the great ironies of the Rome process, the bargaining between like-minded and some nonaligned states was driven to a considerable extent by opposition to positions advanced by the United States. The United States came to Rome with an agenda different in significant respects from many of its closest allies. Initially, the United States saw the Court primarily as a standing body that would reduce the time and expense required to set up ad hoc tribunals with every additional Bosnia or Rwanda, but which in other respects would operate much as the two existing tribunals have done. In particular, the United States argued that the Security Council should be the body to refer situations to the Court for prosecution.[19] In addition, the United States strongly opposed universal jurisdiction, arguing that the effort to give the Court jurisdiction over the nationals of non-party states for official acts amounted to an attempt to bind states to treaty provisions to which they had not consented, in violation of the most fundamental rules of treaty law.[20]

Although the United States position on referral of cases to the Court resembled a prior ILC proposal in many respects, by the time of the Rome Conference few other states were prepared to accept a Security Council veto over the Court's ability to exercise its jurisdiction. Like-minded governments and NGOs saw the United States position as an unwarranted interference with the independence of the Court and its prosecutor. They feared that individual permanent members of the Council would use the veto to block prosecution of their own nationals and the nationals of their allies. Many nonaligned states strongly opposed any role for the Security Council, viewing it as a western-dominated forum in which they exercised little or no influence. Moreover, many states strongly supported universal jurisdiction or some variation that would permit the court to exercise jurisdiction over the nationals of non-party states, for the simple reason that states might otherwise escape the Court's jurisdiction by refusing to ratify the treaty.

As the conference wore on, the United States modified its position on the Security Council by signaling its willingness to accept the so-called "Singapore option," which gave the Security Council the right to suspend prosecutions that might interfere with ongoing Council efforts to manage particular situations. The United States also indicated its willingness to accept automatic jurisdiction over genocide, but pressed for the right to opt out of the Court's jurisdiction over crimes against humanity and war crimes for a period of ten years. The United States continued to oppose universal jurisdiction, but suggested consideration of a provision that would preclude the Court from prosecuting nationals of non-parties for crimes committed in the course of official duties acknowledged as such by the state.[21]

STRIKING A BARGAIN

The shifts in the U.S. position proved to be too little, too late. In a frenzy of last-minute deal making, much of it conducted behind closed doors by the small group of states primarily responsible for the coordination and production of the final draft text, a proposed statute was produced with only a matter of hours left before the final vote was scheduled to take place. The statute that emerged, if ratified by the requisite 60 states, would lead to the establishment of a permanent Court with automatic jurisdiction over genocide, crimes against humanity, and war crimes.[22] Prosecutions could be initiated on referral from the Security Council, states parties, or the prosecutor acting on his or her own initiative, provided in the latter two cases that *either* the state on whose territory the alleged crime was committed *or* the state of nationality of the accused consented to the court's jurisdiction. The Security Council is authorized to suspend a prosecution for a period of twelve months. Nationals of non-party states are subject to prosecution, provided that the jurisdictional requirements noted above are satisfied.

As last-ditch efforts to amend the text were voted down at the closing plenary, many delegates to the conference clapped and cheered. Even the most optimistic recognized that much work remained to be done. Critical issues relating to funding, the definition of aggression, and the specification of the elements of particular crimes were left for future resolution. But for the celebrants, the long struggle to create an international criminal court had finally come to a successful conclusion.

It is too soon, however, to declare the effort to create an international criminal court a success. There is a large difference between a strong treaty and a strong court, and, as discussed below, it is doubtful in any event that the treaty as adopted can be fairly characterized as strong.

DEFINITIONAL HURDLES

To avoid a divisive debate over the definition and elements of the crime of genocide, the drafters of the ICC treaty adopted verbatim the definition contained in the 1948 Genocide Convention. That definition contains at least two inherent weaknesses.[23] First, the Convention deliberately excludes from its reach attempts to destroy political or social groups. Under the Convention, genocide entails any of a series of harmful acts, but only if committed with "intent to destroy, in whole or in part, *a national, ethnical, racial or religious* group, as such."[24] Some of the most egregious cases of mass slaughter in recent memory might not qualify as genocide under that definition. For example, Pol Pot and the Khmer Rouge's murderous assault on their fellow Cambodians, because it did not focus on any particular national, ethnic, racial or religious group, arguably falls outside the definition of genocide.[25] Moreover, determining whether a particular group constitutes a national, ethnic, racial, or religious group poses, at least in theory, contentious issues of group identification and definition.

Second, the Convention definition requires proof of an intent to destroy the group as such, whether in whole or in part. Thus, in addition to demonstrating that an accused intended to commit one of the Convention's predicate acts, such as killing or otherwise causing serious harm to members of the group, prosecutors must also show that the accused was aware of and intended to further a larger policy of genocide, or, at a minimum, that the accused was aware of the larger political context in which his or her predicate act might have been facilitated by or might have furthered a policy or practice of genocide.

Proving the requisite intent is difficult. As Cherif Bassiouni points out, "while this type of intent is more readily identifiable in leaders or decision-makers, it is not always easily demonstrated with respect to the different layers or levels of executors of the policy."[26] Intent can be inferred from contextual evidence, including factors such as "the general context of the perpetration of other culpable acts systematically directed against" a targeted group, "the scale of atrocities committed, their general nature . . . [or] the fact of deliberately and systematically targeting victims on account of their membership in a particular group, while excluding the members of other groups."[27]

Nonetheless, the difficulty of proving specific intent is great enough that prosecutors often shy away from pursuing charges of genocide in favor of more easily demonstrable charges of crimes against humanity and war crimes. Thus, the Office of the Prosecutor for the Yugoslavia tribunal has only occasionally included genocide among the charges brought against the perpetrators of atrocities in the Yugoslav conflicts, and the tribunal has yet to render a verdict of guilty of genocide. As of December 6, 1999, the Rwanda tribunal has rendered six verdicts for the crime of genocide. A recent decision (against Georges Rutaganda) involved life imprisonment for genocide and crimes against humanity.

In some respects, it might be counted as a victory for international humanitarian law that the definition of genocide in the ICC statute is exactly the same as that found in the 1948 Convention. In contrast, the drafters of the statute consciously adopted definitions of crimes against humanity and war crimes more restrictive than those found in other international law instruments. Something similar might easily have happened to the definition of genocide. Still, retaining the 1948 definition perpetuates all the definitional and evidentiary hurdles associated with that definition.

FLAWS IN THE ICC STATUTE

More serious constraints on the effectiveness of the court lie in some of its more controversial provisions, especially those relating to the Court's jurisdiction, and the reactions of individual states, particularly the United States, to those provisions. These constraints may be exacerbated—or ameliorated—by the ultimate resolution of issues that proved too complex or too contentious to decide in Rome, but which are the subjects of the work of a Preparatory Committee established pursuant to a November 1998 resolution of the UN's Sixth Committee.

Problems with the Court's Jurisdiction

As noted earlier, last-minute deal-making produced a jurisdictional regime that fell short of the universal jurisdiction supported by NGOs and some of the "like-minded" states, but that went too far for the United States to support. In some respects, the outcome is the worst of all worlds.

On the one hand, the jurisdictional reach of the court is too narrow. Because jurisdiction requires the consent of the state on whose territory the alleged crime is committed or the state of nationality of the accused, a sitting government can frustrate the Court's exercise of its inherent jurisdiction by the simple expedient of refusing to join the treaty or to consent ad hoc to the prosecution of its nationals for crimes committed on that state's territory. In other words, as the United States has often pointed out, a future Saddam Hussein or Pol Pot can easily escape prosecution for crimes committed on the territory of their home state, in the absence of a Security Council referral. This problem of underinclusion is a serious one, because the vast majority of contemporary cases of genocide, crimes against humanity, and war crimes take place in internal conflicts, and because the governments most likely to order or to tolerate such crimes are precisely the governments least likely to consent to the Court's jurisdiction.

On occasion, the problem might be overcome by Security Council action, pursuant to article 13 of the treaty. But Russian and Chinese support for referral of situations to the Court some years hence is uncertain at best. And ironically, U.S. support is also uncertain. Although it is impossible to predict with confidence the posture the United States will adopt toward the Court in future administrations, it is certainly possible, for reasons elaborated more fully below, that the United States might, in a given situation, block Security Council action.[28]

In some cases, replacement of the regime in power at the time the offenses are committed may permit the state involved to consent to the Court's jurisdiction. The government that assumed power in Rwanda following the 1994 massacres has cooperated with the ICTR, notwithstanding significant concerns about the slow pace of the tribunal's proceedings and its inability to mete out the death penalty (a penalty applied to Rwandans convicted of genocide and other crimes in national courts). In other cases, a change of regime is no guarantee that a state will cooperate with the Court. In Cambodia, for example, the fall of the Pol Pot regime has yet to lead to any genocide prosecutions, international or domestic. In other countries, such as El Salvador, regime changes have been accompanied by amnesties and truth commissions rather than wide-ranging criminal prosecutions. For these reasons, the treaty will not reach some of the worst violators of international humanitarian law.

On the other hand, the treaty's reach is in some respects too broad. The treaty permits the Court to assert jurisdiction over nationals of non-party states, if they commit covered crimes in another state and that state consents to the court's jurisdiction. Although it is a basic principle of treaty law that treaties do not bind non-parties, the legal justification for this approach is that the treaty does not confer jurisdiction over non-party states, but rather over their nationals, and under circumstances that would permit the territorial state to exercise jurisdiction itself. Because the state on whose territory the crime at issue has been committed could itself prosecute the offender, that state arguably has the power to delegate the authority to prosecute to the tribunal, either ad hoc or by virtue of joining the treaty. The validity of this delegation theory is uncertain. The Nuremberg tribunal was established by virtue of a treaty among the four victorious powers at the close of World War II, but the legal justification for the exercise of authority over German nationals rested in part on the fact that the creators of the tribunal were also the occupying powers in Germany, and therefore in a position to claim the right to administer courts of justice in lieu of national courts.

It could be argued that application of the treaty to nationals of a non-party state amounts to the application of the treaty to the state itself, at least insofar as the acts under consideration reflect the policy of the state, and therefore violates the principle that treaties do not bind non-parties.[29] Whether or not one accepts this argument, the problem posed by application of the treaty to non-party nationals for countries such as the United States is clear. Although it is highly unlikely that U.S. military action abroad might bring charges of genocide, it is not at all improbable that such action might generate charges of crimes against humanity or war crimes or (depending on the outcome of continuing negotiations) aggression. As a practical matter, a decision by an international criminal court to prosecute such charges, or even to investigate them, would be highly problematic from a U.S. foreign policy standpoint. The United States has international security interests and responsibilities that require it to deploy troops abroad in a wider range of situations and for a broader variety of purposes than any other country. It is therefore difficult for the United States, practically and politically, to accept the constraints on deployment of forces that might stem from the possibility of an international criminal prosecution for official government actions.

During the negotiations on the ICC treaty, the United States attempted to secure provisions in the treaty that would preclude such prosecutions. Other states refused to accept such provisions, arguing that any protections afforded to the United States would necessarily also insulate the nationals of other states from prosecution, including the egregious offenders that all delegates to the conference agreed should be the focus of the Court.[30] In addition, other states argued that the treaty's complementary provisions would afford adequate protection from any unwarranted international prosecution. Article 17 of the treaty, which is based on the principle of complementarity, requires the Court to defer to national prosecutions of individuals accused of treaty crimes, provided that the state conducting the prosecution is genuinely able and willing to do so and is not engaged in a sham proceeding for the purpose of protecting the offender. Thus, if a U.S. soldier was accused of committing a crime covered by the ICC treaty, the United States could forestall an international prosecution by trying that soldier in a U.S. court. Although this is an important protection against politicized prosecutions, the United States viewed it as inadequate for at least two reasons. First, the Court retains the final authority to determine whether the prosecution at issue is in fact genuine. Second, and more troubling, complementarity does not protect a state that engages in a particular action (e.g. a military strike against a particular target) that the state reasonably believes is legitimate under international humanitarian law but that the Court or the Prosecutor believes is not legitimate.

Any military conflict of significant magnitude is likely to generate instances in which observers after the fact disagree on the propriety of a particular target, the necessity of a particular use of force, the legal status of a particular weapon, or the proportionality of a particular action. Although prosecutors might be expected to avoid close cases when there is an abundance of obvious humanitarian law violations to pursue, a prosecutor seeking "balance" in the work of the Court might well choose to prosecute close cases involving the United States.

Other states, including some of the United States' closest allies, worked hard to persuade the United States that the risk of such prosecutions was minimal, and that it was an unavoidable feature of a court that needed the authority to prosecute nationals of nonconsenting states in order to be more than just a standing court for cases referred by the Security Council. The United States, concerned about the possible implications of international criminal prosecutions for official actions whether undertaken in peacekeeping, peace enforcement, or other conflict situations, disagreed.

The net result, from the U.S. perspective, was doubly unfortunate. Hypothetically, at least, a future Saddam Hussein could escape prosecution for genocide committed on his own territory, while conferring jurisdiction on the ICC to prosecute U.S. peacekeepers sent in to end that same genocide.

Problems with Amendments

Under the amendment procedures stipulated in the treaty, parties to the treaty may expand the list of crimes within the Court's jurisdiction. In what has been justified post hoc as an incentive for treaty ratification, the treaty permits parties to exempt their nationals from the Court's jurisdiction over newly added crimes, even though no such exemption is available for nationals of non-parties.[31] The result is difficult to defend on any principled basis, since there is no substantive reason why nationals of a state that is party to the treaty should be exempt from the Court's jurisdiction for a crime for which nationals of a state that is not party to the treaty would be prosecuted. The incentive argument borders on diplomatic blackmail. States that do not wish to have their nationals subject to the Court's jurisdiction at all are told that they must join the treaty in order to minimize its application to their nationals. (The provision in article 124 of the statute permitting parties—but not non-parties—to opt out of the Court's jurisdiction over war crimes for a period of seven years works in much the same way.)

The ability of party states to exempt their nationals from the effects of an amendment dilutes an important constraint on what amounts to an international legislative power. Ordinarily, states through treaties "legislate" only for themselves and are constrained in their actions by the reciprocal effects of any treaty. The ICC treaty allows party states to create new crimes that will apply to conduct by nationals of non-party states, and to do so through a voting process in which dissenting party states need not worry that newly legislated crimes will apply to them. Thus, for example, two thirds of the members of the Assembly of States Parties might choose to outlaw the use of antipersonnel mines or nuclear weapons, leading to a prosecution of nationals of the United States for violations for which nationals of at least some treaty parties could not themselves be held liable. In this scenario, treaty parties that could ordinarily be expected to oppose vigorously any effort to outlaw such weapons would have a much weaker incentive to do so, given their ability to exempt themselves from the new provision's application.

All of this has no direct bearing on the crime of genocide, since that is already one of the core crimes of the treaty and not likely, in its essentials, to be the subject of an amendment in the foreseeable future. But the amendment process constitutes another feature of the treaty likely to provoke the opposition of states whose cooperation or at least acquiescence is vital to the effective operation of the Court, whether now or in the future. Certainly, the United States has identified the amendment provision as one of the principal flaws of the treaty.

THE EFFECT OF U.S. NONPARTICIPATION

Whether or not U.S. concerns are exaggerated, as many critics have argued, is almost beside the point. The United States has made clear that there is no prospect that it will sign the treaty in its present form. Even if a future administration chose to sign the treaty, the chances that the Senate would ratify it in the foreseeable future are negligible at best. Senator Helms, Chairman of the influential Senate Foreign Relations Committee, has taken various opportunities to announce his implacable opposition to the treaty, and has suggested a number of coercive measures the United States could take in opposition to it.[32] More surprising, there is little support for the treaty even among Democrats in Congress.[33]

Unfortunately, past experience suggests that the capacity of the proposed Court to serve as an effective vehicle for the prevention and punishment of genocide rests in significant part on the cooperation and support of the United States. The United States took the lead role in the initiation, organization, and operation of the two existing international criminal tribunals. More than any other state, the United States has supplied the political impetus, the funding, the intelligence information, and on occasion the military muscle needed by the tribunals, especially the Yugoslavia tribunal, for their existence and day-to-day functioning.

Where will the ICC find comparable support? It is possible that the European states who have championed the present ICC statute will step up to the plate in the absence of the United States and provide the political and financial support needed for an effective tribunal. But there is considerable room for doubt.

Funding for the Court is particularly problematic. Many treaty signatories favor UN funding, at least for the large start-up costs associated with creating a permanent institution of this magnitude. The United States, faced with legislation prohibiting support for treaty bodies created under treaties to which the United States is not a party, strongly opposes funding from the regular UN budget, and is likely to reduce its payments to the UN by any amount assessed for the Court (except perhaps for amounts associated with situations referred to the Court by the Security Council). If the Court is to live up to the aspirations of its supporters, it will cost far more than either of the existing international tribunals, which have mandates limited to specific conflicts. Whether other states will fund the Court at levels adequate for effective performance of its functions remains to be seen.

Political support for the Court is equally vital. Its ability to obtain cooperation, even from treaty parties, in acquiring evidence and custody of suspects requires active assistance from the countries directly involved in particular cases. In many instances, the countries most involved are also the most reluctant to cooperate. Chile's vigorous objections to the arrest of General Pinochet suggest that a proposition attractive to many states in the abstract—that all accused of genocide and crimes against humanity should be brought to trial even if their home country objects—may, for at least some countries, lose some of its luster in the context of actual cases. In such cases, only broad international support for the Court is likely to be able to overcome a state's reluctance to cooperate.

In turn, the Court's ability to shape international humanitarian law, and, more important, to act as a deterrent to the commission of crimes within the Court's jurisdiction, depend on adequate financing and political support. If the Court can prosecute only the occasional case, the deterrent value of the threat of prosecution obviously diminishes. Moreover, sporadic decisions by a Court without broad international support can have only limited effect on the future direction of international humanitarian law.

FUTURE PROSPECTS

The danger that emerges from the inability to achieve a consensus in Rome that included major states such as the United States, China, and India is that the Court will lack both the broad international legitimacy and the political, financial, and logistical support the Court needs to be truly effective. If the Court is to realize its potential, it will need to convince the skeptics that it can operate effectively and (within reason) apolitically. Supporters anticipate that actual operation of the Court will alleviate many of the doubts expressed by the United States and others. They note that the overwhelming majority voted in favor of the Court's statute in Rome, and predict that ratification by the requisite sixty states will come within a few years.

Although the Rome treaty may indeed come into force in the next few years, it is less apparent that in the short term it will command the support of the states most important to its success. While most European and other western democratic states are likely to ratify the treaty in the relatively near future, these are not the states in which the covered crimes are most likely to occur. Moreover, while a significant number of states with shabby human rights records are among the signatories of the Court's statute, it is as yet unclear whether such states will actually ratify the Rome treaty, or cooperate with the Court even if they do ratify.

Of course, to say that the Court will not be all that it could be is not to say that its creation is not an important step in the effort to prevent and punish genocide and related crimes. At a minimum, creation of the Court may help constrain future *genocidaires* and war criminals in their foreign travels, lest they be arrested and extradited to stand trial before the Court. Moreover, when those responsible for the statute's core crimes lose power in their home states, new governments in those states may turn to the Court for assistance in prosecutions. In other situations, the Security Council may choose to refer matters to the Court, as an alternative to creating new ad hoc tribunals. Perhaps most important, countries in transition, that is, countries seeking to leave behind a history of violent political conflict and egregious human rights abuses by adoption of democratic political institutions and norms, may find that ratification of the statute helps protect their gains by sending a message to some of the worst elements in their societies that certain kinds of crimes will not be tolerated in the future.

Still, it is hard not to conclude that the Rome negotiations fell substantially short of what might have been achieved.[34] How far short, time alone will tell. Much depends on whether the concerns of the United States and other key countries can ultimately be satisfied.

NOTES

1. 78 United Nations Treaty Series 277, entered into force December 9, 1948.
2. Statement by the International Commission of Jurists at the Plenary Session of the Rome conference, quoted in 4 The Rome Treaty Conference Monitor (http://www.igc.apc.org/icc/rome/html/rome_monitor/4/rmon4.htm).

3. See David J. Scheffer, "America's Stake in Peace, Security and Justice," *American Society of International Law Newsletter* (September–October 1998).

4. David J. Scheffer, "U.S. Policy on International Criminal Tribunals," *American University Journal of International Law* 13 (1998).

5. Genocide Convention, *supra* note 1, article VI ("Persons charged with genocide or any of the other acts enumerated in article III shall be tried by a competent tribunal of the State in the territory of which the act was committed, or by such international penal tribunal as may have jurisdiction with respect to those Contracting Parties which shall have accepted its jurisdiction").

6. General Assembly Resolution 260 (1948).

7. General Assembly Resolution 489(V) (1950).

8. See Jordan Paust, M. Cherif Bassiouni, Sharon Williams, Michael Scharf, Jimmy Gurule, and Bruce Zagaris, *International Criminal Law: Cases and Materials* (Durham, NC: Carolina Academic Press, 1996), at 845.

9. See Leila Sadat Wexler, "The Proposed International Criminal Court: An Appraisal," *Cornell International Law Journal* 29, 683 note 112 (1996).

10. Security Council Resolution (1993).

11. See Paust et al., *International Criminal Law*, at 847.

12. Report of the International Law Commission, UN GAOR, 49th Sess., Supp. No. 10, UN Doc. A/49/10 (1994).

13. United States Department of State Press Briefing, April 9, 1998 (http://secretary.state.gov/www/briefings).

14. Coalition for an International Criminal Court, *Overview* (http://www.un.org/icc/overview.htm).

15. See Seth Mydans, "Cambodian Leader Resists Punishing Top Khmer Rouge," *New York Times*, December 29, 1998, p. A1.

16. See David J. Scheffer, *Genocide and Crimes Against Humanity: Early Warning and Prevention*, Address at the Holocaust Museum, December 10, 1998 (www.state.gov/www/policy_remarks).

17. Quoted in *Background and Information* (http://www.un.org/icc/overview.htm).

18. Report of the Working Group on the question of an international criminal jurisdiction, Report of the International Law Commission, 44th Session, 74 UN G.A.O.R., Supp. No. 10, annex, at 162, UN Doc. A/47/10.

19. David J. Scheffer, Address before the Carter Center, November 13, 1997 (http://www.state.gov/www/policy_remarks/971113_scheffer_tribunal.html).

20. Statement of David J. Scheffer before the Committee on Foreign Relations of the United States Senate, July 23, 1998.

21. Ibid., see also Theodor Meron, "The Court We Want," *The Washington Post*, October 13, 1998, p. A15.

22. Rome Statute of the International Criminal Court, A/CONF.183/9 (July 17, 1998).

23. See generally Lori F. Damrosch, "Genocide and Ethnic Conflict," in David Wippman, ed. *International Law and Ethnic Conflict* (Ithaca, NY: Cornell University Press, 1998), p. 256.

24. Genocide Convention, article II (emphasis added).

25. See Steven R. Ratner and Jason S. Abrams, *Accountability for Human Rights*

Atrocities in International Law: Beyond the Nuremberg Legacy (Oxford: Clarendon Press, 1997), pp. 243–253.

26. Cherif Bassiouni, *Crimes Against Humanity in International Criminal Law* (Boston: Lumer Academic Publishers, 1992).

27. Prosecutor vs. Jean-Paul Akayesu, Case No. ICTR-96–4-T, 6.3.2, September 2, 1998.

28. Senator Jesse Helms, Chairman of the Senate Foreign Relations Committee, has already stated his intent to seek assurances from the Clinton administration that the United States will never vote in favor of referring a situation to the Court. See Jesse Helms, "We Must Slay This Monster," *Financial Times*, July 21, 1998, p. 18.

29. See Scheffer, *supra* note 20.

30. See Phillipe Kirsch, "The Rome Conference on the International Criminal Court: A Comment," *American Society of International Law Newsletter* (November–December 1998).

31. Under article 121 of the Court's statute, a two-thirds majority of the parties to the statute may amend the statute to provide for jurisdiction over additional crimes beyond those now contained in the Court's statute. Parties may choose to opt out of the Court's jurisdiction over those additional crimes, but that choice is not available to non-parties.

32. Helms, "We Must Slay This Monster."

33. See Ruth Wedgwood, "Fiddling in Rome: America and the ICC," *Foreign Affairs* 76, No. 6 (December 1998).

34. Many states and NGOs, though not fully satisfied with the Rome treaty, nonetheless view it as a historic step forward. In their view, the Court envisioned by the treaty will help establish the rule of law internationally, promote stability and peace, and deter genocide, crimes against humanity, and war crimes. Indeed, many argue that the United States would be among the principal beneficiaries of the new Court. See, for example, Lawyers Committee for Human Rights, "The International Criminal Court: The Case for U.S. Support" *International Criminal Court Briefing Series* (December 1998).

6

A UN Constabulary to Enforce the Law on Genocide and Crimes Against Humanity

Saul Mendlovitz and John Fousek

INTRODUCTION

This chapter concerns itself with two ideas whose time has at last begun to arrive. The older of these ideas, the concept of standing international forces to protect world peace and uphold international law, goes back at least to the period between the two world wars. The newer idea, the concept of "genocide" as a particularly heinous crime that the international community should be obligated to prevent and punish, dates back to the era of World War II. This latter idea was codified in the 1948 Convention on the Prevention and Punishment of the Crime of Genocide. The former idea has never been similarly codified in any binding international agreement. And, of course, the crime of genocide has scarcely been prevented or punished in the half century since the genocide convention was signed.

Both these ideas gained currency and momentum in the wake of World War II. But during the Cold War, it was politically impossible even to discuss these matters, let alone implement them. Indeed, they remained suppressed in the immediate post-Soviet years, as the tragic events in Bosnia and Rwanda testify. But since 1995, they have gained new impetus. It is clear that the establishment of the ad hoc international criminal courts for former Yugoslavia and Rwanda by the Security Council has been a milestone in this regard. Building on the Nuremberg legacy, the Convention on Genocide, the 1949 Geneva Conventions and their protocols of 1977, the creation of these two courts—which marked the formal acceptance of the category of crimes against humanity by the Security Council—supported and laid the foundation for the acceptance of a Permanent International Criminal Court, which was adopted in Rome in July 1998. And beyond that, the Security Council's continuing acceptance of human rights matters (in this instance, genocide and crimes against humanity) as fitting within the context of Chapter VII of the Charter combines establishment of the Court with enforcement measures that include the use of force. As the twentieth century came to a close, the most recent episodes of preventable atrocities, in Kosovo and East Timor, showed that further institutional development is still needed.

We are very much aware that a standing UN force cannot by itself prevent genocide altogether. As long as human beings divide themselves into groups that define members of their own group as inherently more fully human than members of other groups, the possibility of genocide will remain with us. Our presentation here is informed by and sensitive to the immensely important and complex issues of group identity, otherness, dehumanization, mediation, reconciliation, and the building of what Leo Kuper has called "the non-genocidal society."[1] However, these issues are beyond the scope of this chapter. Rather, we focus instead on law enforcement, believing that enforcement is possible without a full understanding of all these issues, much as domestic criminal law is more or less effective while society continues to fathom the causes and prevention of crime.

Two propositions underlie our argument for the establishment of a UN constabulary force. First, the normative or legislative components of an international criminal law on genocide and crimes against humanity are already in place. The Genocide Convention, the two courts set up by the Security Council, as well as the statute of the permanent international criminal court, have defined and codified these crimes. Effective enforcement machinery is still not in place. It is the thesis of this paper that such machinery is both necessary and achievable.

Second, human society now stands at a particularly pivotal and "open" juncture in the evolution of the world's normative and institutional order. Humanity is undergoing an extraordinary shift in its political, economic, and social fabric. What with some six billion people circa the year 2000 in constant touch with one another throughout the globe, and the phenomena of globalization in finance, trade, and perhaps more significantly, communication and cultures, the state system as we have known it is undergoing extraordinary adaptation. In recent years, moreover, the range of images—both descriptive and normative—projecting the evolution of global polity over the first two decades of the twenty-first century has varied widely, from Robert Kaplan's "coming anarchy"[2] to Samuel Huntington's "clash of civilizations"[3] to Francis Fukuyama's "end of history"[4] (not to mention regionalism, functionalism, "small is beautiful," bioregionalism, and more). We believe that this combination of far-reaching global transformations, with such a diversity of views about their directions, allows significant space for consciously shaping new global institutions, including institutions to deal with international criminal law. The creation of a UN Constabulary can therefore be approached as a concrete, pragmatic political project to be promoted and perhaps realized in the early years of the twenty-first century.

THE CONTEXT: THE CREATION OF THE PERMANENT INTERNATIONAL CRIMINAL COURT

The idea of working towards the creation of a UN constabulary force gains credence from the recent adoption of the Rome Statute for the establishment of a permanent international criminal court. The rationale for this court and the crucial role of citizens' groups in promoting its realization both help to illuminate the process by which a UN constabulary force may also be brought into being. In the following discussion of the International Criminal Court (ICC), we highlight the role of the United States. We do so because the United States is generally seen as the most powerful state in the world, and therefore its political position on these matters has a good deal of impact. The unwillingness of the United States to sign the Rome Statute has been seen as evidence that the court will have little influence. Moreover, in invoking the imperatives of state sovereignty in arguing against a fully independent court, the United States expresses fears shared by states throughout the world.

The signing by 120 states of the statute to establish a permanent international criminal court with jurisdiction over the most heinous of violent international crimes—genocide, other crimes against humanity, and war crimes—marks a moment of great promise, despite the statute's imperfections and the failure of the United States to sign on. It took the United States forty years, and sustained political efforts by advocates of the world rule of law, to ratify the 1948 Genocide Convention. Sustained political efforts may also change the present United States position on the ICC. Moreover, it is well worth noting that human rights organizations and other citizens' groups played an essential role in initiating and shaping the political process that led to the Rome treaty. A similar worldwide citizens' campaign aimed at the creation of a standing UN Constabulary could have similar results in the decade ahead. With these two new, global institutions in place, the prospect for enforcing international criminal law and deterring potential criminals in the future would be immeasurably improved.

The outbreak of violent conflict needs ultimately to be dealt with on the ground, in terms of conflict resolution, education for coexistence, competent and humane governance, and resolution of the socioeconomic problems that underlay violent conflict. However, creation of a permanent International Criminal Court and a standing UN Constabulary with police powers to address genocide and crimes against humanity would together go a long way toward breaking the cycle of impunity that has fueled the continuation of genocidal violence in the half century since the Genocide Convention was signed.

The treaty creating the ICC must be ratified by sixty signatory states before it goes into effect as law, and there is reason to believe this can be accomplished in the next few years, some 61 states having already signed. (The genocide convention went into effect in 1951, three years after its initial signing.) If the court is successfully established by, say, 2001, it may have some deterrent effect even initially. To the extent that cases are brought before it, the Court will accelerate the development of case law concerning the crimes under its jurisdiction, particularly concerning genocide, a crime that has rarely even been brought to trial in its fifty years on the books. Yet the problem of apprehending suspects and bringing them to trial will remain problematic, as will the prospect for halting episodes of large-scale criminal violence before they run their tragic course. The Court's efficacy in this regard may very well depend on the use of force as a necessary element of external intervention (as with NATO's role in Bosnia, where, of course, the highest-level war criminals remain at large) or on the victory of the previously victimized side in an internal conflict (as in the Tutsi's return to power in Rwanda). To be fully effective, the Court will need some form of constabulary empowered to arrest suspects and stop nascent or escalating atrocities.

Ironically, the United States government, which likes to represent the rule of law as an American ideal, voted against the Rome treaty (placing itself in the company of China, Iraq, and Libya, as well as Israel, Qatar and Yemen) and would tend to oppose the creation of a standing UN force for similar reasons. The United States has argued that, as the world's sole superpower, it alone has global responsibilities and the obligation to deploy its troops in conflict areas around the world. A strong ICC independent of Security Council control, the argument goes, would lend itself to trumped-up prosecutions of United States soldiers involved in foreign interventions. An independent Court, in other words, is seen as a threat to the freedom of unilateral action, which the United States needs to fulfill its unique global responsibilities.

But in the post-Soviet era, marked as it is by accelerating global economic integration as well as political disintegration, U.S. unilateralism is likely to prove increasingly futile. Most United States citizens do aspire to the rule of law, but few believe the United States should act as the world's policeman in perpetuity. The backlash against the humanitarian intervention in Somalia after American soldiers were killed there reveals the weakness of public support for such policies. Moreover, the effort to maintain the capacity to police the world stretches the solvency of United States foreign policy to its limits and usurps financial resources that might better be directed to social investment in education, worker training, health care, and communications and transportation infrastructure.

We believe that multilateral institution building, specifically in the form of creating a standing UN Constabulary along with rapid reaction brigades for peacekeeping operations, has the potential for greater legitimacy and greater effectiveness than either United States unilateralism or ad hoc multistate interventions under UN auspices. Although creating a permanent international police force of any kind will require a sustained political effort and substantial start-up costs as well as ongoing funding demands, it will ultimately save billions of dollars—and perhaps countless lives. The amount of money spent on post-conflict refugee relief and economic reconstruction by itself constitutes a potent argument for the creation of such a force.

Interestingly enough, in its arguments against the Rome treaty, the United States said that genocide was the one crime in which it would support a doctrine of universal jurisdiction. As a state party to the Genocide Convention, of course, the United States could hardly oppose universal jurisdiction on genocide. Still, the position taken at Rome seems to reflect a recent shift in the Clinton administration's views. In the spring of 1994, the United States and the world stood aside as some 800,000 people were systematically slaughtered in Rwanda inside of three months. Near the end of this episode, which some analysts see as the clearest case of genocide since the Holocaust, the United States Ambassador to Rwanda, David Rawson, explained away his government's inaction, saying "as a responsible Government, you don't just go around hollering 'genocide.' You say that acts of genocide may have occurred and they need to be investigated." Four years later, in his visit to Rwanda as part of a multination African tour in April 1998, President Clinton said plainly that the United States and the rest of the international community had been in error in not recognizing the genocide as a genocide and in failing to take action to stop it. He used the opportunity to publicize a proposal for the creation of a regional readiness corps in Africa to prevent or stop future genocides. Also in the spring of 1998, the Clinton administration disclosed plans for deploying a force into the mountains of Thailand to capture the remaining band of Khmer Rouge leaders, and most particularly to arrest Pol Pot and bring him to trial on charges of genocide and crimes against humanity. Even Senator Jesse Helms, though a vociferous opponent of the ICC, has gone on record in favor of bringing figures like Saddam Hussein and Pol Pot to trial on charges of genocide and crimes against humanity.

In previous essays, we argued for the creation of a standing police force charged solely with enforcing the law on genocide.[5] We have since come to believe that a police body with jurisdiction over that single crime would be severely hamstrung, since specific intent possesses special problems for prosecutors. Conviction requires proof of specific intent to destroy a national, racial, ethnic, or religious group in whole or in part. In many instances, prosecutors may be leery of issuing indictments on genocide even when they suspect it has occurred because of this inherent difficulty in demonstrating specific intent. Indeed, the experience of the ad hoc tribunals on the former Yugoslavia and Rwanda shows that charges of genocide may be hard to prove, and individuals suspected of genocide may more easily be convicted, and more readily indicted, on the related but broader charges of crimes against humanity.

For that reason, we are recommending that the constabulary have competence to deal with crimes against humanity. Genocide is conceptually linked to the category of crimes against humanity and is frequently referred to as a crime against humanity. An effective international constabulary needs to have jurisdiction over crimes against humanity as well as genocide even if the main aim is to use it to halt genocidal violence. As defined in the Rome Statute, crimes against humanity are specific atrocities "committed as part of a widespread or systematic attack directed against any civilian population, with knowledge of the attack."[6] Even more restrictively, such an attack must be a matter of state or organizational policy. This definition sets a high threshold for establishing crimes against humanity, and it is to be hoped that the Court will interpret its mandate broadly in this area. Nonetheless, the efficacy of a UN Constabulary will be enhanced by having police powers for two categories of crimes—genocide and crimes against humanity—rather than just one.

The third category of crimes under the jurisdiction of the proposed International Criminal Court, war crimes, raises complex questions concerning the mandate of the Constabulary we propose here. On the one hand, a police force charged with enforcing the law on the three crimes under the new Court's jurisdiction provides an attractive degree of logical consistency. On the other hand, the law on war crimes has a long history of being enforced by domestic jurisdiction, by victor states, or by battlefield powers. Moreover, war crimes are generally perpetrated by larger numbers of people in lower positions of authority. For these reasons, we are inclined to exclude war crimes from the mandate of the proposed UN Constabulary.

TOWARD A UNITED NATIONS CONSTABULARY FORCE

Calls for the creation of some form of permanent, standing UN force charged with peacekeeping and police functions have become increasingly frequent in the mid- to late 1990s. They have also come from increasingly significant voices. In the wake of the "ethnic cleansing" in Bosnia, Brian Urquhart, the former UN Under-Secretary General, published a widely discussed piece in the *New York Review of Books* (June 1993), calling specifically for a volunteer force.[7] Elsewhere in the American press, even mainstream

commentators like the iconoclastic Eduard Luttwak and the conservative
columnist George Will have argued that a standing UN force is badly
needed. In the wake of the Rwanda genocide, two high profile international
commissions—the Commission on Global Governance and the Carnegie
Commission on Preventing Deadly Conflict—have endorsed the idea. Also
in the wake of the Rwandan tragedy, several states conducted major studies
on the need to improve the rapid reaction capacities of the UN's peacekeeping system. The Danish, Dutch, and Canadian governments put forward specific proposals for the creation of rapid reaction brigades, and a
number of governments from various world regions have supported these
proposals. The Canadian proposal explicitly sees multilateral rapid reaction
brigades as a stepping stone toward the creation of a standing UN volunteer
force. These government-sponsored proposals together constitute a significant shift in the political winds. Over the next five to ten years, a concerted
campaign to create a standing UN Constabulary along with rapid reaction
peacekeeping brigades could bear fruit, just as the Coalition for an International Criminal Court has over the past several years.

The UN Constabulary, as we propose it here, would be a new kind of
force, with assertive police powers dedicated to preventing and halting episodes of genocide and crimes against humanity, and to apprehending the
alleged perpetrators and bringing them to justice. Unlike UN peacekeeping
forces, which have always been formed on an ad hoc basis from *national*
military contingents provided voluntarily by member states, and unlike proposed rapid reaction brigades similarly comprised of state contingents, the
UN Constabulary would be a permanent, *transnational* institution. Its
members would be individually recruited and trained as international civil
servants. They would be employed directly by the UN, rather than by their
national military authorities. Nation-states would have no formal part in the
command structure, allowing the force to operate as an effective global law
enforcement agency, thus avoiding the danger that it would be a captive of
the geopolitical interests of states. Because nation-states and ad hoc peacekeeping forces have shown themselves to be wholly ineffectual in enforcing
the law against genocide and crimes against humanity, we believe such institutional innovation is needed now if the world community is to close the
gap between its normative professions and the grisly realities of criminal
violence.

Unlike other proposals, this essay calls for the creation of a constabulary,
not a peacekeeping force or a UN army or "legion." The constabulary we
propose would be dedicated exclusively to dealing with genocide and other
crimes against humanity. It would be a police arm of the evolving regime
of international criminal law embodied in the Rome Statute for the International Criminal Court. A UN Constabulary would be separate from any
UN forces used to deal with invasions of one state by another (such as Iraq
against Kuwait, or Iran against Iraq) and would not intervene in civil wars

where neither genocide nor crimes against humanity constitute a major component of the conflict (as in Afghanistan or Nicaragua). Its mandate would be clearly limited to genocide and crimes against humanity.

The approval of the Rome Statute by the overwhelming majority of the world's states reflects a general consensus that new means are needed to prevent and suppress the most egregious violations of international humanitarian law. Moreover, the idea of a UN Constabulary may be more politically feasible than it initially appears. Within the present context, we believe, the appropriate composition, mission, financing, command, and control of such a force, as presented in this proposal, could overcome many of the political obstacles that have traditionally blocked the creation of a more general international police force. Equipped with the right arguments, a sustained political campaign, drawing on the experience of the Coalition for an International Criminal Court and the International Campaign to Ban Landmines, could overcome the remaining political obstacles and make this idea a reality.

Some Issues of Jurisdiction

The 1948 Genocide Convention empowers any signatory state to "call upon the competent organs of the United Nations to take such actions under the Charter of the United Nations as they consider appropriate for the prevention and suppression of acts of genocide."[8] Given the failure of the international community to develop any other effective enforcement mechanisms, however, this provision may serve as the basis for creating a UN Constabulary as proposed here. This force could be established under the UN Charter by either the Security Council (under Articles 47 or 27) or the General Assembly (GA) (under Articles 10 or 22). Its legitimacy would be enhanced if it were brought into being by a General Assembly resolution adopted by a substantial majority of member states and, subsequently, a Security Council resolution that, in effect, ratified the GA's proposal. Done in this fashion, the establishment of the force would not necessarily require a new treaty.

Another possible authorization platform would be the notion of humanitarian intervention in instances of grave and egregious deprivations of human rights, particularly where there is reasonable evidence of intent to commit genocide. This has the advantage of following procedures established in customary international law for humanitarian intervention and does not need to be legitimated by a new treaty. We want to follow agreed-upon rules of humanitarian intervention, so long as the intervention is carried out by a UN force, and so long as that force has built-in safeguards to prevent big powers from using it as an instrument of their own policies, whatever the authorizing agency.

In making these suggestions, we wish to underscore that present UN practice in peacekeeping, peacemaking, and peace enforcement would not be altered. To be sure, the procedures we are proposing for creating and controlling the constabulary move beyond the UN experience, but they are rooted in it. Under our program, Chapter VII of the UN Charter would still allow the Security Council to require member states to take coercive measures against any threat to or breach of international peace. The Security Council could also continue to ask member states to volunteer their national forces for UN measures. Although the Uniting for Peace Resolution has questionable legal and political validity, the General Assembly might well decide to recommend forces to deal with genocide and other crimes against humanity when disagreement among permanent members of the Security Council prevents the Council from discharging its responsibility. These mechanisms of enforcement would not be altered by the present proposal.[9]

Deciding When to Deploy the UN Constabulary

The UN Constabulary proposed here would perhaps play a role in preventing genocides and crimes against humanity and a significant role in halting them when they do occur. In the course of intervening to prevent or suppress these atrocities, this force would also play a role in apprehending suspects, incarcerating them, and bringing them to justice. As already noted, in speaking of prevention here we are not looking at underlying root issues, such as human nature, culture and socialization; rather, we are examining what a UN Constabulary could do to prevent future episodes of genocide.

The actual decision to deploy UN constabulary personnel would be delegated to the Secretary-General. Because this is obviously a major departure from the existing system, we will now sketch out the manner in which the Secretary-General's authority would be defined and implemented. We begin with depicting the processes that would be needed to provide effective prevention.

As an initial matter, some sort of early warning system needs to be developed to provide guidelines that indicate when the police force would be brought onto the scene. Developing these guidelines remains a challenging problem, but the challenge can be met by a global community committed to detecting early signs. According to former Secretary-General Boutros-Ghali, "Genocide does not happen spontaneously." Some observers might debate that statement, though it seems to be based on the reasonable view that specific intent to destroy a group necessarily involves calculation or planning. But Secretary-General Boutros-Ghali was certainly correct to assert that "in most cases there are abundant danger signs long before the killing begins."[10] The same can be said for crimes against humanity as defined in the Rome Statute for the International Criminal Court.

We recommend that an International Crime Watch Advisory Board be established under the Secretary-General of the UN. This Board should be charged with (1) developing a detailed early warning system to identify advance signs of any incipient episodes of genocide or other crimes against humanity, (2) monitoring conflict situations in which even a latent threat of these crimes seems present, and (3) overseeing the Constabulary's activities to protect against potential abuse of police powers. In these tasks, this new Board should work in conjunction with transnational citizens' groups, such as Human Rights Watch and Amnesty International, already engaged in similar pursuits.

The Crime Watch Advisory Board could be established and selected by the Security Council and would be composed of respected, senior members of the world diplomatic community and prominent moral authority figures. Its membership should be constitutionally structured to ensure gender equality and adequate representation of the world's cultural, socioeconomic, linguistic, and religious diversity, and to prevent it from serving simply as a policy instrument of permanent members of the Security Council. As its name suggests, the Crime Watch Advisory Board would have an advisory role only, with no binding authority. That would be retained by the Secretary-General, and thus this board would not be subject to the vetoes of the permanent members of the Security Council. After studying a given situation, the Board could vote either to approve or disapprove the Secretary-General's decision, or, alternately, it could vote to recommend action in a situation that the Secretary-General has failed to heed. But again, the ultimate authority would rest with the Secretary-General.

Both Bosnia and Rwanda are examples of situations for which early warning signs existed but went essentially unheeded. In the case of Bosnia, as soon as the international community recognized Bosnia-Herzegovina as an independent state in April 1992, it was clear that the Serbs and Croats alike aimed to destroy it. The subsequent Serb policy of "ethnic cleansing" clearly seems to have signaled genocidal intent. Western Europe, the United States, or the UN could have stopped the atrocities at that point but lacked the political will to do so.[11] The UN also lacked the proper instrument. An independent, standing UN Constabulary deployed to Bosnia in the spring of 1992, before the fighting escalated, might have saved tens if not hundreds of thousands of lives.

In the case of Rwanda, where upwards of one million people were massacred in just three months—between April and June 1994—there was abundant evidence before the killings began.[12] Human Rights Watch reported government-sponsored massacres of members of the Tutsi minority more than a year before the wholesale genocide began. In August 1993, a Rwandan television station with close ties to the government began to broadcast open incitements, first to hate, and then to kill. Local human rights groups told members of the diplomatic community that genocide seemed likely to occur. At the same time, evidence suggests that a militia was being recruited, organized, and trained to kill. Guns were distributed wholesale to members of the Hutu majority. And all Rwandans were required to carry ethnic identity cards, which were subsequently used to identify those to be killed. Such a mass of evidence would have set off any early warning system designed to prevent genocide or crimes against humanity.

In cases where genocide or other crimes against humanity do occur, the creation of the International Criminal Court will make available a new and very clear set of guidelines for deciding when to deploy a UN Constabulary. Under the Rome Statute, the prosecutors of the Court will have considerable independence to issue indictments for individuals they reasonably suspect to have committed any of the crimes under the Court's jurisdiction. We believe a UN Constabulary should be empowered to apprehend those individuals indicted by the ICC prosecutors on charges of genocide or crimes against humanity.

Functions of the Proposed UN Constabulary

Once deployed in the field, the proposed UN Constabulary would assume the following functions:

1. *Keep the peace—prevent the killing.* There is some ambiguity here, especially as related to prevention. At this moment in history, it is not clear at what point preventive deployment of a transnational police force would be possible, feasible, or sensible. In instances of intergroup tensions within nation-states—such as those between Moslems and Hindus in India, Jews and Arabs in Israel or the West Bank, and blacks and whites in the United States—police and paramilitary forces are often called in when some outbreak of violence seems imminent, not simply after it happens. The proposed International Crime Watch Advisory Board, which we described earlier, would have responsibility for monitoring such potential conflict situations— much as citizens' human rights groups do today—and informing the Secretary-General when the threat of genocide or other crimes against humanity seems to require UN action. At this stage of global political development, it might prove difficult to initiate preventive police intervention, but U.N. monitoring and judicial intervention might well be possible. Clearly, early intervention is crucial to enforcing both the Genocide Convention and the evolving law on crimes against humanity. Most crucially, it is necessary to save innumerable lives.

2. *Create assertive safe havens—stop the killing.* Once the UN Constabulary has intervened to halt the alleged criminal behavior, some outside force will need to occupy the territory where the behavior occurred, often for quite some time. We recommend that the occupation policy be guided by the doctrine of assertive safe havens.[13] Specifically, in such instances the UN Constabulary in conjunction with rapid reaction forces with greater military capacity would have an "assertive" mandate and power of enforcement. These forces would be authorized to:

1. demilitarize the area surrounding each safe haven, placing heavy weapons under effective supervision;

2. disarm the populations in the areas designated as safe havens;

3. seek out and lead to safety those individuals outside the protected area who are targets of the criminal behavior and who desire entry into a safe haven; and

4. use appropriate force to defend itself and its charges, and to carry out its mandate.

3. *Apprehend alleged criminals, complying with appropriate legal procedures, and assist in gathering evidence for prosecution.* As soon as it has established its position in the field, the force would be empowered to arrest and incarcerate alleged perpetrators of acts punishable under the definitions of genocide and crimes against humanity in The Statute of the International Criminal Court. It would also assist prosecutors in gathering evidence and identifying and protecting witnesses.

4. *Arrange for the presence of humanitarian relief agencies.* Both United Nations and voluntary citizens groups (such as the Red Cross, church and medical groups) will generally need to be brought in. These agencies would initially take over basic needs functions and initiate civil society processes of health and housing. The police presence would make this possible.

5. *Initiate processes of competent, humane governance.* As a corollary to halting criminal behavior, UN representatives will have to assume a central role in initiating governance processes among the local population and ensuring that these processes are competent, just and humane. These efforts at initiating humane local governance should utilize a wide variety of individuals and techniques. Again, the police presence would make this possible.

Structure of the Proposed UN Constabulary

The structure of the proposed UN Constabulary is crucial to making it both workable and feasible. By structure, we mean in particular the rules and procedures guiding the force's size and location, command and control, financing and operations.[14]

1. Size and Location. A standing Constabulary of 10,000 to 15,000 members should be housed in perhaps three or more base camps. These camps should be strategically located so that at least part of the force could be deployed anywhere in the world in the event of genocide or crimes against humanity or early warning signs of incipient outbreaks of these crimes. The force housed at each base camp would be best prepared for action in the sociocultural, linguistic, and climatic conditions of its particular region. A force based in the Western Hemisphere, for example, should include many Spanish-speaking as well as English-speaking officers. Yet each base unit would also be available as necessary for deployment beyond its primary area. To the extent possible, these bases should be located in rela-

tively isolated areas, where they would be least subject to interference from any host nation, and where they themselves would be least likely to interfere in the life of the local community. The force could also be made available for disaster relief missions.

2. Control. The procedures we propose for controlling the UN Constabulary are rooted in but move beyond UN experience with ad hoc forces throughout the postwar era. Our proposal would not diminish the UN's present authority to engage in enforcement and peacekeeping actions in any way. Under Chapter VII of the UN Charter, the Security Council can legally require member states to take coercive measures against any threat to or breach of international peace. The Security Council can also ask member states to volunteer their national forces for UN missions. Under the Uniting for Peace Resolution, the General Assembly can recommend sending peace-keeping forces into action in instances where disagreement among permanent members of the Security Council prevents the Council from discharging its responsibility for peacekeeping. These mechanisms of enforcement would not be altered by the present proposal. Indeed, the Constabulary could be placed at the disposal of the Council or the Assembly under these established procedures.

But as noted above, we propose that the primary decision-making control concerning the deployment of the UN Constabulary should be vested in the Secretary-General of the United Nations, as the chief executive accountable to the member states. This would require a delegation of authority by the Security Council. However, the Secretary-General would be authorized to deploy this force only in two types of situations: first, after consulting with a standing International Crime Watch Advisory Board, which would be duly constituted for that purpose, as discussed above; and second, when individuals have been indicted on charges of genocide or crimes against humanity by the prosecutors of the ICC. Decision-making powers and day-to-day command and control of the Constabulary would rest with the Secretary-General. Following the principle of a "war powers" clause, however, the Security Council would retain the authority to withdraw the police force thirty to forty-five days after its initial deployment if it disagreed with the initial decision, or of if it deemed that the genocide had been effectively prevented or suppressed.

3. Financing. Financing might be obtained through conventional UN budgetary procedures and allotments. An alternative formula might also be considered. Total costs for the UN Constabulary could be divided among all UN member states on a scale proportional to each country's portion of total global military expenditures. Each country's quota could be figured over the preceding five-year period, to avoid wide fluctuations. Insofar as military expenditures contribute to international tension and violence, and thus to the context in which most egregious violations of international humanitarian law occur, it seems appropriate that the biggest military spenders

should pay the largest share of the cost of a UN Constabulary. Another alternative method of financing a UN Constabulary, along with other enhanced global institutions, is through a modest tax of 1/100th of one percent of all international financial transactions over $10,000.

4. Operations. Unlike armies, the force we are proposing would aim simply to uphold the law against genocide and crimes against humanity, rather than to achieve the political objectives of a belligerent state. It should be outfitted and trained in the manner of a highly professional national guard. Members of the force should be specifically trained to identify, apprehend, and incarcerate individuals engaged in acts punishable under the Genocide Convention and the Statue of the International Criminal Court, and to restore order and establish assertive safe havens as outlined above.

The weapons employed by the force should be limited as strictly as possible, because the purpose is to prevent or suppress criminal behavior and reduce human suffering. To fulfill an assertive mandate for enforcing the Genocide Convention and establishing safe havens for members of targeted groups, the police force will likely need light tanks and state-of-the-art infantry equipment, again comparable to well-equipped national guard forces. It would also require advanced aircraft for transportation and logistical support. Yet field operations should be guided by the principle of using the least lethal means possible to enforce the law. Wherever possible, the force should rely on relatively humane, nonlethal weaponry, such as rubber bullets, tranquilizers, stun-guns, and tear gas. Where necessary, the UN Constabulary could be augmented or supported by more extensive forces authorized by the Security Council or the General Assembly under existing procedures. That is, the standing police force could be deployed rapidly for specific law enforcement purposes, but additional forces could be sent in later, first from newly created rapid reaction brigades, and then, for longer-term operations, from ad hoc forces assembled from member states.

POLITICAL OBSTACLES

Today, several major political obstacles stand in the way of establishing a UN Constabulary. These include the imperatives of state sovereignty and the reluctance of states to relinquish authority to transnational actors; "body bags"—domestic objections to any casualties incurred through participation in a transnational force (or any force not deemed to be in service of "the national interest"); financing (the dimensions of this problem are presumably self-evident); and, finally, the inherent weaknesses of the present Genocide Convention. We believe that the structure and functions of the proposed force presented in this essay go a long way toward overcoming these obstacles.

The rather gruesome and tragic image of the body bag conveys perhaps the greatest obstacle to effective UN actions to halt the recent killings in both the former Yugoslavia and Rwanda. That is to say, the major states of the world—the United States, Britain, France, and perhaps Russia—had the capacity to intervene in these situations and could have done so in a manner that would have saved countless lives. But these powerful states failed to act because their chief executives were fearful of an irate domestic backlash should any of their military personnel be killed in carrying out humanitarian intervention. Thus, for example, the killing of eighteen U.S. military personnel in Somalia prompted a major public uproar, which led President Clinton to set a termination date for the deployment of U.S. forces in that country. Similarly, although the French government had a clearer mandate with regard to its intervention in Rwanda, French leaders feared casualties that the electorate at home would criticize vehemently. At least from the viewpoint of western society, then, policing the world has become a highly suspect endeavor in the post-Soviet era, except where an overwhelming national interest is seen to be at stake, as in the case of oil in the Middle East.

It may well be true that some societies do not have this obstacle—certain small and medium-sized states in other parts of the world. But these states are inhibited from volunteering troops for humanitarian actions because of their own lack of financial resources. That, of course, raises the crucial problem of how any international police force would be financed. Beyond, or perhaps beneath, the problems of body bags and dollars, however, lies a third problem: the issue of sovereignty. States fear that if they agreed to the establishment of a transnational police force, it would lead to an erosion of their sovereignty in two distinct ways. First, states fear that any UN police force might be used against the interests of a member state, and that this would erode the general principle of state sovereignty. Second, they fear that the UN, for whatever reasons, might intervene directly into their own territory, thereby undermining their own sovereignty quite specifically.

Is there a way to deal with these problems of sovereignty, money, and body bags? We believe there is. Suppose that the UN has a constabulary some 10,000 to 15,000 members strong. Suppose further that the members of this force are individually recruited, highly trained for intervention, well-educated, with decent salaries and benefits, including postpolice career opportunities and retirement funds. These individuals would be international civil servants. Rather than being appointed by their governments, they would apply for these positions directly, just as individuals apply to join the local police force in Toledo, Harare, or Kyoto. No more than 3 to 5 percent of the personnel should come from any one member state. There would be no nationally organized units within the force, and citizens from each member state should be dispersed as widely as possible throughout the force.

It would be regrettable, of course, if members of such a force were wounded or killed while engaged in efforts to halt or prevent genocide. But such casualties would not raise issues of national interest, national security, or injury to the state of any kind. Nor would they provoke the kind of nationalist sentiments and hostile backlash that swept through U.S. public opinion when U.S. soldiers were killed in Somalia. Because these individuals would serve as UN police, no country's honor or dignity would be at stake. No local community would feel that its national government had needlessly sacrificed its sons. The point, then, is that a UN Constabulary structured as a transnational or global entity would bypass the politically volatile issues of national identity.

The question of financing remains a difficult one. Proposals for various types of international rapid reaction forces range considerably both in force size and in cost. In a recent, thorough analysis of the problem, George Rathjens and Carl Kaysen conclude that a force of 15,000 members would allow 10,600 deployable personnel and 4,400 support staff (including training, logistics, and headquarters staff). Such a force, they argue, could send out two contingents simultaneously while keeping a third contingent in reserve. Rathjens and Kaysen calculate the cost of such a force at $1.5 billion annually.[15] (The annual UN peacekeeping budget now runs $2 to $3 billion per year, and much of that could be saved by the successful operation of the UN Constabulary we propose.) Even at a higher cost level, such a force would ultimately prove cost-effective for the international community and for leading UN member states. Suppose that such a force had been available early on in Rwanda or in the former Yugoslavia situation. The costs to the UN of intervening in these areas with an established, standing force might well have been less than the total costs the various states have subsequently incurred for both humanitarian relief and long-delayed, largely unsuccessful military deployments.

CONCLUSION

Fifty years after the liberation of the Nazi death camps, genocide and other crimes against humanity are very much still with us—to the shame of all the nations of the world. But today genocide is universally recognized as a high crime under international law, and crimes against humanity have been codified authoritatively in the Statute of the International Criminal Court. The challenge the world community now faces is how to enforce the evolving body of international criminal law, particularly the 1948 Genocide Convention. The successful creation of the proposed International Criminal Court will mark an important but unfortunately inconclusive step toward meeting that challenge.

With the tragic events of recent years in Somalia, Bosnia, Rwanda, and Burundi, and most recently in Kosovo and East Timor, the world today is forced to confront its failure to prevent genocidal episodes all too reminiscent of Nazi horrors. For a host of reasons, intervention by individual powers or by ad hoc coalitions of nation-states, whether formed regionally or under UN auspices, has not provided a workable solution. Rapid reaction peacekeeping forces are needed, but the force proposed here has a more specific purpose. Diplomacy and sanctions, of course, must always be employed fully before force is deployed. But in too many instances since 1948, they have failed to provide effective enforcement of the Genocide Convention adopted that year.

In cases of genocide and other crimes against humanity, as for heinous crimes committed within nation-states, effective law enforcement requires effective police operations. We believe the time has come for the world community to confront this fact, and deal with these crimes by establishing a special transnational police force, under the UN, dedicated to halting, preventing, and punishing these grave and egregious offences.

NOTES

1. Leo Kuper, *Genocide: Its Political Use in the Twentieth Century* (New Haven: Yale University Press, 1981).

2. Robert Kaplan, "The Coming Anarchy," *The Atlantic Monthly* 273, No. 2 (1994); see also Kaplan, *The Ends of the Earth: A Journey to the Frontiers of Anarchy* (New York: Vintage Books, 1997).

3. Samuel Huntington, "The Clash of Civilizations?," *Foreign Affairs* 72, No. 3 (1993): 22–49; see also Samuel Huntington, "The West Unique, Not Universal," *Foreign Affairs* 75, No. 6 (1996): 28–46.

4. Francis Fukuyama, "The End of History?," *The National Interest* 16 (Summer 1989): 3–18; see also Fukuyama, *The End of History and the Last Man* (New York: Free Press, 1992).

5. See Saul H. Mendlovitz and John Fousek, "The Prevention and Punishment of the Crime of Genocide," in *Genocide, War, and Human Survival*, eds. Charles B. Strozier and Michael Flynn (Lanham, MD: Rowman & Littlefield, 1996); and Mendlovitz and Fousek, "Enforcing the Law on Genocide," *Alternative* 21 (1996): 237–258.

6. The Rome Statute of the International Criminal Court (July 17, 1998).

7. Brian Urquhart, "For a UN Volunteer Military Force," *New York Review of Books*, June 10, 1993; see also his more recent, sobering discussion, "Looking for the Sheriff," *New York Review of Books*, July 16, 1998.

8. Convention of the Prevention and Punishment of the Crime of Genocide, December 9, 1948, 78 U.N.T.S. 277. Entered into force, January 12, 1951; for the United States, February 23, 1980.

9. See also the discussion below under the heading "Deciding When to Deploy the UN Constabulary."

10. Barbara Crossette, "U.N.: Reason, in Small Doses, May Stop Genocide," *New York Times*, April 9, 1995, p. 16, quoting Boutros-Ghali's opinion piece in the *International Herald Tribune*, April 1, 1995.

11. See Misha Glenny, "Yugoslavia: The Great Fall," *New York Review of Books*, March 23, 1995; and Misha Glenny, "Letter from Bosnia: The Age of the Parastate," *The New Yorker* (May 8, 1995); see also David Rieff, *Slaughterhouse: Bosnia and the Failure of the West* (New York: Simon & Schuster, 1995), p. 22.

12. This review of events in Rwanda is drawn largely from Helen Fein, "An Interview with Alison L. Des Forges: Genocide in Rwanda was Foreseen and Could Have Been Deterred," in *The Prevention of Genocide: Rwanda and Yugoslavia Reconsidered*, ed. Helen Fein, a Working Paper of the Institute for the Study of Genocide, 1994; see also Milton Leitenberg, "U.S. and U.N. Actions Escalate Genocide and Increase Costs in Rwanda," in *The Prevention of Genocide: Rwanda and Yugoslavia Reconsidered*; and Milton Leitenberg, "Rwanda, 1994: International Incompetence Produces Genocide," *Peacekeeping and International Relations* (November/December 1994).

13. This discussion of assertive safe havens is largely drawn from a statement written to the editor from the Citizens' Committee on Bosnia-Herzegovina. See "Safe Havens in Bosnia," *New York Review of Books*, May 13, 1993. The senior author was a member of that committee and helped to formulate the proposal presented in that statement.

14. The following discussion draws on material presented in Robert C. Johansen and Saul H. Mendlovitz, "The Role of Enforcement of Law in the Establishment of a New International Order: A Proposal for a Transnational Police Force," *Alternatives* 6 (1980): 320–24; and Saul H. Mendlovitz and John Fousek, "Enforcing the Law on Genocide," *Alternatives* 21 (1996): 237–258.

15. Carl Kaysen and George W. Rathjens, "Send in the Troops: A UN Foreign Legion," *Washington Quarterly* (Winter 1997); see also Lionel Rosenblatt and Larry Thompson, "The Door of Opportunity: Creating a Permanent Peacekeeping Force," *World Policy Journal* (Spring 1998).

7

On Humanitarian Intervention

Michael Joseph Smith

INTRODUCTION

By the time we have come to the point of discussing intervention of one kind or another, we are on the edge of failure. The situation has become desperate. Identification, prevention, and deterrence have failed, and we are on the edge of the abyss of genocide—indeed, the horror may already have begun. Events have overtaken foreign office contingency plans, diplomatic consultations, Security Council meetings; a people is in danger. At this point, we (and who, exactly, constitutes that "we" is a point to which I shall return) face a stark choice: acquiescence or action. More and more, as ethnic violence rips through the post–cold-war world, the international community, individual states, and the array of nongovernmental organizations will face choices like this. Do we intervene, if necessary with military force, or do we continue to temporize and rationalize our collective inaction?

Most recently, the grim situations in Rwanda, Kosovo, and East Timor, provide all-too-concrete reminders that our topic concerns real people, struggling to survive in desperate situations of conflict. But as we learn throughout this volume, much about this subject of preventing genocide is complex, difficult, and controversial—all the more reason, of course, to keep in mind our central purpose of preventing genocide by whatever means possible. So as I lead us through some of the difficult and contested territory here, I shall try my best to keep in mind this central goal—though I warn you in advance that at times it may seem distant and utopian. The danger is to turn the imperative of a "creative breakthrough" in world politics into a pious wish expressed by those who live in the safety of a rich and stable state.

PRELIMINARY PROBLEMS: LANGUAGE

The difficulties begin even with language. One may well question how easily one can join the terms "just" and "humanitarian" to the militaristic notion of intervention, redolent as it is of marines, gunboat diplomacy, or, say, the Vietnam War. That war, we should remember, produced a feast of Orwellian obfuscation: brutal removal and resettlement of villagers became "forced draft urbanization," civilians were bombed and killed if they failed to leave "free fire zones," and, most famously, the invasion of Cambodia in 1970 was more politely called an "incursion." Given Orwell's injunction about clear language, and with respect to those with misgivings about the militarized notion of the term, I think justice and lucidity require us to insist on the blunt term of "intervention." Why? Because all too often, more than "humanitarian action," peacekeeping, or some form of "intercession" will be required. The NATO bombing of Serb positions in Sarajevo in summer 1995 can only with difficulty be called an "intercession"; yet I would argue that this military action ("intervention" in plain language) was essential for creating the conditions for the Dayton Peace Accord.

Traditional international law defines "intervention" as "forcible interference in the domestic affairs" of another state. As I have argued elsewhere, it makes most sense to think of intervention as involving a spectrum of possible actions, ranging from a mild diplomatic protest to military invasion, even occupation.[1] (Think of the first United States intervention in Haiti, which occurred in July 1915 and resulted in United States military presence until August 1934.) When we are considering forcible action for the purpose of preventing genocide, we may need to do more (or less) than separate presumed combatants. As in Sarajevo, we may need to bomb the positions of one party in a conflict in an effort not so much to "win" as to change the calculations of one set of actors—to raise the cost to them of continuing on the path of genocide. Indeed, we may need to "intercede" with a peace-keeping force until a political settlement may be negotiated; but more than this, we may need to monitor procedures and/or establish institutions that follow from that negotiation. As in Cambodia, we may need to stay and supervise elections; as in both Bosnia and Rwanda, we may need to establish an International War Crimes Tribunal. In short, "just humanitarian intervention" can include a whole range of actions occurring over an indeterminate period of time.

There is another difficulty of language that we must admit from the start: the very meaning and implications of the term "genocide" itself. Because the 1948 Convention on the Prevention and Punishment of the Crime of Genocide (finally ratified by the United States in 1985) directs its signatories to take action "appropriate for the prevention and suppression of acts of genocide," states are often reluctant to employ the term even when acts that plainly amount to "acts committed with intent to destroy, in whole or in part, a national, ethnical, racial, or religious group"[2] are occurring. The experiences of Bosnia and Rwanda have taught us that getting accurate, real-time information about these events is not as straightforward as we consumers of news tend to think. Governments and parties to the conflict seek to mislead and suppress such information; they clearly have a stake in whether a conflict is or is not termed a genocide in progress. Official UN agencies and representatives must balance their needs to stay in contact with, and to seem impartial between, parties in conflict against their own (often flawed) sources of information, directives from their bureaucratic superiors, and their real sense of the dangers involved. Nongovernmental humanitarian organizations (NGOs) face dilemmas of how to characterize events in which they are involved and in which full information is often difficult, even impossible, to obtain and verify; they have become acutely conscious of their roles both on the front lines of unfolding disasters and as the sentinels of the international conscience. As the Head of Communications of the International Committee of the Red Cross (ICRC) put it in a 1997 speech, "Probably never before has the fine art of communication had so much power of life and death over so many people. . . . We [in the ICRC] are increasingly aware of the phenomenal weight a word, a sentence, an expressed belief can have."[3] Humanitarian organizations are learning to come to terms with this new role and with the real possibility that their very presence—and the safety of their personnel—can be caught up in the political calculations of the parties in conflict. Accounts of the experience of the NGO community in Bosnia, Rwanda, and, most recently, Kosovo make this very clear. In the process it also seems that NGOs are, perhaps, losing their sense of political innocence; not only can they be manipulated by combatants, they may find themselves accused of manipulating information for purposes of fund-raising and international visibility.

If the NGO community is only now learning this lesson, thoughtful members of the international news media have known it for some time. Whether, when, and how a particular conflict is reported in the international media has made an enormous difference in the response of the international community to the event. In fact, there has been rather too much facile citation of a so-called "CNN effect" as inspiring—and constraining—United States participation in humanitarian conflicts.[4] We do know that the character and quality of the reportage from an event strongly influences the nature of the international response, as recent reports on the genocides in Bosnia and Rwanda have shown. One such report, on Rwanda, asserts that "the international media played a mixed role in the Rwanda crisis. While the media were a major factor in generating worldwide humanitarian relief support for the refugees, distorted reporting on events leading to the genocide itself was a contributing factor to the failure of the international community to take more effective action to stem the genocide."[5] And it is by now commonplace to cite the images of the "dead American soldier being dragged through the streets of Mogadishu" as pivotal to ending United States support for the humanitarian operation in Somalia.[6]

Awareness of the importance of international reporting of conflicts has grown among all the interested parties surrounding a deadly, potentially genocidal, conflict. News professionals, relief workers, UN personnel, diplomats, and military personnel—all of these actors now appreciate that even the most brutal and crude killers have become extraordinarily sophisticated in their attempt to manipulate information. Nor should this really surprise us, given that the founder of modern propaganda techniques was the Nazi Josef Goebbels. As one learns more about the cunning manipulations of General Mladic in the course of the massacre at Srebenica, one realizes that modern perpetrators of genocide have learned from earlier evil masters.[7]

Outside governments and their diplomats have also been tiptoeing around the issue of calling a genocide by its name. Why? Because to apply the term to the event is to set in motion a demand for concerted action. Thus if one wishes to temporize or actively to avoid action of any sort, one denies that a "genocide" is in progress. This denial was the reason President Clinton apologized to the people of Rwanda on his spring 1998 visit there, and this denial explains the considerable soul-searching even among states like Canada, Denmark, and Norway, who have traditionally supported humanitarian operations.

When reports first surfaced about an unfolding genocide in Rwanda in 1994, senior United States officials in the White House apparently sought more information from the United States intelligence community. On one authoritative account by a senior official, the report delivered to the White House rated the chances of a genocidal massacre by Hutus as "remote." Only later did the inadequacy of CIA sources—or, perhaps, the disingenuous character of the intelligence reports—become painfully clear.[8] Studies and articles about the quality and character of the information gathered and then disseminated by outside governments and within the UN itself are beginning to appear. To a disinterested observer, what seems clear in these emerging reports is a reluctance to recognize and release information that almost certainly would have led to demands for action. In October 1996, the Canadian diplomat dispatched by the UN to investigate new reports of genocide in Rwanda said "we would all lose a piece of our soul to accept another genocide" of the kind that occurred in 1994. Would that more of his colleagues in the international diplomatic community felt the same way when the story first broke.

These experiences suggest that even before we discuss the possibility of just humanitarian intervention to prevent genocide, we must monitor potential conflicts, seek and maintain a stream of reliable information, and insist that such information provide the basis of an honest application of terminology. If the international community is really to do nothing to stop a genocide in progress, we ought at least to be honest about the costs of our inaction. In Rwanda, even the President has admitted our culpability by inaction. Throughout 1998, in Kosovo, we may have been participants (reluctant, perhaps, but surely not unwitting) in an exercise of collective denial. In this world of denial, genocide is not genocide, but "civil conflict"; murderous removal of people not genocidal ethnic cleansing but "population resettlement"; and merciless bombing of civilians not terrorism but "civil war." Responsibility to gather accurate information and to face the worst of its grim implications must be shared among all the players in the global arena, and we must all be vigilant about the possibility of manipulating both images and negotiations for purposes of hiding, or continuing to perpetrate, awful horrors. To these pitfalls of manipulation, we must add our own constant temptation willfully to avert our gaze from events that shock our collective conscience. The formula of "civil war" between faraway peoples divided by "ancient hatreds" allows us to look the other way in a pretense of powerlessness. When we say that "well, apparently, there have been atrocities on both sides," without seeking honestly to assign responsibility, we make excuses for our inaction. What can we, over here, do about such people, over there, who act so badly toward each other? To call these events "genocide" is to demand that we act; it is to assert our common humanity against those who deny it and seek to negate its existence. When we allow softer words to stand in for grim reality, we allow the horror to continue. An evocative title of a recent book about Bosnia is *This Time We Knew*.[9] Sometimes what we know demands that we intervene to stop it.

INTERVENTION: PROBLEMS OF JUSTIFICATION, AGENCY, AND CAPABILITY

The first questions to ask about interventions concern justification and agency. To put it most simply, when is humanitarian intervention justified? Who should undertake it, on what basis, and for what purpose? I would suggest an answer that, in principle, is relatively straightforward. Humanitarian intervention is justified, first, when the condition or behavior of a state results in grave threats to the peace and security of other states and peoples, and, second, in cases of egregious and potentially genocidal violations of human rights—even if those violations occur entirely within the borders of a given state. A genocide is no less "a common threat to humanity" (the characterization of former UN Secretary-General Boutros Boutros-Ghali) if it occurs within borders than if it crosses them.[10] The basic principle that should guide international intervention is this: Individual state sovereignty can be overridden whenever the behavior of the state—even within its own territory—threatens the existence of elementary human rights abroad, and whenever the protection of the basic human rights of its own citizens can be assured only from the outside. On this interpretation, then, state sovereignty, in short, is a contingent value: its observance depends upon the actions of the state that seeks its protection. Members of the international community are not obliged to "respect the sovereignty" of a state that egregiously violates human rights. If the international community were to adopt this standard, this would indeed constitute a "creative breakthrough" in politics of the sort specified at the outset of this volume by Professor Riemer.

Note that in defining these "just causes" for humanitarian intervention, the standards for decision are, first, security and the maintenance of peace, and second, protection against egregious or genocidal violations of human rights. One could question the traditional, state-centric character of the first justification. Is, say, a response to traditional aggression really a case of "just humanitarian intervention"? To put it differently, does a "collective security" intervention undertaken under Chapter VII of the UN Charter—to address threats to peace and security—count as "humanitarian"? To these questions, I have two answers that bear further consideration. First, a world where aggression can proceed without penalty is a world that invites the violation of human rights. If an Iraqi dictator can help himself to the territory of another state with impunity, an international regime that respects human rights is but a distant chimera. Conversely, we can treat massive violations of human rights as constituting in themselves a threat to peace and security. Thus I see no intrinsic conflict between pursuing peace and security on the one hand, and human rights on the other.

The willingness of the Security Council to treat massive violations of human rights as a *prima facie* threat to peace and security, and to frame its resolutions largely in terms of the latter seems to me to reflect its history and the nature of the UN as an organization of states. States are still reluctant to recognize norms and institutions that scrutinize "internal" behavior and constrain their actions toward their own citizens. Therefore, in a time of evolving norms of sovereignty, it may be easier to frame humanitarian operations essentially aimed at preventing or ending human rights disasters as interventions to preserve peace and security. And, of course, it is also true that "traditional" aggression *does* violate human rights—by mistreatment of people in the invaded territory, by the massive production of refugees, and by the threat to regional stability such operations inevitably entail. One need only look to the example of Rwanda and the civil war in the Republic of Congo, where the failure to act in the face of the original genocide continues to play itself out at the cost of many innocent lives.[11]

The attentive reader will note that I qualified the second just cause for humanitarian intervention by preceding "violations of human rights" with the adjectives "egregious" and "potentially genocidal." Why "egregious"? The sad answer is that the world presents a far too rich array of human rights violations that might justify outside intervention. We must choose among the evils we seek to end. To much of the world, for example, capital punishment violates human rights. Yet few disinterested observers would urge or welcome the forcible landing of an international military force to prevent Virginia's next execution. However one regards capital punishment after due process of law—to me an unjustifiable atavism—it does not compare with the scale of violations that occurred in Rwanda or in the Cambodia of Pol Pot. If the international community has had difficulty mobilizing against documented acts of genocide, it seems unlikely that it will embark on wholesale interventions in cases on a lower level of violation. Nevertheless, as President Clinton put it in his speech justifying the NATO action in Bosnia, "We cannot stop all war for all time. But we can stop some wars. . . . There are times and places when our leadership can make the difference between peace and war."[12] So we must make some judgments about the scale of evil we face, and about the capacities we have to address it.

Who should undertake the intervention, and with what mandate? I think we must begin by recognizing the vital role of the UN, both as an actor itself and as an agency to coordinate the efforts of international humanitarian relief agencies. (And here I note, with qualified approval, that the United States has finally agreed, although with troubling reservations, to pay a substantial amount of US arrears for past UN operations and assessed dues. Repeated polls have demonstrated that the citizens of the United States believe that the UN is the most appropriate agency for peacekeeping and—despite some notable UN-bashing from United States politicians—hold the UN in much higher regard than they do the U.S. Congress.)[13]

Why emphasize the UN? Perhaps the most obvious reason is that despite some well-publicized failures, it has responded to the human needs presented by conflicts throughout the world. In the period from 1988–1994, the UN initiated nearly twice the number of peacekeeping missions than it initiated during its entire existence until then. The budget for peacekeeping operations rose from $230 million in 1988 to $3.61 billion in 1994. In 1994, seventy-six countries contributed police and military units for seventeen peacekeeping operations that involved some 75,500 personnel. Currently, the UN has fifteen ongoing peacekeeping operations.[14]

At the same time, it is widely recognized that the capacities of the UN are in no way equal to the magnitude of the need for them. Without going into great detail, there is currently a wide range of proposals for improving the ability of the UN to identify, seek to prevent, and, if necessary, move on to intervene in areas where humanitarian disasters are unfolding.[15] Three kinds of international forces have been identified as necessary:

1. Unarmed or lightly armed peace-keepers, to be deployed after an agreement by all parties has been reached;

2. Peace-enforcers, whenever there is no genuine consent among all parties, and the operation, or the execution of the agreement reached under international jurisdiction, requires the use of force to protect the international contingents from attack and to allow them to carry out their mission;

3. Genuine war fighting forces, under Article 43, "useful . . . in meeting any military force" other than that of a major modern army. Such forces ought to be capable of resorting to air strikes against military targets in a variety of "domestic" cases (genocide, dangerous nuclear buildups, state terrorism, etc.).

Not all of these forces must necessarily be under the direct aegis of the UN.

A detailed study by Carl Kaysen and George Rathjens offers suggestions along these lines. They conclude that a volunteer force, though "requir[ing] a mobilization of political will in a way that goes against the current tide," could enable the international community to respond quickly in ways that could save human lives, reduce human suffering, and facilitate political settlements between contestants. Moreover, "it would also have a broader deterrent effect, which in some cases would make diplomatic intervention alone effective in preventing armed conflict, and give a weight to the resolutions of the Security Council that they now lack."[16]

Note that the point of such a force is as much to act as a *deterrent* to genocidal actions as to act as an automatic global rescue force. No one is advocating a UN "army" as a kind of Global 911. But it does seem clear that some kind of force, in place, could act to deter a would-be perpetrator, presuming that there is the political will to deploy it. Recall that the basic components of deterrence, whether nuclear or conventional, are capability, credibility, and communication. For more than forty years, states and analysts studied the requirements of nuclear deterrence in minute detail. We built many quite redundant weapons systems because we (or, more precisely, those representing us and making the procurement decisions) decided that credibility required a so-called strategic triad of weapons systems, missiles of every range and launch capability, and tactical weapons for possible battlefield use. We amassed these weapons, we were told, because we needed them to have robust deterrence.[17] Compare this level of energy and commitment of resources to the current discussion in the United States on preventing genocide and equipping forces for humanitarian interventions.

We have only just begun to scratch the surface of this challenge; we remain too focused on traditional interstate conflict. Yet of the ninety-six armed conflicts during the years 1989–1996 that have been documented, only *five* were traditional interstate wars. All the others were internal, often reflecting ethnic and religious differences, and often involving mass abuses of human rights.[18] We must devote far greater attention than we have thus far to the problem of how to *deter* such conflicts. It seems obvious that a standing force at the disposal of the UN Security Council could help. The essay by Saul Mendlovitz and John Fousek elsewhere in this volume makes what I take to be a compelling case for what they call an international "constabulary." The terminology obviously matters a good deal less than the fact of existence. An international policing force has the potential to make a huge difference in our capacity to prevent genocide.

Of course, many have pointed to the failure of the UN in the case of the breakup of Yugoslavia and to its problems regarding Serb brutality in Kosovo and the consequent NATO intervention in spring 1999. Much of the discussion here seems to have been shallow or marred by recrimination, so it may be useful, as we consider the possibility of just humanitarian intervention, to reflect on the experience in Bosnia. The fact that at least two of my coauthors in this volume feel the same need to consider this case in itself indicates its importance as an example of where the international community is today on the issue of just humanitarian intervention.

What are the lessons to be learned from this conflict? Perhaps the initial imperative is to engage in some thoughtful and self-critical examination. Some have already resisted the effort to draw lessons for the international community, for Europe, and for the United States, preferring instead to blame the conflict on "ancient hatreds and rivalries" within Yugoslavia, and have asserted a kind of moral equivalence among all the parties to the conflict.[19] As Timothy Garton Ash has written in a penetrating essay, these assertions are willfully blind to important distinctions in the kind and degree of responsibility held by the parties: "Bosnia and the Bosnians have suffered most, lost most, and are still most likely to lose more."[20] So let us not avoid the attempt to assign relative responsibility and to assess the reasons for the international failures.

The UN and earlier European attempts at collective intervention remind one uncomfortably of the League of Nations' policy toward Italy's aggression in Ethiopia in 1935. From the beginning, the policy was crippled by ambiguity. On the one hand, the UN first imposed an arms embargo on all sides, and negotiated with all the parties, first in order to obtain a cease-fire between Serbia and Croatia and, in March 1992, to establish the United National Protection Force (UNPROFOR) in Bosnia-Herzegovina, Croatia, and the former Yugoslav Republic of Macedonia. The embargo and the UN presence were supposed to move the parties to agree to the Vance-Owen plan for a settlement of the Bosnian war. This procedure emphasized "evenhandedness" and impartial conflict resolution. It avoided "taking sides in the conflict" and sought to negotiate between the parties as equals.[21]

On the other hand, as the atrocities committed by the Serbs increased along with their hostility toward a peaceful resolution, the UN shifted from an approach that attempted to treat the parties fighting within Bosnia as factions in a civil war (with the Serbs and Croats described as outside interferers in the civil strife) to an approach far more characteristic of the provisions of the UN Charter that deal with interstate aggression: in other words, the imposition of economic sanctions against Serbia, and the creation of a war crimes tribunal. Each of these two procedures can be (and were) defended. But one cannot pursue both at the same time; the simultaneous pursuit of both weakens each. The application of the model of aggression made the overall arms embargo look absurd and unfair to the Bosnians, and certainly did not help to induce compromise from the Serbs while they held a military advantage. The pursuit of the negotiations by the parade of impotent international mediators merely delayed attempts to get tougher with Serbia—and thus largely removed any incentive for Serbia to compromise and give up force. The pursuit of peaceful settlement by mutual compromise when one party believes it can reach all its objectives by force is hardly likely to succeed. Conversely, the attempt at treating Serb behavior as a form of aggression was terminally hampered by the unwillingness to use force either against the Serbs or to enforce the "safe haven" agreements later. Even collective intervention must have a clear goal backed by a credible capacity to reward or punish.

Thus, the first lesson to be drawn from this unhappy conflict is, in fact, an old lesson taught by realists reaching back to E. H. Carr and Hans Morgenthau. Force and diplomacy must be skillfully integrated if either is to work. This is no less true for the international community than for individual states. Looking back, it seems clear that a key turning point was the failure of the West to respond to the Serb bombing of Dubrovnik in December 1991. It has been reliably reported that the commander of NATO in Europe requested the Chairman of the Joint Chiefs in Washington, General Colin Powell, to authorize air strikes against Serbia in response to this bombing. General Powell allegedly responded that "we do deserts, we don't do mountains," and his decision was confirmed by his civilian superiors in the Bush administration. The chance to deter future Serb atrocities passed.

What should the goal of international intervention have been? "Even-handed conflict resolution" or "collective punishment of an aggressor"? Because Serbia decided to go to war—rather than attempt a negotiation in good faith—over the secession of several member states of Yugoslavia, and thus resolve its dispute with Croatia and Bosnia over the fate of Serbs in these areas by force; and because of the brutal methods used by the Serbs to impose their will, the international community would have been morally justified in rapidly and decisively treating Serbia as an aggressor. But given the political and military difficulties of actually compelling the Serbs (i.e., forcing them to give up conquered lands and undo the effects of their "ethnic cleansing") an early resort to deterrence through credible military threats would have had a better chance of impressing the Serbs than belated, vague, and obviously reluctant hints about the possibility of using force. Deterrence in advance, before stakes escalate and before "new realities" are created, is much to be preferred to *post hoc* efforts to compel agreement. And yet no serious effort was made to deter the Serbs from escalating the conflict. Despite all the theories concocted about deterrence during the forty-year superpower conflict, and despite the ubiquitous "Munich analogy," the obvious point was not drawn: diplomacy in the absence of a credible threat of force swims against a strong current.

The chances of getting the Serbs to accept either the Vance-Owen plan or any of its subsequent variants since, or, indeed, of getting them to honor any negotiated settlement short of wholesale partition, were slim to non-existent as long as the major powers (France, Britain, the United States and, of course, Russia) fiercely refused to countenance a serious threat of or use of force. By the time these powers began to discuss air strikes against Serbia and a possible lifting of the arms embargo on Bosnia, there wasn't enough of Bosnia left to make that threat very intimidating. The kind of collective military measures that were necessary to compel the Serbs to cease and desist and to accept a compromise settlement—in short, the sustained NATO bombing of July/August 1995—were resisted for far too long by all the members of the Security Council. Serbia quite consistently acted on the good Leninist maxim: "if you meet steel, stop; if you meet mush, push."

Thus, the second international lesson is, in effect, a variant of the first (concerning the necessity of integrating force and diplomacy): a credible *threat* of force made in advance may well obviate the necessity actually to *use* force, or at least may require a lesser degree of force. The obvious re-luctance of the West even to threaten seriously to use force simply encour-aged the Serbs to push harder and longer, and led them to believe that they could engage in genocidal war crimes—like those that occurred after the fall of the "safe haven" of Srebenica—with impunity.

At bottom, the reluctance, or inability, to integrate force and diplomacy as well as the failure to deter Serbia reflected a crippling conceptual hesitancy on the part of all the outside parties. Was this a civil war or an act of ag-gression by an outside state? There seemed to be just enough factual un-certainty about the situation to excuse the attempt to split the difference. Moreover, even though it was undertaken with the best intentions, the hu-manitarian operation entrusted to UNPROFOR in Bosnia turned out to reinforce the refusal to choose between the two models (civil war or ag-gression) concurrently used by the UN. Although it occasionally, and under very difficult circumstances, succeeded in providing food and aid to besieged and starving civilians, the UN and European Union (EU) missions failed to protect civilians from bombs, bullets, and the systematic murders directed by General Mladic. And quite often it put the UN in the humiliating situ-ation of dependence on the good graces of the attacking and contemptuous Serbs.[22] The European and UN humanitarian missions also made the switch to the model of collective security against aggression more difficult. It pro-vided the countries whose military forces were in UNPROFOR (mainly Brit-ain and France) with the argument that the UN operation would become a target for Serbian violence if NATO or the UN decided at last to get tough with the Serbs.

A third lesson, therefore, is that a "humanitarian" mission cannot be undertaken in isolation from the political circumstances of a conflict. Without a clear sense of political direction, such humanitarian aid may even prolong the conflict if the combatants make pawns of the deliverers of aid. A manmade war, or massive and deliberate violations of human rights, simply cannot be treated in the same way as a natural disaster. The killing must stop or be stopped before effective humanitarian assistance like food aid can begin. Relief work cannot be undertaken merely as a sop to the international conscience. Regrettably, this seems to have been the case for much of the Bosnian war.

At no point was the reluctance—or unwillingness—to choose between the "punish the aggressor" model and the "even-handed peacekeeper" model more apparent than in the disaster of Srebrenica in July of 1995.[23] In April 1993, the UN declared Srebrenica to be a "safe area" in which refugees, mainly Muslims, could be assured of protection from persecution. The concept of a "safe haven" or "safe area" was deeply problematic and controversial from the start. When first proposed in October 1992 by Cornelio Sommaruga, the president of the International Committee of the Red Cross, the idea met almost universal skepticism. Sommaruga argued that internationally guaranteed "safe zones" could at once protect innocent people from becoming the victims of ethnic cleansing and at the same time limit the geographic liability of the international community.

An apparent model was the safe area established—belatedly—to protect Kurds in the aftermath of the Gulf War. But the conditions that made the concept work in 1991 Iraq were not present in post-1992 Bosnia. In Iraq, a victorious outside power, the United States, was willing to enforce the protection of this zone against a defeated Iraqi army, even if the army were still led by a defiant Saddam Hussein. In Bosnia, the armies were intact and the willingness of the UN to enforce the protection of a safe area was, from the very beginning, nonexistent. David Owen and Cyrus Vance vocally warned UN members that a safe area would, in effect, enable all areas not so defined to be open without resistance to ethnic cleansing. Most of the major states of the so-called "contact group" (i.e., United States, Britain, France, and Russia) opposed the idea.

Despite this opposition, the idea resurfaced in the spring of 1993 as the situation in the Serb-surrounded town of Srebrenica deteriorated. Its main advocates, besides Sommaruga, were Austrian foreign minister Alois Mock and Dutch Defense Minister Joris Voorhoeve. Their efforts finally resulted in Security Council Resolution 819, adopted on April 16, 1993. As Honig and Both argue, the "resolution was dangerously inconsistent" in that it declared a safe haven without specifying precisely where this haven would be and how it would be guaranteed as safe:

Resolution 819 created high expectations. Many, both in Bosnia and elsewhere, believed that the United Nations from now on would protect Srebrenica against the

Serbs. In reality, the resolution carefully avoided creating new military obligations for UNPROFOR either to establish or even to protect the safe area. The Council firmly placed the onus on the Serbs and Muslims to make Srebrenica safe. UNPROFOR's role would be simply to "monitor" the humanitarian situation.[24]

The rest of this ghastly story we know all too well. When the Serbs attacked and took Srebrenica, General Ratko Mladic announced on Serb television that he now stood in Serbian Srebrenica, and, as a "present to the nation," the moment for revenge against the "Turks" had arrived. Then, launching the operation for which he has since been indicted by the International War Crimes Tribunal, he personally oversaw the forced expulsion of over 23,000 Bosnian Muslim women and children and the cold-blooded murder of over 8,000 Muslim men. And he did so under the eyes of the UN-authorized troops sent to monitor the humanitarian situation. Thus "the largest single war crime in Europe since the end of World War II" took place literally under the eyes of internationally placed monitors.[25] This kind of "humanitarian intervention" endangered peoples obviously do not need. It surely must stand among the darkest moments of international (in)action in postwar history. And it happened as a result of a noxious combination of flawed analysis and lack of political will among all the great powers.

For the United States, the lesson may simply be that there is no escape from the responsibilities of being the sole remaining superpower. An official of the Bush administration, who did not spare his criticism of the Bush policy in the former Yugoslavia, called the acquiescence of the United States to the massacres in Srebrenica perhaps the most dishonorable episode in the history of United States foreign policy.[26] The responsibilities of the United States should include, at the least, a willingness to be lucid about the criteria for defining its interests in the world. And it must, at the same time, be realistic about the costs of pursuing that definition of interests. American leaders have only just begun to address these questions, and they continue to do so within the narrow context of "risking the lives of American boys." Surely, a great power must occasionally risk the lives of its soldiers in the service of its wider interests; and surely the wider interests of a great power include enforcing the existing minimum rules of international behavior, helping to prevent avoidable conflicts, indeed helping to avoid a slide into genocide. Few would disagree that NATO's military actions in August 1995 to end the siege of Sarajevo could just as easily and, arguably, more effectively, have been undertaken in 1992—*before* the worst atrocities; before the wholly preventable horror of Srebrenica.

The same logic may well apply to NATO's spring 1999 intervention in Kosovo. The lack of firm international action in response to escalating Serb atrocities in Kosovo after the Dayton accords, as well as the failure to apprehend indicted war criminals like Mladic and Karadzic, had serious consequences. Serb dictator Milosevic, who throughout 1997 and 1998 continued to be treated as a sincere partner in the Dayton peace process, apparently came to believe that the international community would not act to prevent further abuses in Kosovo. When the NATO powers finally did get serious about Kosovo, it was already too late to affect his calculations. The diplomacy that culminated in the Rambouillet meetings in February/ March of 1999 resulted in embarrassing failure, when initially even the Kosovar Albanians did not sign the accord and the Serbs used the time of negotiations to reinforce their troop deployments in Kosovo. Throughout this period the situation in Kosovo was rapidly deteriorating. "Between the end of December and mid-March 1999, some 80,000 Albanians were driven from their homes by Serbian forces, while the death toll for the period March 1998 through mid-March 1999 stood at more than 2,000."[27] Note that these figures apply *before* the NATO bombing campaign.

What followed was a double miscalculation, tragically played out at the expense of the innocent inhabitants of Kosovo and, paradoxically, of Belgrade. NATO leaders apparently believed that a brief episode of aerial bombardment would change Milosevic's mind about Kosovo; Milosevic failed to behave as scripted. Instead he used the bombing as the occasion for a genocidal campaign of expulsions—and worse—in Kosovo, apparently thinking that the NATO alliance lacked the will either to sustain the air campaign or to launch an intervention with ground troops. Although he was right on the latter point, his horrific actions within Kosovo in effect allowed NATO to pursue its increasingly costly air campaign, despite widespread misgivings in the West about the civilian casualties it caused within Serbia. In the end, of course, NATO prevailed, but not before the wholesale violations of human rights within Kosovo and the devastating attacks on the fabric of social and economic life within Serbia. Compelling moral reasons dictated that Serbian atrocities in Kosovo could not be tolerated; but surely the whole sorry episode shows yet again that firm deterrence is far superior to belated and costly compulsion. And the character of the NATO intervention—airstrikes designed primarily to minimize the casualties of the intervenor—must surely raise questions about the morally acceptable means of humanitarian interventions.

The underlying ethical principle here remains sound and straightforward: There *is* a duty of mutual aid, and the fact that one cannot do everything does not mean that one should do nothing. This duty of aid becomes deeply compelling in the case of an unfolding genocide. For the United States, the lesson is that a democratic power devoted to peaceful change must exert its will and effort to enhance such change and to resist a slide into war and anarchy. International relations do constitute, in the phrase of the late Hedley Bull, an "anarchical society"; in this post-Cold War era the clear responsibility of democratic states—whether in Europe, Asia, or North America—is to enhance the element of "society" and resist, by whatever means, the element of anarchy. In the case of Yugoslavia, the United States, Europe, and the broader international community took far too long to reassert the element of society. That element of society, I have argued, requires us to have a capability for just humanitarian intervention.

For the purposes of this volume, considering as it does the daunting mission of preventing genocide, the overarching lesson I have hoped to impart is that we can prevent genocide only if we muster the collective will and create the capabilities to do so. This will, and these capabilities, need not be limited to the institutions and practices of the UN; but I do think we should work to make the application of just humanitarian intervention a genuinely collective process, and, in most cases, this will mean a strong UN role. The UN may choose in effect, as it eventually had to in Bosnia, to subcontract to an effective regional organization like NATO, or even, as in Haiti, to a single state. But in general, I think we should work through the norms and institutions of the UN because, for all its failures and contradictions, it remains the preeminent international body able to embody cosmopolitan and supranational norms simultaneously.

As we reflect upon the fiftieth anniversary of the Universal Declaration on Human Rights, we should recommit ourselves to its insistence that "all human beings are born free and equal in dignity and rights." And let us remember that this commitment can take many forms: participation in human rights organizations, lobbying congressmen, leading community discussions, even teaching classes. The history of the Genocide Convention itself can offer us some encouragement. The devoted work of a single professor, Raphael Lemkin, who lost most of his family to the Nazi Holocaust, not only gave us the term genocide, but resulted—largely through his determined efforts—in the Convention on the Prevention and Punishment of the Crime of Genocide, adopted at the same time as the Universal Declaration.

Each of us can make some difference. We can learn to act rapidly and decisively against the purveyors of genocidal hatred and violence. We may debate the means of effecting such action, and recognize, sadly, that the international instruments of pacification remain, at this point, inadequate and underdeveloped. But the inadequacy of our current means does not excuse a refusal to see the problems of ethnic conflict and civil wars for what they truly are—major threats to peace, order, and human rights. We ignore them at the cost of denying our common humanity.

NOTES

1. Michael Joseph Smith, "Ethics and Intervention," *Ethics and International Affairs* 3 (1998): 1–26.

2. Ian Brownlie, ed., *Basic Documents on Human Rights*, 3rd ed. (Oxford: Clarendon Press, 1992), 31, 32.

3. Nik Gowing, "Dispatches from Disaster Zones: The Reporting of Humanitarian Emergencies," unpublished paper presented at a London Conference on "New

Challenges and Problems for Information Management in Complex Emergencies,"
May 1998, p. 21.

4. For discussion of this issue see Amir Pasic and Thomas G. Weiss, "Yugoslavia's
Wars and the Politics of Rescue," *Ethics and International Affairs* 11 (1997): 128;
and the many references in note 58, especially Robert I. Rotberg and T. G. Weiss,
eds., *From Massacres to Genocide: The Media, Public Policy, and Humanitarian Crises*
(Washington, D.C.: Brookings Institution, 1996).

5. Gowing, "Dispatches from Disaster Zones," p. 35. The quotation is from the
five-volume report by the Steering Committee of Emergency Assistance to Rwanda,
*The International Response to Conflict and Genocide: Lessons from the Rwanda Ex-
perience*, published by the Danish Foreign Ministry, 1996.

6. Carnegie Commission on Preventing Deadly Conflict, *Preventing Deadly Conflict: Final Report* (Washington, D.C.: Carnegie Corporation, December 1997),
p. 121.

7. On this point see the eighth and most recent article in the remarkable series
on Bosnia by Mark Danner, "The Killing Fields of Bosnia," *New York Review of
Books*, September 24, 1998, pp. 63–77; and the many sources cited there. Earlier
articles in the same series appeared in the same journal on November 20, December
4, and December 18, 1997; and on February 5, 19, March 26, and April 23, 1998.

8. My source for these remarks was a conference held at the Carnegie Council
on Ethics and International Affairs in May 1998; by the rules of the conference
specific attributions to particular people cannot be made. But for other accounts see
the Carnegie Commission on Preventing Deadly Conflict, *Preventing Deadly Conflict: Final Report*, pp. 4–7; the account provided by Helen Fein in her paper also
(quite plausibly) questions the notion that good, real-time information was lacking.
Nevertheless, this is what the senior official claimed.

9. Thomas Cushman and Stjepan G. Mestrovic, eds., *This Time We Knew: Western Responses to Genocide in Bosnia* (New York: New York University Press, 1996).

10. Charles F. Kegley, "International Peacemaking and Peacekeeping," *Ethics and
International Affairs* 10 (1996): 40.

11. On these points see the exchange of views between Robert C. Johansen and
Stanley Hoffmann in Hoffmann, *The Ethics and Politics of Humanitarian Intervention* (Notre Dame: University of Notre Dame Press, 1996), pp. 68–86, 97–99.

12. *New York Times*, November 28, 1995, A12.

13. Jessica Matthews, "The UN and the Congress," *Washington Post*, March 5,
1995.

14. See Kegley, "International Peacemaking and Peacekeeping," p. 26; other data
are taken from this article. Also see Carnegie Commission on Preventing Deadly
Conflict, *Preventing Deadly Conflict: Final Report*, pp. 174–179.

15. See Brian Urquhart, "For a UN Volunteer Military Force," *New York Review
of Books*, June 10, 1993; and "Looking for the Sheriff," *New York Review of Books*,
July 16, 1998.

16. Carl Kaysen and George Rathjens, "Peace Operations by the United Nations:
The Case for a Volunteer UN Military Force," (1996), pp. 51, 52; available from
the American Academy of Arts and Sciences, Cambridge, MA.

17. On the history of deterrence, see McGeorge Bundy, *Danger and Survival:
Choices about the Bomb in the First Fifty Years* (New York: Random House, 1988).

18. Peter Wallensteen and Margaret Sollenberg, "The End of International War?

Armed Conflict 1989–1995," *Journal of Peace Research* 33, No. 3 (August 1996): 353–370. This study is cited by the Carnegie Commission, *Preventing Deadly Conflict.*

19. See, for example, General Charles G. Boyd, "Making Peace with the Guilty," *Foreign Affairs* (September/October 1995).

20. Timothy Garton Ash, "Bosnia in Our Future," *New York Review of Books,* December 21, 1995, p. 30.

21. For a brief, penetrating account of the Vance-Owen Plan, see Sabrina P. Ramet, *Balkan Babel: The Disintegration of Yugoslavia from the Death of Tito to the War for Kosovo,* 3rd ed. (Boulder, CO: Westview Press, 1999), pp. 207–210. This book is an outstanding treatment of the whole conflict.

22. An eloquent account of this point of view can be found in David Rieff, *Slaughterhouse: Bosnia and the Failure of the West* (New York: Simon and Schuster, 1995, 1996). See, especially, the afterword to the paperback edition, pp. 226–262.

23. In what follows I rely on the account provided by two Dutch journalists, Jan Willem Honig and Norbert Both, *Srebrenica: Record of a War Crime* (New York and London: Penguin Books, 1996), especially chapter 5.

24. Ibid., p. 104.

25. Ibid., pp. xviii–xix.

26. The official was Philip Zelikow in a lecture to my University of Virginia students on December 3, 1998.

27. Ramet, *Balkan Babel,* pp. 317–318.

8

Conclusion

Neal Riemer

INTRODUCTION

In this concluding chapter I should like to recapitulate the argument I advanced in Chapter 1 on behalf of the probability of the possibility of a Global Human Rights Regime to protect against genocide; and to address, especially, the adverse critique that skeptics of a breakthrough to a Global Human Rights Regime advance.[1] My response will benefit from the keen analysis and insights of my coauthors in Chapters 2–7.

I argued that a creative breakthrough to a genocide-free world demands attention to four interrelated needs: (1) the need to strengthen the institutions and actors in a Global Human Rights Regime, (2) the need to articulate a cogent philosophy of prudent prevention, (3) the need to craft a policy of wisely targeted sanctions, and (4) the need to develop a wise theory of just humanitarian intervention. Addressing these needs, I argued, will lead to a responsible, courageous, and effective Global Human Rights Regime capable of protecting against genocide.

But what now of the adverse critique of this argument and a response to that critique? This critique took on urgent meaning in the light of developments in Kosovo in the spring of 1999.

THE CRITIQUE: FOUR DIFFICULTIES

Let me attempt to summarize some of the criticism that might be made of the proposed creative breakthrough to a Global Human Rights regime capable of protecting against genocide. Any breakthrough must come to grips with four interrelated difficulties.

Difficulty 1: Strengthening the Institutions and Actors of a Global Human Rights Regime

Adverse critics contend that a Global Human Rights Regime can neither develop the institutions needed nor the will to curtail genocide. They note that the Global Human Rights Regime is currently very loosely structured and lacks the power or the will to do the very ambitious job sketched for it. They underscore the point that there is no convincing evidence that the UN, for example, is able to go beyond its own attractive rhetoric in protecting against such admitted evils as genocide. The veto of permanent members of the UN Security Council makes UN action impossible in controversial cases, such as Kosovo. Even on issues that do not divide the permanent members of the UN Security Council, the UN lacks the coherent policy and resources to protect against genocide. Moreover, efforts to strengthen the power of the Secretary-General to make that office more effective in combatting genocide will not be successful.

These critics highlight the previous failures of the UN, regional organizations (such as European Union or NATO), and major powers such as the United States, France, and Britain to act swiftly and effectively in deeply troubled areas. They note that the UN's preventive power is nil, and its actual power to stop genocide negligible. The evidence in support of this contention is found, for example, in a number of UN failures—in Bosnia and Rwanda, as well as in earlier failures to take any action against Pol Pot and the Khmer Rouge in Cambodia (Kampuchea) or against other genocidal attacks. Such major powers as the United States and France also failed to anticipate, prevent, or stop the genocidal slaughter in Rwanda. And in Bosnia and Kosovo, regional organizations such as NATO proved unable to stop dreadful ethnic cleansing early on.

Such critics contend that strengthening the powers of the UN High Commissioner for Human Rights or the UN Commission on Human Rights is politically unrealistic, and so is the proposal to put into place a UN Human Rights Protection Force. Such critics also highlight the difficulties of enabling the new Permanent International Criminal Court to become effective in either preventing and punishing genocidal perpetrators.

These critics also note that a Global Human Rights Regime lacks clearly authorized, agreed-upon principles, policies, practices, and resources; and that there is no compelling evidence that these will come into existence in the near or even distant future.

Finally, in their argument against the reality and sense of strengthening UN institutions, adverse critics point to the dominance—in international law, at the UN, and in custom and practice—of the view of sovereignty that precludes outside interference in a nation's domestic affairs and is hostile to outside "meddling." This view of national sovereignty, critics argue, militates against strengthening the institutions of a Global Human Rights Regime that has the power to intervene against genocide.

Difficulty 2: Prudent Prevention

Several troubling questions must be addressed here. Is it utopian to think that it is possible to move all countries of the world toward mature constitutional democracy, democracy characterized—crucially—by respect for basic human rights? And does this long-range concern deflect attention from the immediate, difficult task of stopping contemporary genocide? Can a policy of deterrence be put into place and will it work? Is preemptive action realistic?

Difficulty 3: Articulating the Theory and Practice of Wisely Staged Implementation

Here critics note that monitoring of egregious violations has not been systematic, strong, and effective, and that resourceful action has not been forthcoming in response to clear warnings of genocide. Efforts to make monitoring stronger and more effective—such as a proposal to place a UN human rights monitor in every world region for surveillance of suspect countries—will not be accepted by the nations most in need of watching. Critics note, too, that early warning will be futile in the absence of actors with the resources and will to act expeditiously on such warning. Such critics also contend that publicity is an impotent weapon against a determined and callous offending nation, particularly if it is a big and powerful nation, or a nation allergic to "illegitimate interference" in its domestic affairs. Political actions will simply not prevail against a determined violator. Judicial remedies are laughable: offending nations or offending leaders, particularly, if they are powerful, will not be deterred by the threat of trials for crimes against humanity. Economic sanctions will not work, and are frequently counterproductive, harming innocent civilians while leaving genocidal perpetuators in power. Some critics even contend that sanctions themselves—as in Iraq after the Gulf War—are, ironically, genocidal! Military intervention is always risky, difficult, costly, and perilous. And, as the crisis in Kosovo demonstrated, even NATO was reluctant to insert ground troops early on in order to defeat Serb forces engaged in ethnic cleansing and to ensure the safe return of Kosovar refugees. Moreover, these critics conclude, there is little confidence that after successful intervention, a human rights-respecting regime can come into play. Again, the crisis in Kosovo illustrates the difficulty of the long-term problem of securing a Serbian regime that will respect the rights of Kosovar Albanians.

Difficulty 4: Just Humanitarian Intervention

Here critics raise a number of troubling questions about the principles of just humanitarian intervention.

(1) Is it really possible to get agreement on the appropriate authority to take action? And will there be a will to take action? And will the appropriate authority have adequate forces to do the job? Will nations be willing to contribute to a regional or UN Human Rights Protection Force? Is it realistic to rely upon a volunteer Human Rights Protection Force? Is unilateral action by a regional actor such as NATO, or by a strong nation, acceptable?

(2) Is it possible to get agreement on the meaning of "just cause," on the meaning of "genocide," or on the basic human rights that are to be protected against egregious violations? How many slaughtered or maltreated victims constitute "genocide"? (And how easy or difficult will it be to know who to protect, particularly in complex situations such as Bosnia and Rwanda, where horrendous violations of human rights have been attributed to both sides?)

(3) How easy or difficult will it be to ascertain a "last resort," so that military intervention to protect against genocide can be invoked because all pacific means have been tried and found wanting? May not early intervention—rather than intervention as a last resort—be the prudent course in many cases? And how early should early intervention be?

(4) At what conclusions will a "reasonable" person arrive after calculating painful costs and desired benefits? Particularly if that "reasonable person" is a political realist dedicated conscientiously to the prudent protection of the nation's vital interests, and not to a regional or global vital interest? And particularly if intervention threatens a Vietnam-style "quagmire" or is directed at a powerful nation-state (such as China)?

(5) How easy or difficult will it be to determine whether the intervention, especially if military, has a reasonable chance of stopping the immediate egregious violations? Can air power alone, as in Kosovo, do the job, or are ground troops always required to complete the job?

(6) What, indeed, are humane and proportionate means? How much unintended, collateral damage is acceptable?

(7) Assuming that military intervention momentarily stops the egregious violations, what confidence can the interceding force have that a human rights-respecting regime will be put into place to ensure ongoing protection of human rights? Will a UN or other protectorate be required, and for how long?

All of these questions—all of which imply skepticism about the doctrine of just humanitarian intervention—emphasize that it may be easier to articulate a theory of just humanitarian intervention than to employ it in real international situations.

These four difficulties, critics charge, add up to a disturbing conclusion:

The endeavor to establish a strengthened Global Human Rights Regime incorporating the ideas of prudent prevention, wisely staged implementation, and just humanitarian intervention, is unrealistic, foolish, and utopian. It betrays an ignorance of the realities of international politics, of the meaning of prudent protection of vital national interests, and of international law.

What, then, can be said in response to this adverse criticism?

THE FULLER DEFENSE OF A BREAKTHROUGH TO A GLOBAL HUMAN RIGHTS REGIME

Let me initially preface my fuller defense of a breakthrough to a Global Human Rights Regime by reflecting candidly on the difficulties revealed by NATO's intervention in Kosovo in 1999. (1) Although NATO is a strong actor and was characterized by a will to act to prevent or stop genocidal ethnic cleansing in Kosovo, it was not successful in preventing a great deal of ethnic cleansing or in stopping it early on. (2) Prevention, based on the existence of a mature constitutional democracy in Serbia, crucially respectful of human rights, was irrelevant, and deterrence and preemption did not work. (3) Political, economic, legal, and military sactions were not effective early on; and military intervention, after seventy-eight days of air strikes, succeeded only after great human and material cost. (4) Just humanitarian intervention is essential and, in my view, was justified in Kosovo and Serbia; but a careful assessment of the principles of just humanitarian intervention reveals troubling problems of interpretation: especially of such principles as appropriate authority, timely resort, reasonable chance of initial success, prudent balancing of costs and benefits, humane and proportionate means so as to minimize harm to innocent civilians, and the long-run chance of success.

Nonetheless, despite these sobering conclusions, it does seem probable that NATO's military intervention in the crisis in Kosovo may have sent a clear signal to all of southeastern Europe that genocide will not be tolerated any longer in the new Europe of the twenty-first century. The high price paid in Serbia and Kosovo may perhaps be justified if NATO's military intervention succeeds in getting that signal sent, recorded, and respected. If so, NATO's military intervention, despite its difficulties, problems, costs, may have contributed modestly to a creative breakthrough in Europe on protection against genocide.[2]

Although it would be foolish to ignore the difficulties posed by the adverse critics, it would be equally foolish to ignore the four badly neglected needs previously outlined and the possibility of a creative breakthrough. A creative breakthrough along the lines outlined is, I maintain, a theoretical possibility; consequently, the real question is the actual probability of that possibility. I shall argue that a fuller defense suggests a more convincing case for the probability of that possibility than the critics are willing to concede.

This case is by no means fool-proof; but it does suggest that modest progress can be made on behalf of protection against genocide.

The fuller defense starts with the strong ethical appeal of a Global Human Rights Regime able to to prevent and stop genocide. Narrow-minded realists may scoff about the significance of this appeal in international politics, but broad-minded realists will affirm its importance. Most certainly this ethical factor operates to keep open the commitment to a Global Human Rights Regime along the lines I have suggested, even if there are doubts about its full functioning in today's world.

The ethical promise of global protection against egregious violations of human rights does not, therefore, need extended defense. What may need defense, however, is the ethical priority to be given to the prevention of and protection against genocide. However, a strong case can be made for this priority once two things become clear: first, that the priority given to the battle against genocide does not necessarily prejudice action in protection of a wide range of human rights less severe than genocide; and second, that the battle against genocide necessarily involves protecting a range of human rights violations that are often premonitory (or early warning) signals of a coming genocide. Such human rights violations, for example, are exemplified by gross maltreatment of ethnic and political opponents, religious persecution, racial discrimination, and violations of other basic human rights, including freedom of speech, press, and association.

Moreover, the priority to be given to the battle against genocide is premised on the argument that a breakthrough against genocide prepares the way for breakthroughs in the protection of human rights less severe than genocide. Thus, the breakthrough against genocide—itself a highly defensible ethical goal—should make possible the development of those institutions, actors, principles, policies, and practices that can subsequently be used in the protection of less egregious violations of human rights than genocide.

It should also be clear that protection against genocide can be coherently and persuasively related to the protection of a country's broader, enlightened national interests. Genocide threatens the fabric of constitutional global order and, therefore, inevitably, impinges on the fabric of all countries that are a part of that global order. The tie between genocide and threats to international peace—for example, peace between countries that made up the former Yugoslvaia, or peace between Rwanda and Burundi or between Rwanda and the Congo—should be clear to perceptive observers. Beyond the vital, enlightened interest of nations in enhancing protection of human rights and averting international conflicts, there is the economic self-interest of nations in averting genocide. Economically, as Helen Fein has argued in Chapter 3, the cost of humanitarian assistance to countries and peoples afflicted by genocide (including the trauma and cost of caring for refugees caused by genocidal conflict) is considerably higher than the estimated cost of early intervention to prevent or stop genocide. This point has again been poignantly brought home in the dreadful conflict in Kosovo.

Candidly, those who seek a breakthrough to a strengthened Global Human Rights Regime—incorporating a guiding theory of prudent prevention, effectively staged implementation, and just humanitarian intervention—confront a past and present seemingly hostile to such a breakthrough. Yet a closer look at past and present may offer some encouraging empirical evidence that a brighter future than the skeptics envision may lie ahead. It is, I suggest, foolish to remain stuck in the "realities" of the conventional wisdom when there is good reason to believe that it may be possible to create new "realities" more in tune with a more adequate protection against genocide. Let us, then, take another look at the probability of the possibility of strengthening the institutions and actors of our Global Human Rights Regime and of pursuing policies of prevention, of effective staged implementation, and of just humanitarian intercession in the battle against genocide.

Most significant in the effort to strengthen the institutions of a Global Human Rights Regime, as Douglas Simon has emphasized in his Chapter 2, is the end of the Cold War and the relative empowerment of the Security Council of the UN. This relative empowerment was dramatically illustrated by the UN's action (with, of course, strong U.S. leadership, will, and commitment) in defeating Iraq's effort to gobble up Kuwait. UN action, however incomplete, at least signalled that the UN Security Council—a key actor in a Global Human Rights Regime—could act decisively under certain conditions free of the restraints of the Cold War. Subsequent efforts, led largely by the United States, to police and protect groups at risk in northern and southern Iraq have been—unfortunately—less than satisfactory. In Kosovo, despite Russia's opposition to NATO's military intervention, NATO was able to act. It is highly doubtful that such NATO action would have taken place if the Cold War had continued.

Despite undeniable difficulties in Somalia, Bosnia, Cambodia, Rwanda, and Haiti, there is evidence that the end of the Cold War makes stronger institutions possible at the UN and elsewhere. Of course, it remains to be seen whether the newly established position of UN High Commissioner for Human Rights can be developed along the lines I have suggested. Similarly, the empowerment of the UN Commission on Human Rights still has to be accomplished. But the probability of the possibility of the development of some strengthened institutions—including UN Human Rights Monitors—is not a distant and foolish utopian dream but a distinct prospect.

Existing institutions for monitoring (many of them highly effective)—at the UN, within such nations as the United States, and including a number of very effective nongovernmental organizations—suggest that an even more effective monitoring establishment can be put into place. It is not naive to expect to see in place in the very near future a most effective program of

global monitoring of human rights. The problem, then, will not lie with
effective monitoring and early warning of genocide, but with a resourceful
and effective response by those actors in the Global Human Rights Regime
who are willing to protect against genocide.

The establishment of a UN Human Rights Protection Force will be much
more difficult. Whether such a force should combine the functions of both
police and/or military intervention to stop genocide *and* consolidation of
a human rights-respecting regime in the offending country is a question that
can profitably be debated. Similarly, debate on the feasibility of a voluntary
UN Constabulary to enforce the law on genocide and crimes against humanity (as proposed by Saul Mendlovitz and John Fousek in Chapter 5)
may be profitable. Mendlovitz and Fousek have at least stimulated us to
think creatively about a volunteer antigenocidal police force. Given the right
circumstances (a crucial qualification), the possibility—indeed, the probability—of a UN Human Rights Protection Force, in whatever shape it eventually takes, is then an idea not impossible of fulfillment in the near future.
The right circumstances would call for an evolving global culture respectful
of human rights and a genuine great power commitment to honor the UN's
Convention on the Prevention and Punishment of the Crime of Genocide.
In the short term—as military intervention in East Timor in the fall of 1999
made clear—regional actors may, with UN approval (and the reluctant approval of the involved government), intervene in certain cases to protect
against egregious violations of human rights. Reliance on regional actors
and regional organizations may serve, temporarily, until a more fully established and funded UN Human Rights Protection Force can come into existence.[3]

Next, the case for prudent prevention is not as unrealistic as critics maintain. Take the difficult and long-range problem of encouraging the development of mature constitutional democracies, countries crucially dedicated
to protection of basic human rights. There is now considerable evidence to
suggest that steps can realistically be taken to enhance the growth and development of democratic and constitutional countries, and thus create a firm
future foundation for the prevention of genocide. This task is not foolishly
utopian. We have in fact seen the growth and development of democratic
and constitutional countries in post-World War II Germany, Italy, and Japan—remarkable constitutional developments in major, powerful, offending
nations in history. Of course, important circumstances (unconditional surrender, military occupation) may have encouraged such democratic and constitutional development in the defeated foes of the allies in World War II.
Yet we cannot deny that fascist and militarist regimes were in fact replaced
by democratic and constitutional countries. The fuller story of this replacement may not always be apt for other authoritarian, despotic, and spuriously
"democratic" regimes; but certainly some relevant lessons can be learned

from that experience. Importantly, the current democratic and constitutional status of Germany and Japan indicate that significant democratic and constitutional transformation can occur even in great powers once given over to persistent, systemic, egregious violations of human rights.

Today, of course, circumstances in other countries—China, Iran, Iraq, Vietnam, North Korea, Sudan, Russia, the Congo, and Serbia, for example—may make the path of transformation different and more difficult than in the cases of a defeated Germany, Italy, and Japan. (And we should not forget the tragic fact that it took a dreadful war to bring about the transformations in Germany, Italy, and Japan.) Yet it would be defeatist and unrealistic to deny the possibility of change in authoritarian countries, even in such powerful states as China and Russia. Moreover, it would be unrealistic to ignore the voices in Montenegro and in Serbia that hold out hope for the truly democratic and constitutional transformation of Serbia.[4]

Moreover, we must not forget the remarkable transformations of other authoritarian regimes. For example, Greece, Spain, and Portugal moved away from right-wing regimes (Greece) and fascist regimes (Spain and Portugal) and are now functioning as constitutional democracies—all within the framework of the European Union. These changes occurred without military defeat in war and military occupation.

Similarly, right-wing authoritarian regimes in Latin America have been replaced by governments committed to constitutional democracy—for example, in Brazil, Argentina, and Chile. The path to constitutional democracy in these countries has often been rocky, and the advent of really mature constitutional democracy has still to be achieved. But it is unrealistic to deny the partial progress that has been made in Latin America.

Most significantly, a powerful communist state, the Soviet Union, has been peacefully replaced by the Commonwealth of Independent States, and the guiding ideology of the Soviet Union, communism—an ideology hostile to the protection of human rights—has been repudiated. This transformation has also included the emergence of Russia as a power that has significantly, if not fully, repudiated its oppressive human rights heritage and is seeking, amidst great difficulty, to develop into a constitutional democracy. Again, it would be foolish to assert that mature constitutional democracy has emerged in Russia. Yet it would be even more foolish to close one's eyes to the remarkable change in Russia that has occurred, and may—painfully, and with some setbacks—still occur.

Movements in a democratic and constitutional direction have also occurred in other formerly communist nations in Eastern Europe, once dominated by the Soviet Union. These transformations include the reunification of formerly communist East Germany with democratic and constitutional West Germany, and the slow, halting, painful progress of other former Soviet-dominated countries of Eastern Europe toward constitutional democracy. Some of these countries—for example, the Czech Republic and Poland—have made greater progress than others. But the changes from old-style repressive communist regimes are undeniable.

These developments—with their great portent for the protection of human rights—occurred despite the conventional wisdom, which affirmed that it was utopian to think of the breakup of the Soviet Union, of the demise of communism, and of a day when all countries of Eastern and Central Europe would be moving—however painfully and slowly—toward constitutional democracy. It now remains to be seen whether Serbia will, in time, move toward genuine constitutional democracy.

Most recently, we have also seen another seemingly unbelievable event: a free general election, and Nelson Mandela's election as president, in a South Africa once dedicated to apartheid and white rule forever. Moreover, the protection of basic human rights for all South Africa citizens has become a cardinal feature of the new South Africa. This transformation (still in its difficult early stages), once deemed utopian by the conventional wisdom, is another piece of evidence supporting the proposition that movement toward constitutional democracy can occur even in regimes that were once stuck in the most authoritarian systems. Genocide, per se, may not have characterized all such authoritarian systems, but a wide range of other human rights were clearly violated in persistent, systemic, and egregious ways.

These developments, then—especially in Germany, Japan, Italy, Spain, Greece, Portugal, Brazil, Argentina, Russia, and South Africa—provide a genuinely realistic hope for movement toward genuine democracy and constitutionalism in other countries and other parts of the world. Clearly, then, a Global Human Rights Regime can profit from a study of these remarkable transformations and developments. Such a regime can encourage constructive policies derived from that study as well as from other policies derived from a general knowledge of the necessary and sufficient conditions of mature constitutional democracy.

The case for deterrence as a more immediate instrument of prevention is not easy to make, but the ethical sense of stopping egregious violations before they occur is so overwhelming that the study of the policy and machinery of deterrence must not be undermined by short-sighted realists and other advocates of a timid conventional wisdom who affirm that little or nothing can be done to deter offenders.

Theoretically, it should not be difficult to identify all those national regimes that should be subjects of scrutiny as case studies for possible deterrence of genocide. They are authoritarian regimes of the Left or Right and spurious "democratic" regimes that currently maltreat political opponents or people of certain races, religions, and ethnic backgrounds.

To argue on behalf of a theory of deterrence to prevent egregious violations before they occur is not to argue that prudence will easily dictate the application of deterrence in connection with each and every offending regime. I argue only that we must *begin* to develop a theory of deterrence, so that we shall be clear-headed about its application in the first few test cases in which we activate the theory. Clearly, protection against genocide will be enormously advanced if this second aspect of a theory of protection via prevention can become an operational reality in the global community. It will take time to develop the policy and machinery of deterrence. It would be probably be wise to employ deterrence, at the start, in cases where success is guaranteed, or almost guaranteed. Then, gradually and prudently, the range of cases in which the doctrine of deterrence would come into play could be extended.

Much of the argument and strategy articulated above about deterrence is relevant to the argument on behalf of preemptive action. Here, however, the case for a preemptive strike to forestall genocide is even more difficult to make; the stakes are higher, because such strikes could involve military or police intervention. Such preemptive military or police intervention should, in my judgment, be rarely used. But, again, given the ethical sense of saving lives before egregious violations occur, in other words, given the logic of prevention over "cure," the weapon of the preemptive strike should be included in the arsenal of weapons to be employed—rarely, prudently, and carefully—as occasion demands. Very careful consideration should be required to demonstrate that a just preemptive intervention is in order. The threat of preemptive humanitarian intervention may often serve as a deterrent and make actual military intervention necessary. But in those normally rare cases where there is a clear and present danger of genocide, the policy and machinery of preemption should be ready for use. The UN Secretary-General, who would normally be in charge of recommending a preemptive strike to the Security Council of the United Nations, would have to have an overwhelmingly compelling case before making such a recommendation, and the Security Council would have to concur only on being convinced that such an overwhelming case exists. Clearly, these precautions against easy and loose preemptive strikes may deny the interceding force of the element of surprise in its action against a potential offender. Yet this loss may well be justified if it ensures that the most careful and thorough justification for action is established prior to any preemptive strike. This UN scenario is a preferable scenario.

The difficulties facing unanimity among the permanent members of the UN Security Council (and avoidance of a veto that would prevent Security Council action) strongly suggest the need for alternatives at the regional level. The North Atlantic Treaty Organization is one such regional alternative in Western and Central Europe. Other sound regional alternatives are, frankly, sorely lacking, but clearly need to be developed. Other difficulties facing this option will be addressed when I consider the doctrine of just humanitarian military intervention *after* genocidal violations have occurred.

Next, we come to the difficult and crucial task of effective staged implementation, the task of enforcing an escalating strategy for protecting human rights. Fortunately, as we have already noted, there is already a good deal of policy and machinery in place. Monitoring, investigating, and reporting are already modest realities and can be significantly enhanced. Acting on behalf of the Global Human Rights Regime, a committed and resourceful UN High Commissioner for Human Rights can coordinate much of the work now being done by NGOs, individual nations, regions, and the UN itself. Even more information can be obtained, especially if a Human Rights Monitor can be established in every region of the world. There will, of course, be some resistance to such monitoring in general, and to a Human Rights Monitor in every world region; but the prospects for effective monitoring are, nonetheless, promising.

Similarly, publicity with regard to the results of findings on violations of human rights can be enhanced and can increasingly serve as a powerful weapon in the creation of a supportive public opinion on human rights. The use of modern means of communication to get the word out on protection against genocidal violations will be increasingly effective.

Our creative political imaginations should not be limited to some of the usual political or diplomatic pressures that can be brought to bear against offending parties. Here, too, the test of success will be a pragmatic one. Withdrawal of diplomatic recognition, ending of foreign aid, other political and economic pressures (including freezing or seizure of assets and limitations on travel) can be brought to bear on offending countries and their leaders. And it should be clear that nations (generally acting pursuant to UN Security Council decisions) will normally be the political actors making enforcement decisions effective. Nations will normally make decisions to assess fines, seize or freeze assets, and limit the travel of egregious violators of human rights. Moreover, as Michael Smith has crucially emphasized in Chapter 7, diplomacy and the credible threat of force must be intelligently integrated if either is to work effectively.

One often hears that economic sanctions do not work to protect human rights. As George Lopez has argued in Chapter 4, we do need to be careful when working out a policy of carefully targeted economic sanctions to minimize harm to innocent civilians. The story on economic sanctions may be a mixed one, but limited successes in South Africa and Zimbabwe (Rhodesia) suggest that economic sanctions may sometimes play a more important role than is often thought. The case of Bosnia certainly suggests that economic sanctions alone against the former Yugoslavia did not bring an end to "ethnic cleansing" and other violations of human rights. Ironically, military sanctions affecting Croatia and Bosnian Muslims may have actually favored Serbia and adversely affected Croatia and Bosnian Muslims in their struggles to protect themselves against military action by Bosnian Serbs. Yet we do not know with certainty what limited effect economic sanctions may have had in curtailing, to some extent, the brutal activities in the countries of the former Yugoslavia. Clearly, more research is in order on the effectiveness of economic sanctions—what kind, how administered, and so on—in protecting against genocidal violations.

It is especially important to keep in mind the effect of sanctions on innocent children, women, and men. The harm to innocent civilians created by economic sanctions in Iraq cannot, in my judgment, be deemed genocidal—as some critics allege—primarily because the UN Security Council (and those supporting sanctions against Iraq) clearly had no genocidal intent in imposing sanctions on Iraq. Moreover, efforts (sometimes inadequate) were made to enable food and medical supplies to reach Iraq to avert unnecessary suffering. It is also clear that the major responsibility for harm to innocent Iraquis rests with the regime of Saddam Hussein. Nonetheless, it is still vital that sanctions policy—if sometimes needed—be very carefully targeted to avoid harm to innocent civilians.

The effectiveness of judicial trials in enhancing protection against genocidal violations needs to be more fully explored. The beneficial results of the Ad Hoc International Criminal Tribunals for the former Yugoslavia and for Rwanda have still to be ascertained. It is important to develop judicial trials as a plausible tool in the human rights arsenal. Their effectiveness will, in turn, depend upon the development of a constitutional global culture strongly supportive of human rights and willing to act on information of genocidal violations. Experience will also demonstrate whether, for example, the newly established Permanent International Criminal Tribunal to try genocidal offenders (analyzed by David Wippman in Chapter 7) will be effective in apprehending, trying, and punishing genocidal offenders. This Tribunal, as Wippman has emphasized, faces a number of obstacles, not the least of which is U.S. lack of support. It is ironic, indeed, that the United States, which took a leadership role in establishing the ad hoc tribunals for the former Yugoslavia and Rwanda, has grave reservations about the new Permanent International Criminal Tribunal. It is encouraging, however, that key human rights NGOs such as Human Rights Watch, although not perfectly satisfied with the Rome treaty, nevertheless see the Rome treaty as a most significant step forward in the effort to protect against genocide.

Finally, we come to the ultimate sanction, the use of police and/or military force in humanitarian intervention. This is a concededly difficult and dangerous weapon in the battle to protect human rights. It should normally be employed as a last resort and used very sparingly, although early military intervention may sometimes be wise. As such cases as Bosnia, Rwanda, and Kosovo strongly indicate, early police and/or military intervention may be wisely dictated in cases where it is clear that genocide is imminent or already in process, and where diplomacy and other sanctions will not work. Used prudently, police and/or military force can be an effective weapon in stopping genocide. I repeat: it is a difficult and dangerous weapon and must be used accordingly. Its use will always involve an agonizingly tough, prudential decision based on balancing costs and benefits.

The task of those concerned with a creative breakthrough in this domain is to minimize the perils and maximize the promise of humanitarian military intervention. Very difficult questions must be faced here: What actor—for example, the UN, NATO, another regional organization, the United States or another military power—will make the commitment to employ military force? What should the character of military intervention be? Ground troops alone? Ground troops in conjunction with air power? Or, as in the Kosovo crisis, air strikes, to be followed by ground troops—but only when a "permissive" environment has been established? These questions are not easily answered, and answers may vary from genocidal situation to genocidal situation. But, clearly, policy must pose them and have an appropriate strategy at the ready.

Since just humanitarian police and/or military intervention are such important parts of a Global Human Rights Regime, let me recapitulate the compelling argument on wise guidelines to be followed in such interventions, and emphasize how such guidelines may serve to distinguish between just humanitarian intercession and illegitimate intervention.

The doctrine of just intervention would require (1) that the decision to intervene be made by an appropriate authority (preferably the UN Security Council), normally on the recommendation of the UN Secretary-General (as he is advised by the UN High Commissioner for Human Rights, or a comparable Watch Group such as the International Crime Watch Advisory Board recommended by Saul Mendlovitz and John Fousek in Chapter 6), (2) that a just cause for intervention be clearly established (based on reliable, authentic information of genocidal violations—or, in the case of preemptive intervention, on reliable, authentic information of a clear and present danger of such violations), (3) that police and/or military intervention normally be a last resort without, however, precluding early intervention when clearly required to stop genocide that is imminent or beginning (after pacific means of intervention have been tried and found wanting), (4) that the military intervention be based on a careful calculation of costs and benefits, (5) that military intervention have a strongly reasonable chance of immediate success, (6) that the means of intervention be humane and proportionate to the end sought (protection against genocide), (7) that the end results (protection against genocide) are not temporary or transient but durable, that—in brief—just results be accomplished and be as permanent as human affairs can permit.

Next, let me address the argument that "just humanitarian intervention" is a cover for illegitimate intervention. Historically, we must concede that so-called humanitarian intervention has often, in fact, been a cover for illegitimate intervention in the internal affairs of other states. Consequently, great care is required to avert illegitimate intervention and to protect nation-states from unwarranted meddling. Such great care can be advanced if a strong case is made—as I have argued—for following the principles of just humanitarian intervention outlined above. The making of such a strong case can provide the safeguards to guard against illegitimate intervention.

Nations have a crucial role to play in the protection against genocide, and they should be encouraged to play this valuable role. However, protecting against illegitimate intervention and securing the development of global constitutionalism call for primary use of global (UN) and regional organizations. Action by the UN, or by regional organizations or actors with UN approval, can serve to some extent to counter the argument that just humanitarian intervention is simply a cover for illegitimate intervention by big, bullying states acting in their own selfish interests. Intervention can be ill- or well-advised, depending on fulfillment of the principles of just humanitarian intervention. Buttressed by a convincing doctrine of just humanitarian intervention and by an effective Human Rights Protection Force, intervention—in the very rare cases in which it will be invoked—can prudently go forward. Intervention will almost always—but not necessarily—be a difficult enterprise. This difficulty is a powerful reason for considering it carefully and employing it only on very limited and very special occasions. Nonetheless, carefully conceived and executed, it can be less costly than failing to intervene—less costly in human lives, time and effort, and monetary expenditures.[5]

The idea of protection of basic human rights against genocidal violations is not a diabolic Western invention. I affirm the universality of basic human rights, reject the arguments of radical cultural relativists on human rights, yet recognize the historical particularity of some aspects of human rights. Basic human rights (at least on the rhetorical level) are recognized globally. Their protection makes great sense. Even if human rights are not always adequately protected—especially by authoritarian, despotic, or spuriously "democratic" regimes—or are not always respected by political, religious, and tribal fanatics around the globe, there is considerable global support for the protection of life against genocidal attacks. Moreover, the evidence revealed by the collapse of the Soviet Union and Soviet communism and by the replacement of other authoritarian regimes of the Left or Right strongly suggests that large numbers of people in the countries that underwent these transformations understand the meaning of human rights and want them respected and adequately protected. There is also considerable evidence to support the proposition that human rights, even though they clearly owe a great debt to the western constitutional tradition, are deeply rooted in human needs and find support in all the world's great religions.

It is most important that individual nations act to protect basic human rights in their own polities. Clearly, they must also avoid giving aid and comfort to nations that engage in persistent, systemic, egregious violations of human rights. Moreover, it is important for them to take other prudent actions against violators of human rights. Having said this, it is important, nonetheless, also to declare that sometimes—in a modest and careful and constitutional way—nations may also have an ethical obligation, related to their constitutional obligation, to support regional and global policies and measures to protect against genocidal violations beyond national borders. Indeed, the effectiveness of a Global Human Rights Regime will depend upon the support that individual nations in the UN—pursuant to an enlightened view of their national self-interest in a constitutional global order—can bring to that regime. Individual nations must appreciate the important role they have to play in building on national, regional, and UN precedents, and thus furthering the protection against genocide.

Regional declarations and practices deserve special attention. Here, developments in Western Europe can serve as a model for other regions of the world that have been less effective in protecting human rights. The irony here is that although Western Europe has the most effective regional human rights regime in place, there has been less need for a Western European regime to act in the post-World War II world because of the absence of egregious human rights violations in Western European countries during this period. Nonetheless, the experience of these regional human rights regimes in dealing with lesser human rights violations provides valuable empirical lessons for the development of constitutional machinery to protect against egregious violations elsewhere in the world.

NATO's military intervention in the Serbian-Kosovo conflict illustrates both the promise and the peril of action by a regional organization whose original purpose was to function as a defensive alliance against a potential threat by the Soviet Union. The promise of its action is the end of genocidal "ethnic cleansing" in Kosovo and the achievement of respect there for the political and human rights of Kosovar Albanians. The peril of its action lies in the human and material costs to all sides in the conflict and the uncertainty about respect for human rights—of Serbs as well as Kosovar Albanians—after the initial military intervention ends.

We must also take note of other significant developments, apropos the protection of human rights, that have occurred or are occurring in international law. Fernando Tesón, in his book, *Humanitarian Intervention: An Inquiry Into Law and Morality* (1988), makes one of the strongest cases for the protection of human rights under international law.[6] Tesón makes both legal and moral arguments on behalf of just humanitarian intervention. International law, and the theory and practice of the UN, Tesón contends, are compatible with such intervention. Fundamentally, those who argue on behalf of just humanitarian intervention maintain that such intervention to deal with persistent, systemic, egregious violations of human rights—such as genocide—trumps the principle of Article 2, Paragraph 7 of the UN Charter (no interference in the internal affairs of a sovereign state). Tesón insists that international law and moral philosophy are essentially linked. He holds that the rights of states derive from human rights and, consequently, wars in defense of human rights are just. He maintains that the right of humanitarian intervention is consistent with the UN Charter and supported by state practice. More recently, Beth Van Schack, in a 1997 *Yale Law Review* article, has advanced a powerful argument on behalf of the *jus cogens* prohibition of genocide, which again provides a basis in international law for just humanitarian intervention.[7]

Clearly, the effectiveness of a Global Human Rights Regime will be immensely enhanced if a clear basis in international law is established for prudent prevention and just humanitarian intervention.

The foregoing arguments underscore the prudential judgments that have to be made by an effective Global Human Rights Regime. Bold and successful prudential judgments are required on a number of key issues: strengthening global institutions and actors, prudent prevention, staged implementation, and just humanitarian intervention. Such prudential judgments must be capable of grappling with the dangers of illegitimate intervention, on one hand, and cowardly failure, on the other. Such prudential judgments must also help with the real problems encountered in dealing with the costs and benefits of prudent prevention, with effective implementation of sanctions, and with just humanitarian intervention. Only careful assessment of actual practice will inform us of the success of the difficult prudential judgments required to make a Global Human Rights Regime an operational reality.

CONCLUSION

The arguments on behalf of an effective Global Human Rights Regime partake of key elements of a "thought experiment." A thought experiment can only point the general way toward a prophetic breakthrough to a Global Human Rights Regime capable of preventing and stopping genocide. Only time will tell if this future breakthrough occurs and is then consolidated. The breakthrough, however, depends significantly on imaginative, creative leaders and imaginative, creative followers. Thought experiments—and a creative breakthrough is always, early on, a thought experiment—can be transformed into reality only when they are taken seriously by creative leaders and when they make sense to thoughtful followers. It is easy to be pessimistic or skeptical about the possibilities of creative breakthroughs in politics in a political world that does not lend itself readily to change of the right kind, in a world in which it is so easy to be overwhelmed by external forces—powerful forces beyond our control. I hope, however, that the arguments made in this book lead one to be skeptical about the skeptics—skeptical about the overwhelming cogency of the arguments of the adverse critics.

We conclude, then, that a creative breakthrough to a Global Human

Rights Regime capable of protecting against genocide is a theoretical possibility. What will be tested in the future is the probability of that possibility. As we explore this probability, we can be encouraged by other creative breakthroughs in politics (for example, to religious liberty in key areas of the world, to the concept of the federal republic in the United States, or to European Union).

We may also be encouraged by the insights of other penetrating observers of the political scene. Machiavelli, for example, often viewed as the crown prince of political realists, observed that although "there is nothing more difficult to carry out, nor more doubtful of success, nor more dangerous to handle, than to initiate a new order of things," it is also the case that although "fortune is the ruler of half our actions," "she allows the other half or thereabouts to be governed by us."[8] Machiavelli's emphasis, of course, is on what humans can do in their fifty-percent zone of freedom!

James Madison, the brilliant architect of the creative breakthrough to the American federal republic, observed in Number 14 of the *Federalist*:

Hearken not to the voice which petulantly tells you that the form of government recommended for your adoption is a novelty in the political world; that it has never yet had a place in the theories of the wildest projectors; that it rashly attempts what it is impossible to accomplish. . . . But . . . is the experiment of an extended republic to be rejected, merely because it may comprise what is new? Is it not to the glory of the people of America, that whilst they have paid a decent regard to the opinions of former times and other nations, they have not suffered a blind veneration for antiquity, for custom, or for names, to overrule the suggestion of their own good sense, the knowledge of their own situation, and the lessons of their own experience. To this manly spirit, posterity will be indebted for the possession, and the world for the example, of the numerous innovations displayed on the American theatre, in favor of private rights and public happiness. Had no important step been taken by the leaders of the Revolution for which a precedent could not be discovered, no government established of which an exact model did not present itself, the people of the United States might, at this moment, have been numbered among the melancholy victims of misguided councils, must at best have been laboring under the weight of some of those forms which have crushed the liberties of the rest of mankind.[9]

Madison clearly saw the need to move beyond the conventional wisdom, beyond precedent, and to experiment and innovate in order to advance human liberties.

Madison and Machiavelli thus emphasize the importance of human creativity, purposeful will, and bold action. This emphasis can reinforce those who believe that creative breakthroughs are as possible and probable in the future as in the present and the past.

Mission impossible? No. Mission probable but extraordinarily difficult? Yes.

NOTES

1. See, again, my earlier appraisal, in Neal Riemer, "Protection Against Genocide: Toward a Global Human Rights Regime," *Creative Breakthroughs in Politics* (Westport, CT: Praeger, 1996), Chapter 7.

2. See my paper, "Political Scientists and Protection Against Genocide in Kosovo: Critical Reflections on Political Theory and Public Policy," American Political Science Association, Annual Meeting, Atlanta, Georgia, September 2, 1999.

3. See, here, UN Secretary-General Kofi Annan's opening speech on September 20, 1999, to the UN General Assembly in favor of humanitarian intervention. Subsequent debates reveal that objections to intervention by the UN, NATO, or regional multinational forces remain strong in countries such as China, India, Malaysia, Iraq, North Korea, and Libya.

4. See the op-ed article by Milo Djukanovic, President of Montenegro, and Zoran Djindjic, head of the Democratic Party in Serbia, in *The New York Times*, May 8, 1999, A 15. (Montenegro and Serbia constitute the two states that make up Yugoslavia today.) They wrote: "Despite the current conflict, we remain committed to Yugoslavia's integration into Europe, and eventually into the European Union." They held that "Democracy can be established in our country only with a complete political transition in Serbia and the rest of Yugoslavia." They recognized the need for "an outside body to help monitor the political change." They called for "long-term international support" to aid in "democratic and economic reconstruction in Yugoslavia."

5. Currently, a volunteer Human Rights Protection Force is not in existence; and, even if it were in existence, it is by no means clear that it could be strong enough to stop a major genocidal onslaught. It could, however, conceivably stop a minor genocidal danger; and, if reinforced by a credible, bigger, and stronger military force, it could even deter a major genocidal danger.

6. Fernando Tesón, *Humanitarian Intervention: An Inquiry Into Law and Morality* (Dobbs Ferry, NY: Transnational Publishers, 1988).

7. Beth Van Schaack, "The Crime of Political Genocide: Repairing the Genocide Convention's Blind Spot," *Yale Law Journal* 106, No. 7 (May 1997); 2259–2291.

8. Niccolo Machiavelli, *The Prince* (New York: Modern Library, 1940), Chapter 7, p. 21, and Chapter 25, p. 91.

9. James Madison, *The Federalist*, (No. 14 New York: Modern Library, 1937), pp. 84–85.

Appendix 1

United Nations Convention on the Prevention and Punishment of the Crime of Genocide

(Adopted 1948; in force 1951)

The Contracting Parties

Having considered the declaration made by the General Assembly of the United Nations in its resolution 96 (1) dated 11 December 1946 that genocide is a crime under international law, contrary to the spirit and aims of the United Nations and condemned by the civilized world;

Recognizing that at all periods of history genocide has inflicted great losses on humanity; and

Being convinced that, in order to liberate mankind from such an odious scourge, international co-operation is required;

Hereby agree as hereinafter provided

ARTICLE I

The Contracting Parties confirm that genocide[,] whether committed in time of peace or in time of war, is a crime under international law which they undertake to prevent and to punish.

ARTICLE II

In the present Convention, genocide means any of the following acts committed with intent to destroy, in whole or in part, a national, ethnical [sic], racial or religious group, as such:
(a) Killing members of the group;
(b) Causing serious bodily or mental harm to members of the group;

(c) Deliberately inflicting on the group conditions of life calculated to bring about its physical destruction in whole or in part;

(d) Imposing measures intended to prevent births within the group;

(e) Forcibly transferring children of the group to another group.

ARTICLE III

The following acts shall be punishable:
    (a) Genocide;
    (b) Conspiracy to commit genocide;
    (c) Direct and public incitement to commit genocide;
    (d) Attempt to commit genocide;
    (e) Complicity in genocide.

ARTICLE IV

Persons committing genocide or any of the other acts enumerated in article III shall be punished, whether they are constitutionally responsible rulers, public officials or private individuals.

ARTICLE V

The Contracting Parties undertake to enact, in accordance with their respective Constitutions, the necessary legislation to give effect to the provisions of the present Convention and, in particular, to provide effective penalties for persons guilty of genocide or any of the other acts enumerated in article III.

ARTICLE VI

Persons charged with genocide or any of the other acts enumerated in article III shall be tried by a competent tribunal of the State in the territory of which the act was committed, or by such international penal tribunal as may have jurisdiction with respect to those Contracting Parties which shall have accepted its jurisdiction.

ARTICLE VII

Genocide and other acts enumerated in article III shall not be considered as political crimes for the purpose of extradition.

The Contracting Parties pledge themselves in such cases to grant extradition in accordance with their laws and treaties in force.

ARTICLE VIII

Any Contracting Party may call upon the competent organs of the United Nations to take such action under the Charter of the United Nations as they consider appropriate for the prevention and suppression of acts of genocide or any of the other acts enumerated in article III.

ARTICLE IX

Disputes between the Contracting Parties relating to the interpretation, application or fulfillment of the present Convention, including those relating to the responsibility of a State for genocide or any of the other acts enumerated in article III, shall be submitted to the International Court of Justice at the request of any of the parties to the dispute.

ARTICLE X

The present Convention, of which the Chinese, English, French, Russian and Spanish texts are equally authentic, shall bear the date of 9 December 1948.

ARTICLE XI

The present Convention shall be open until December 1949 for signature on behalf of any Member of the United Nations and of any non-member State to which an invitation to sign has been addressed by the General Assembly.

The present Convention shall be ratified, and the instruments of ratification shall be deposited with the Secretary-General of the United Nations.

After January 1950, the present Convention may be acceded to on behalf of any Member of the United Nations and of any non-member State which has received an invitation as aforesaid.

Instruments of accession shall be deposited with the Secretary-General of the United nations.

ARTICLE XII

Any Contracting Party may at any time, by notification addressed to the Secretary-General of the United Nations, extend the application of the present Convention to all or any of the territory for the conduct of whose foreign relations that Contracting Party is responsible.

ARTICLE XIII

On the day when the first twenty instruments of ratification or accession have been deposited, the Secretary-General shall draw up a *proces-verbal* and transmit a copy of it to each Member of the United Nations and to each of the non-member States contemplated in article XI.

The present Convention shall come into force on the ninetieth day following the date of deposit of the twentieth instrument of ratification or accession.

Any ratification or accession effected subsequent to the latter date shall become effective on the ninetieth day following the deposit of the instrument of ratification or accession.

ARTICLE XIV

The present Convention shall remain in effect for a period of ten years as from the date of its coming into force.

It shall thereafter remain in force for successive periods of five years for such Contracting Parties as have not denounced it at least six months before the expiration of the current period.

Denunciation shall be effected by a written notification addressed to the Secretary-General of the United Nations.

ARTICLE XV

If, as a result of denunciations, the number of Parties to the present Convention should become less than sixteen, the Convention shall cease to be in force as from the date on which the last of these denunciations shall become effective.

ARTICLE XVI

A request for the revision of the present Convention may be made at any time by any Contracting Party by means of a notification in writing addressed to the Secretary-General.
The General Assembly shall decide upon the steps, if any, to be taken in respect of such request.

ARTICLE XVII

The Secretary-General of the United Nations shall notify all Members of the United Nations and the non-member States contemplated in article XI of the following:

(a) Signatures, ratifications and accessions received in accordance with article XI;
(b) Notifications received in accordance with article XII;
(c) The date upon which the present Convention comes into force in accordance with Article XIII;
(d) Denunciations received in accordance with article XIV;
(e) The abrogation of the Convention in accordance with article XV;
(f) Notification received in accordance with article XVI.

ARTICLE XVIII

The original of the present Convention shall be deposited in the archives of the United Nations.
A certified copy of the Convention shall be transmitted to all Members of the United Nations and to the non-member States contemplated in article XI.

ARTICLE XIX

The present Convention shall be registered by the Secretary-General of the United Nations on the date of its coming into force.

Appendix 2

United Nations Universal Declaration of Human Rights

(Adopted 1948)

PREAMBLE

Whereas recognition of the inherent dignity and of the equal and inalienable rights of all members of the human family is the foundation of freedom, justice and peace in the world,

Whereas disregard and contempt for human rights have resulted in barbarous acts which have outraged the conscience of mankind, and the advent of a world in which human beings shall enjoy freedom of speech and belief and freedom from fear and want has been proclaimed as the highest aspiration of the common people,

Whereas it is essential, if man is not to be compelled to have recourse, as a last resort, to rebellion against tyranny and oppression, that human rights should be protected by the rule of law,

Whereas it is essential to promote the development of friendly relations between nations,

Whereas the peoples of the United Nations have in the Charter reaffirmed their faith in fundamental human rights, in the dignity and worth of the human person and in the equal rights of men and women and have determined to promote social progress and better standards of life in larger freedom,

Whereas Member States have pledged themselves to achieve, in co-operation with the United Nations, the promotion of universal respect for and observance of human rights and fundamental freedoms,

Whereas a common understanding of these rights and freedoms is of the greatest importance for the full realization of this pledge,

Now, Therefore THE GENERAL ASSEMBLY proclaims THIS UNIVERSAL DECLARATION OF HUMAN RIGHTS as a common standard of achievement for all peoples and all nations, to the end that every individual and every organ of society, keeping this Declaration constantly in mind, shall strive by teaching and education to promote respect for these rights and freedoms and by progressive measures, national and international, to secure their universal and effective recognition and observance, both among the people of Member States themselves and among the peoples of territories under their jurisdiction.

Article 1.

All human beings are born free and equal in dignity and rights. They are endowed with reason and conscience and should act towards one another in a spirit of brotherhood.

Article 2.

Everyone is entitled to all the rights and freedoms set forth in this Declaration, without distinction of any kind, such as race, color, sex, language, religion, political or other opinion, national or social origin, property, birth or other status. Furthermore, no distinction shall be made on the basis of the political, jurisdictional or international status of the country or territory to which a person belongs, whether it be independent, trust, non-self-government or under another limitation of sovereignty.

Article 3.

Everyone has the right to life, liberty and security of person.

Article 4.

No one shall be held in slavery or servitude; slavery and the slave trade shall be prohibited in all their forms.

Article 5.

No one shall be subjected to torture or to cruel, inhuman or degrading treatment or punishment.

Article 6.

Everyone has the right to recognition everywhere as a person before the law.

Article 7.

All are equal before the law and are entitled without any discrimination to equal protection of the law. All are entitled to equal protection against any discrimination in violation of this Declaration and against any incitement to such discrimination.

Article 8.

Everyone has the right to an effective remedy by the competent national tribunals for acts violating the fundamental rights granted him by the constitution or by law.

Article 9.

No one shall be subjected to arbitrary arrest, detention or exile.

Article 10.

Everyone is entitled in full equality to a fair and public hearing by an independent and impartial tribunal, in the determination of his rights and obligations and of any criminal charge against him.

Article 11.

(1) Everyone charged with a penal offence has the right to be presumed innocent until proven guilty according to law in a public trial at which he has had all the guarantees necessary for his defence.

(2) No one shall be held guilty of any penal offence on account of any act or omission which did not constitute a penal offence, under national or international law, at the time when it was committed. Nor shall a heavier penalty be imposed than the one that was applicable at the time the penal offence was committed.

Article 12.

No one shall be subjected to arbitrary interference with his privacy, family, home or correspondence, nor to attacks upon his honour and reputation. Everyone has the right to the protection of the law against such interference or attacks.

Article 13.

(1) Everyone has the right to freedom of movement and residence within the borders of each State.

(2) Everyone has the right to leave any country, including his own, and to return to his country.

Article 14.

(1) Everyone has the right to seek and enjoy in other countries asylum from persecution.

(2) This right may not be invoked in the case of prosecutions genuinely arising from non-political crimes or from acts contrary to the purposes and principles of the United Nations.

Article 15.

(1) Everyone has the right to a nationality.

(2) No one shall be arbitary deprived of his nationality nor denied the right to change his nationality.

Article 16.

(1) Men and women of full age, without any limitation due to race, nationality or religion, have the right to marry and to found a family. They are entitled to equal rights to marriage, during marriage and at its dissolution.

(2) Marriage shall be entered into only with the free and full consent of the intending spouses.

(3) The family is the natural and fundamental group unit of society and is entitled to protection by society and the State.

Article 17.

(1) Everyone has the right to own property alone as well as in association with others.
(2) No one shall be arbitrarily deprived of his property.

Article 18.

Everyone has the right to freedom of thought, conscience and religion; this right includes freedom to change his religion or belief, and freedom, either alone or in community with others and in public or private, to manifest his religion or belief in teaching, practice, worship and observance.

Article 19.

Everyone has the right to freedom of opinion and expression; this right includes freedom to hold opinions without interference and to seek, receive and impart information and ideas through any media and regardless of frontiers.

Article 20.

(1) Everyone has the right to freedom of peaceful assembly and association.
(2) No one may be compelled to belong to an association.

Article 21.

(1) Everyone has the right to take part in the government of his country, directly or through freely chosen representatives.
(2) Everyone has the right to equal access to public service in his country.
(3) The will of the people shall be the basis of the authority of government; this will shall be expressed in periodic and genuine elections which shall be by universal and equal suffrage and shall be held by secret vote or by equivalent free voting procedures.

Article 22.

Everyone, as a member of society, has the right to social security and is entitled to realization, through national effort and international co-operation and in accordance with the organization and resources of each State, of the economic, social and cultural rights indispensable for his dignity and the free development of his personality.

Article 23.

(1) Everyone has the right to work, to free choice of employment, to just and favourable conditions of work and to protection against unemployment.
(2) Everyone, without any discrimination, has the right to equal pay for equal work.
(3) Everyone who works has the right to just and favourable remuneration ensuring for himself and his family an existence worthy of human dignity, and supplemented, if necessary, by other means of social protection.

Article 24.

Everyone has the right to rest and leisure, including reasonable limitation of working hours and periodic holidays with pay.

Article 25.

(1) Everyone has the right to a standard of living adequate for the health and well-being of himself and of his family, including food, clothing, housing and medical care and necessary social services, and the right to security in the event of unemployment, sickness, disability, widowhood, old age or other lack of livelihood in circumstances beyond his control.
(2) Motherhood and childhood are entitled to special care and assistance. All children, whether born in or out the wedlock, shall enjoy the same social protection.

Article 26.

(1) Everyone has the right to education. Education shall be free, at least in the elementary and fundamental stages. Elementary education shall be compulsory. Technical and professional education shall be made generally available and higher education shall be equally accessible to all on the basis of merit.
(2) Education shall be directed to the full development of the human personality and to the strengthening of respect for human rights and fundamental freedoms. It shall promote understanding, tolerance and friendship among all nations, racial or religious groups, and shall further the activities of the United Nations for the maintenance of peace.
(3) Parents have a prior right to choose the kind of education that shall be given to their children.

Article 27.

(1) Everyone has the right to freely to participate in the cultural life of the community, to enjoy the arts and to share in scientific advancement and its benefits.
(2) Everyone has the right to the protection of the moral and material interests resulting from any scientific, literary or artistic production of which he is the author.

Article 28.

Everyone is entitled to a social and international order in which the rights and freedoms set forth in this Declaration can be fully realized.

Article 29.

(1) Everyone has duties to the community in which alone the free and full development of his personality is possible.
(2) In the exercise of his rights and freedoms, everyone shall be subject only to such limitations as are determined by law solely for the purpose of securing due recognition and respect for the rights and freedoms of others and of meeting the just requirements of morality, public order and the general welfare in a democratic society.

(3) These rights and freedoms may in no case be exercised contrary to the purposes and principles of the United Nations.

Article 30.

Nothing in this Declaration may be interpreted as implying for any State, group or person any right to engage in any activity or to perform any act aimed at the destruction of any of the rights and freedoms set forth here.

[Adopted by the General Assembly of the United Nations on December 10, 1948.]

Select Bibliography

Adeney, Bernard T. *Just War, Political Realism, and Faith*. Metuchen, NJ: Scarecrow Press, 1988.

Alnasrawi, Abbas. "Does Iraq Have an Economic Future?" *Middle East Executive Reports* 19, No. 3 (March 1996).

Arnison, Nancy D. "International Law and Nonintervention: When Humanitarian Concerns Supersede Sovereignty." U.S. Government, Hearing . . . 1992, *Humanitarian Intervention: A Review of Theory and Practice*. Washington, DC: U.S. Government Printing Office, 1993.

Baldwin, David A. *Economic Statecraft*. Princeton, NJ: Princeton University Press, 1985.

Bassiouni, M. Cherif. *Crimes Against Humanity in International Criminal Law*. Boston: Klumer Academic Publishers, 1992.

Boutwell, Jeffrey, Klare, Michael T., and Reed, Laura W., eds. *Lethal Commerce: The Global Trade in Small Arms and Light Weapons*. Cambridge, MA: Committee on International Security Studies, American Academy of Arts and Sciences, 1995.

Boyd, Charles G. "Making Peace with the Guilty: The Truth About Bosnia." *Foreign Affairs* 74 (September/October 1995).

Brown, Michael, and Rosecrance, Richard, eds. *The Cost of Conflict: Prevention and Cure in the Global Arena*. Report to the Carnegie Commission on Preventing Deadly Conflict. Washington, DC: Carnegie Commission, 1998.

Brownlie, Ian, ed. *Basic Documents on Human Rights*. Oxford: Clarendon Press, 1992.

Bull, Hedley, ed. *Intervention in World Politics*. Oxford: Clarendon Press, 1984.

Bundy, McGeorge. *Danger and Survival: Choices About the Bomb in the First Fifty Years*. New York: Random House, 1998.

Burg, Steven L. *War or Peace? Nationalism, Democracy and American Foreign Policy in Post-Communist Europe*. New York: New York University Press, 1996.

———. "Ethnic Nationalism, Breakdown, and Genocide in Yugoslavia." In Helen Fein, ed., *The Prevention of Genocide: Rwanda and Yugoslavia Reconsidered*. New York: Institute for the Study of Genocide, 1994.

Burg, Steven L., and Shoup, Paul S. *The War in Bosnia-Herzegovina: Ethnic Conflict and International Intervention*. Armonk, NY: M. E. Sharpe, 1998.

Burkhalter, Holly. "The 1994 Rwandan Genocide and U.S. Policy." Testimony, Physicians for Human Rights, U.S. Subcommittee on Human Rights and International Operations, Washington, DC, May 5, 1998.

———. "US Failure in Rwanda—And How to Prevent Future Genocides." *Institute for the Study of Genocide Newsletter*, No. 21 (Summer/Fall 1998).

Buzan, Barry, Jones, Charles, and Little, Richard. *The Logic of Anarchy: Neorealism to Structural Realism*. New York: Columbia University Press, 1993.

Carnegie Commission on Preventing Deadly Conflict. *Preventing Deadly Conflict*. Final Report. New York: Carnegie Corporation, 1997.

Cassese, Antonio. *Human Rights in a Changing World*. Philadelphia, PA: Temple University Press, 1990.

Center for Economics and Social Rights. *UN Sanctioned Suffering: A Human Rights Assessment of United Nations Sanctions on Iraq*. New York: Center for Economic and Social Rights, 1996.

Charny, Israel W., ed. *Genocide: A Critical Bibliographic Review*. New York: Facts on File, 1988.

———. "Early Warning, Intervention, and Prevention of Genocide." In Michael N. Dobkowski and Isidor Wallimann, eds., *Genocide in Our Time: An Annotated Bibliography with Analytical Introductions*. Ann Arbor, MI: Pierian Press, 1992.

———, ed. *The Widening Circle of Genocide. Genocide: A Critical Bibliographic Review*, vol. 3. New Brunswick, NJ: Transaction Publishers, 1994.

Citizens' Committee on Bosnia-Herzegovina. "Safe Havens in Bosnia." *New York Review of Books*, May 13, 1993.

Coalition for an International Criminal Court. *Overview*. [http://www.un.org/icc/overview.htm].

Cohen, Roger. *Hearts Grown Brutal: Sagas of Sarajevo*. New York: Random House, 1998.

Cooper, Belinda. "U.S. Courts a Loss of Leadership." *Newsweek*, July 29, 1998, A37.

———. "Criminal Court for the World." *The Economist*, December 6, 1997, 18–19.

Corradi, Juan E., Fagen, Patricia Weiss, and Garreton, Manuel Antonio, eds. *Fear at the Edge: State Terror and Resistance in Latin America*. Berkeley: University of California Press, 1992.

Cortright, David, and Lopez, George A. "Sanctions and Contending Views of Justice: The Problematic Case of Iraq." *Journal of International Affairs* 52, No. 2 (Spring 1999).

———. "Trouble in the Gulf: Pain and Promise." *The Bulletin of the Atomic Scientists* 54, No. 3 (May/June 1998).

———, eds. *Economic Sanctions: Panacea or Peacebuilding in a Post-Cold War World?* Boulder, CO: Westview Press, 1995.

Cross, Cairin. *The Death of Distance*. Boston: Harvard Business School Press, 1997.

Cushman, Thomas, and Mestrovic, Stjepan G., eds. *This Time We Knew: Western Responses to Genocide in Bosnia.* New York: New York University Press, 1996.

Damrosch, Lori Fisler. "Genocide and Ethnic Conflict." In David Wippman, ed., *International Law and Ethnic Conflict.* Ithaca, NY: Cornell University Press, 1998.

———, ed. *Enforcing Restraint: Collective Intervention in Internal Conflicts.* New York: Council on Foreign Relations, 1993.

Danner, Mark. "The Killing Fields of Bosnia." *New York Review of Books* 45, No. 14, September 24, 1998.

Davidowicz, Lucy S. *The War Against the Jews.* New York: Bantam, 1975.

Davies, John L., and Gurr, Ted Robert, eds. *Preventive Measures: Building Risk Assessment and Crisis Early Warning Systems.* Lanham, MD: Rowman and Littlefield, 1998.

Des Forges, Alison. *The Killing Campaign: The 1994 Genocide in Rwanda.* New York: Human Rights Watch, 1998.

———. *"Leave None To Tell The Story:" Genocide in Rwanda.* New York/Paris: Human Rights Watch/Internatinal Federation of Human Rights, 1999.

———, and Plattner, Marc F., eds. *Nationalism, Ethnic Conflict, and Democracy.* Baltimore, MD: The Johns Hopkins University Press, 1994.

Diamond, Larry. "Is the Third Wave Over?" *Journal of Democracy* 7, No. 3 (1996): 1–13.

Dobkowski, Michael N., and Wallimann, Isidor. *Genocide in Our Time: An Annotated Bibliography.* Ann Arbor, MI: Pierian Press, 1992.

Donnelly, Jack. *Universal Human Rights in Theory and Practice.* Ithaca, NY: Cornell University Press, 1998.

———. *International Human Rights.* Boulder, CO: Westview Press, 1993.

———. "Human Rights, Humanitarian Intervention, and American Foreign Policy: Law, Morality and Politics." *Journal of International Affairs* 37 (Winter 1984).

Dugger, Ronnie. "To Prevent or to Stop Mass Murder." In Charles B. Strozier and Michael Flynn, eds. *Genocide, War, and Human Survival.* Lanham, MD: Rowan & Littlefield, 1996.

Elman, Miriam Fendius. *Paths to Peace: Is Democracy the Answer?* Cambridge, MA: MIT Press, 1997.

Elshtain, Jean Bethke, ed. *Just War Theory.* Oxford: Basic Blackwell, 1992.

Eriksson, John. "The International Response to Conflict and Genocide: Lessons from the Rwanda Experience." Steering Committee of the Joint Evaluation of Emergency Assistance to Rwanda. *Journal of Humanitarian Assistance* (March, 1996).

Farer, Tom J., ed. *Beyond Sovereignty: Collectively Defending Democracy in the Americas.* Baltimore and London: Johns Hopkins University Press, 1996.

———. "Intervention in Unnatural Humanitarian Emergencies: Lessons of the First Phase." *Human Rights Quarterly* 18, No. 1 (February 1996).

Feil, Scott R. *Preventing Genocide: How the Early Use of Force Might Have Succeeded in Rwanda.* A Report to the Carnegie Commission on Preventing Deadly Conflict. New York: Carnegie Corporation, April 1998.

Fein, Helen. *Accounting for Genocide: National Responses and Jewish Victimization*

During the Holocaust. New York: Free Press, 1979; Chicago: University of Chicago Press, 1984.

———. "Accounting for Genocide After 1945: Theories and Some Findings." *International Journal of Group Rights,* Vol. 1 (1993).

———, ed. *Ever Again?: Evaluating The United Nations Genocide Convention on Its 50th Anniversary and Proposals to Activate the Convention.* New York: Institute for the Study of Genocide, 1999.

———. *Genocide: A Sociological Perspective.* London: Sage Publications, 1990/1993.

———. *Lives at Risk: A Study of Life Integrity Violations in 50 States in 1987.* New York: Institute for the Study of Genocide, 1990.

———. "More Murder in the Middle: Life-Integrity Violations and Democracy in the World, 1987." *Human Rights Quarterly* 17, No. 1 (February 1995).

———, ed. *The Prevention of Genocide: Rwanda and Yugoslavia Reconsidered.* New York: Institute for the Study of Genocide, 1994.

———. "Scenarios of Genocide: Models of Genocide and Critical Responses." In I. Charney and S. Davidson, eds., *The Book of the International Conference on Holocaust and Genocide: Towards Understanding, Intervention and Prevention of Genocide,* vol. 2. Boulder, CO: Westview Press, 1984.

———. "Tools and Alarms: Uses of Models for Explanation and Anticipation." *Journal of Ethno-Development* (July, 1994).

———, and Apsel, Joyce F., eds. *Teaching About Genocide: A Guidebook for College and University Teachers: Critical Essays, Syllabi, and Assignments.* Washington, DC: American Sociological Association, 1998.

Forsythe, David P. *Human Rights and World Politics,* 2d ed. Lincoln: University of Nebraska Press, 1989.

———. *Human Rights and Peace: International and National Dimensions.* Lincoln: University of Nebraska Press, 1993.

Forsythe, David P., and Pease, Kelly Kate. "Human Rights, Humanitarian Intervention, and World Politics." *Human Rights Quarterly* 15, No. 2 (May 1989).

Freedman, Lawrence, ed. *Military Intervention in European Conflicts.* Oxford: Blackwell, 1994.

Freedom House. *Freedom in the World: The Annual Survey of Political and Civil Liberties, 1990–91, 1991–92, 1992–93, 1993–94, 1994–95.* New York: Freedom House, 1996.

Fromkin, David. *Kosovo Crossing: American Ideals Meet Reality on The Balkans Battlefields.* New York: The Free Press, 1999.

Fukuyama, Frances. "The Beginning of Foreign Policy." *The New Republic* 207 (August 17 and 24, 1992): 24–32.

Gillespie, Thomas R. "Unwanted Responsibility: Humanitarian Military Intervention to Advance Human Rights." *Peace and Change* 18, No. 3 (July 1993).

Goldhagen, Daniel J. "A New Serbia." *The New Republic* (May 17, 1999).

Gordon, Joy. "Using a Pick-Axe for Brain Surgery: The Ethics of Economic Sanctions and Their Predictable Consequences." *Ethics and International Affairs* 13 (March 1999).

Gourevitch, Philip. "The Genocide Fax." *The New Yorker,* May 11, 1998.

———. *"We Wish to Inform You That Tomorrow We Will Be Killed with Our Families": Stories from Rwanda.* New York: Farrar, Straus, and Giroux, 1998.

Gow, James. *Triumph of the Lack of Will: International Diplomacy and the Yugoslav War.* New York: Columbia University Press, 1997.

Gowing, Nik. "Dispatches from Disaster Zones: The Reporting of Humanitarian Emergencies." Unpublished paper presented at London Conference on New Challenges and Problems for Information Management in Complex Emergencies, May 1998.

Gurr, Ted R., and Harff, Barbara. *Early Warning of Communal Conflict and Genocide: Linking Empirical Research to International Responses.* Tokyo: United Nations University Press, 1996.

———. *Ethnic Conflict in World Politics.* Boulder, CO: Westview, 1994.

———, et al. *Minorities at Risk: A Global View of Ethnopolitical Conflict.* Washington, DC: Institute for Peace Press, 1993.

Haass, Richard, ed. *Economic Sanctions and American Diplomacy.* New York: Council on Foreign Relations, 1998.

Hannum, Hurst. *Autonomy, Sovereignty, and Self-Determination: The Accommodation of Conflicting Rights.* Philadelphia; University of Pennsylvania Press, 1990.

Harff, Barbara. "Bosnia and Somalia: Strategic, Legal, and Moral Dimensions of Humanitarian Intervention." *Philosophy & Public Policy* 12, Nos. 3 and 4 (Summer/Fall 1992).

———. "Systematic Early Warning of Humanitarian Emergencies." *Journal of Peace Research* 35, No. 5 (1998).

———. "A theoretical Model of Genocides and Politicides." *Journal of Ethno-Development* 4, No. 4 (July 1994).

———, and Gurr, Ted R. "Victims of the State: Genocides, Politicides and Group Repression Since 1945." *International Review of Victimology* (1989).

Harvard Study Team. "The Effect of the Gulf Crisis on the Children of Iraq." *New England Journal of Medicine* 325, No. 13 (1991).

Hilberg, Raoul. *The Destruction of the European Jews.* Chicago: Quadrangle Press, 1963.

Hirsch, Herbert. *Genocide and the Politics of Memory.* Chapel Hill: University of North Carolina Press, 1985.

Hoffmann, Stanley. "What Is to Be Done?" *The New York Review of Books* 46, No. 9 (May 20, 1999).

———. "Principles in the Balkans, But Not in East Timor?" *New York Times,* September 11, 1999.

———, Johansen, Robert C., Sterba, James P., and Vayrynen, Raimo. *The Ethics and Politics of Humanitarian Intervention.* Notre Dame, IN: University of Notre Dame Press, 1996.

Holbrooke, Richard. *To End A War.* New York: Random House, 1998.

———. "Battles After the War." *New York Times,* September 14, 1999.

Holmes, Robert L. *On War and Morality.* Princeton, NJ: Princeton University Press, 1989.

Honig, Jan Willem, and Both, Norbert. *Srebrenica: Record of a War Crime.* New York and London: Penguin Books, 1996.

Horowitz, Donald. *Ethnic Groups in Conflict.* Berkeley: University of California Press, 1985.

Horowitz, Irving Louis. *Taking Lives: Genocide and State Power*, 4th ed. New Brunswick, NJ: Transaction Publishers, 1997.

Hoskins, Eric, and Nutt, Samantha. *The Humanitarian Impact of Economic Sanctions*. Occasional Paper #29. Providence, RI: The Thomas J. Watson Institute for International Studies, Brown University, 1997.

———. "The Humanitarian Impacts of Economic Sanctions and War in Iraq." In Thomas Weiss et al., *Political Gain and Civilian Pain: Humanitarian Impacts of Economic Sanctions*. Lanham, MD: Rowman & Littlefield, 1997.

Hufbauer, Gary C., Schott, Jeffrey J., and Elliott, Kimberly Ann. *Economic Sanctions Reconsidered: History and Current Policy*, 2d ed. Washington, DC: Institute for International Economics, 1990.

Human Rights Watch. *Slaughter Among Neighbors: The Political Origins of Communal Violence*. New Haven, CT: Yale University Press, 1995.

———. "Bosnia-Hercegovina: The Continuing Influence of Bosnia's Warlords." *Human Rights Watch* 8, No. 7 (December 1996).

———. *Bosnia-Hercegovina: A Dark and Closed Place—Past and Present Abuses in Foca*. New York: Human Rights Watch, June 1998.

———. *Human Rights Watch World Report, 1995*. New York: Human Rights Watch, December 1994.

———. *Human Rights Watch World Report*. New York: Human Rights Watch, 1998.

———. *War Without Quarter: Columbia and International Humanitarian Law*. New York: Human Rights Watch, 1998.

Human Rights Watch/Africa. *Shattered Lives: Sexual Violence during the Rwandan Genocide and Its Aftermath*. New York: Human Rights Watch, 1996.

Ignatieff, Michael. "Balkan Physics." *The New Yorker* 75, No. 10 (May 10, 1999).

International Commission of Jurists at the Plenary Session of the Rome Conference. *The Rome Treaty Conference Monitor*, No. 4, (1998) [http://www.igc.org/icc/rome/html/rome_monitor/4/rmon4.htm].

"International Criminals Beware." *The Economist* (December 6, 1997): 47.

Johansen, Robert C., and Mendlovitz, Saul H. "The Role of Enforcement of Law in the Establishment of a New International Order: A Proposal for a Transnational Police Force." *Alternatives*, VI (1980).

Joint Evaluation of Emergency Assistance to Rwanda. *The International Response to Conflict and Genocide: Lessons from the Rwandan Experience*, 5 vols. Copenhagen: Steering Committee of the Joint Evaluation of Emergency Assistance to Rwanda, 1996.

Jonassohn, Kurt. *Genocide and Gross Human Rights Violations in Comparative Perspective*. New Brunswick, NJ.: Transaction Publishers, 1997.

Joyner, Christopher. "When Human Suffering Warrants Military Action." *Chronicle of Higher Education*, January 27, 1993.

Kaburahe, Antoine. "Africa-Economy: Burundi Bows under Weight of Economic Sanctions." *Interpress Service*, September 10, 1998 [http://www.oneworld.org/ips2/sept98/17_21_062.html].

Kaysen, Carl, and Rathjens, George W. "Peace Operations by the United Nations: The Case for a Volunteer UN Military Force." "Cambridge, MA: American Academy of Arts and Sciences, 1996.

———. "Send in the Troops: A UN Foreign Legion." *Washington Quarterly* 20 (Winter 1997).

Kegley, Jr., Charles W. *Controversies in International Relations Theory*. New York: St. Martin's Press, 1995.

———. "International Peacemaking and Peacekeeping." *Ethics and International Affairs* 10 (1996).

———. "The Neoidealist Moment in International Studies: Realist Myths and the New International Realities." *International Studies Quarterly* 37 (June 1993).

Kelsay, John, and Turner, James, eds. *Just War and Jihad: Historical and Theoretical Perspectives on War and Peace in Western and Islamic Traditions*. Westport, CT: Greenwood Press, 1991.

Kirsch, Phillipe. "The Rome Conference on the International Criminal Court: A Comment." *American Society of International Law Newsletter*, November-December 1998.

Kober, Stanley. "Idealpolitik." *Foreign Policy* 79 (Summer 1990).

Krasner, Stephen, ed. *International Regimes*. Ithaca, NY: Cornell University Press, 1993.

Kressel, Neil J. *Mass Hate: The Global Rise of Genocide and Terror*. New York: Plenum Press, 1996.

Kull, Steven, Destler, I. M., and Ramsay, Clay. *The Foreign Policy Gap: How Policymakers Misread the Public*. College Park: Center for International and Security Studies at the University of Maryland, October 1997.

Kuper, Leo. *Genocide: Its Political Use in the Twentieth Century*. New Haven, CT: Yale University Press, 1981.

———. *The Pity of It All*. Minneapolis: University of Minnesota Press, 1977.

———. *The Prevention of Genocide*. New Haven, CT: Yale University Press, 1985.

Lawyers Committee for Human Rights. "The International Criminal Court: The Case for U.S. Support." *International Criminal Court Briefing Series*, No. 2, December 1998.

LeBlanc, Lawrence J. *The United States and the Genocide Convention*. Durham, NC: Duke University Press, 1991.

Leitenberg, Milton. "U.S. and U.N. Actions Escalate Genocide and Increase Costs in Rwanda." In Helen Fein, ed., *The Prevention of Genocide: Rwanda and Yugoslavia Reconsidered*. New York: Institute for the Study of Genocide. 1994.

———. "Rwanda, 1994: International Incompetence Produces Genocide." *Peacekeeping and International Relations* (November/December 1994).

Lewy, Guenter. "The Case for Humanitarian Intervention." *Orbis* (Fall 1993).

Lillich, Richard B., ed. *Humanitarian Intervention and the United Nations*. Charlottesville: University Press of Virginia, 1973.

Lopez, George A. "More Ethical Than Not: A Response to Joy Gordon's Claims Regarding Sanctions." *Ethics and International Affairs* 13 (March 1999).

———. "The Sanctions Dilemma: Hype Doesn't Help." *Commonweal*, September 2, 1998.

———, and Cortright, David. "Getting Smart About Sanctions." *Chicago Policy Review* 3 (Spring 1999).

———. "Sanctions as Instruments of Global Governance." In Raimo Vayrynen, ed., *New Thinking in Global Governance: U.S. and Canadian Perspectives*. Lanham, MD: Roman & Littlefield, 1999.

————. "Trouble in the Gulf: Pain and Promise." *The Bulletin of the Atomic Scientists* 54, No. 3 (May/June 1998).

————. "What to Do About Iraq? The Moral Dilemma of Sanctions." *Sojourners* 27, No. 2 (March–April 1998).

————. "Economic Sanctions and Human Rights: Part of the Solution or Part of the Problem?" *The International Journal of Human Rights* 1, No. 2 (May 1997).

————. "The Sanctions Era: An Alternative to Military Intervention." *The Fletcher Forum on World Affairs* 19, No. 2 (Summer/Fall, 1995).

Lute, Douglas E. *Improving National Capacity to Respond to Complex Emergencies: The US Experience.* Report to the Carnegie Commission on Preventing Deadly Conflict. New York: Carnegie Corporation, April 1998.

Malloy, Michael P. "Economic Sanctions and Human Rights: A Delicate Balance." *The Human Rights Brief.* Washington, DC: The Center for Human Rights and Humanitarian Law at Washington College of Law, American University, 1995.

Mandelbaum, Michael. "The Reluctance to Intervene." *Foreign Policy* 95 (Summer 1994).

Mayall, James, ed. *The New Interventionism, 1991–1994: United Nations Experience in Cambodia, Former Yugoslavia and Somalia.* Cambridge, UK: Cambridge University Press, 1996.

Mendlovitz, Saul H, and Fousek, John. "Enforcing the Law on Genocide." *Alternatives* 21 (1996).

————. "The Prevention and Punishment of the Crime of Genocide." In Charles B. Strozier and Michael Flynn, eds., *Genocide, War, and Human Survival.* Lanham, MD: Rowman & Littlefield, 1996.

Meron, Theodor. "The Court We Want," *The Washington Post*, A15, October 13, 1998.

Metzl, Jamie. "Information Intervention." *Foreign Affairs* 76, No. 6 (November/December 1997).

Meyer, William H. *Human Rights and International Political Economy in Third World Countries: Multinational Corporations, Foreign Aid, and Repression.* Westport, CT: Praeger, 1998.

Mills, K. "Sovereignty Eclipsed?: The Legitimacy of Humanitarian Access and Intervention." *Journal of Humanitarian Assistance* (July 1997).

Miroslav, Nincic, and Wallensteen, Peter, eds. *Dilemmas of Economic Coercion: Sanctions and World Politics.* New York: Praeger, 1983.

Morsink, Johannes. *The Universal Declaration of Human Rights: Origins and Intent.* Philadelphia: University of Pennsylvania Press, 1999.

Natsios, Andrew S. *U.S. Foreign Policy and the Four Horseman of the Apocalypse: Humanitarian Relief in Complex Emergencies.* Westport, CT: Praeger, 1997.

Newcombe, Hanna. "The Ethics of Economic Sanctions." *Peace Magazine* (January/February, 1998).

O'Brien, William V. *The Conduct of Just and Limited War.* New York: Praeger, 1981.

Pasic, Amir, and Weiss, Thomas G. "Yugoslavia's Wars and the Politics of Rescue." *Ethics and International Affairs* II (1997).

Paust, Jordan, Bassiouni, M. Cherif, William, Sharon, Scharf, Michael, Gurule, Jimmy, and Zagaris, Bruce. *International Criminal Law: Cases and Materials.* Durham, NC: Carolina Academic Press, 1996.

Pejic Jelena. "What Is an International Criminal Court?" *Human Rights* 23, No. 4 (Fall 1996).

Phillips, Robert L., and Cady, Duane L. *Humanitarian Intervention: Just War vs. Pacifism.* Lanham, MD: Rowman & Littlefield, 1996.

Picco, Giandomenico. "The U.N. and the Use of Force." *Foreign Affairs* 73, No. 5 (September/October 1994).

Prunier, Gerard. *The Rwanda Crisis: History of a Genocide.* New York: Columbia University Press, 1995, 1997.

Ramet, Sabrina P. *Balkan Babel: The Disintegration of Yugoslavia from the Death of Tito to the War in Kosovo,* 3d ed. Boulder, Co: Westview Press, 1999.

Ramsay, Paul. *The Just War: Force and Political Responsibility.* New York: Praeger, 1981.

Ramsbotham, Oliver, and Woodhouse, Tom. *Humanitarian Intervention in Contemporary Conflict: A Reconceptualization.* Cambridge, UK: Polity Press, 1996.

Ratner, Steven R., and Abrams, Jason S. *Accountability for Human Rights Atrocities in International Law: Beyond Nuremberg.* New York: Oxford University Press, 1997.

Report of the International Law Commission. U.N. GAOR, 49th sess., Supp. No. 10, U.N. Doc. A/49/10, 1994.

Report of the Working Group on the Question of an International Criminal Jurisdiction. Report of the International Law Commission. 44th sess., 74 U.N. GAOR, Supp. No. 10, annex, at 162, U.N. Doc. A/47/10.

Rieff, David. *Slaughterhouse: Bosnia and the Failure of the West.* New York: Simon and Schuster, 1995.

———. "A New Age of Liberal Imperialism." *World Policy Journal* 16, No. 2 (Summer 1999).

Riemer, Neal. *Creative Breakthroughs in Politics.* Westport, CT: Praeger, 1996.

———. *The Future of the Democratic Revolution: Toward a More Prophetic Politics.* New York: Praeger, 1984.

———, ed. *Let Justice Roll: Prophetic Challenges in Religion, Politics, and Society.* Lanham, MD: Rowman & Littlefield, 1996.

———. "Political Theory and Protection Against Genocide: A Thought Experiment." Paper, Meeting of the Northeastern Political Science Association, Philadelphia, PA, November 13–15, 1997.

———. "Political Scientists and Protection Against Genocide in Kosovo: Critical Reflections on Political Theory and Public Policy." Paper, Meeting of the American Political Science Association, Atlanta, GA, September 2, 1999.

Roberts, Adam. "Humanitarian War: Military Intervention and Human Rights." Edited text of the first John Vincent Memorial Lecture, Keele University, February 26, 1993.

Rome Statute of the International Criminal Court. A/CONF. 183/9 (July 17, 1998).

Rosenblatt, Lionel, and Thompson, Larry. "The Door of Opportunity: Creating a Permanent Peacekeeping Force." *World Policy Journal* 15, No. 1 (Spring 1998).

Rosenthal, Joel H. *Righteous Realists: Political Realism, Responsible Power, and American Culture in the Nuclear Age.* Baton Rouge: Louisiana State University Press, 1991.

Rothberg, Robert I., and Weiss, Thomas G. *From Massacres to Genocide: The Media, Public Policy, and Humanitarian Crises.* Washington, DC: Brookings Institution, 1996.

Scheffer, David J. Address before the Carter Center, November 13, 1997. [http://www.state.gov/www/policy_remarks/97lll3_scheffertribunal.html].

———. "America's Stake in Peace, Security and Justice." *American Society of International Law Newletter*, September–October 1998.

———. *Genocide and Crimes Against Humanity: Early Warning and Prevention.* Address at Holocaust Museum, December 10, 1998. [www.state.gov/www/policy_remarks].

———. Statement before the Committee on Foreign Relations of the U.S. Senate. July 23, 1998.

———. "U.S. Policy on International Criminal Tribunals." *American University Journal International Law* 13 (1998).

Schmeidl, Susan. *Selected Efforts: Research in the Area of Early Warning.* [http://www.yorku.ca/research/crs/prevent/eweffort.htm].

Scully, Gerald W. "Murder by the State." National Center for Policy Analysis, September 1997. [http/www.ncpa.org/studies/ss211/figure12d.html].

Simmons, P. J. "Learning to Live With NGOs." *Foreign Policy* 12 (Fall 1998).

Sivard, Ruth Leger, ed. *World Military and Social Expenditures*, 14th ed. Washington, DC: World Priorities, 1991.

Slater, Jerome, and Nardin, Terry. "Nonintervention and Human Rights." *The Journal of Politics* 48 (1986).

Smith, Michael J. "Ethics and Intervention." *Ethics and International Affairs* 3 (1989).

———. *Realist Thought from Weber to Kissinger.* Baton Rouge: Louisiana State University Press, 1986.

Smith, Roger W., ed. *Genocide: Essays Toward Understanding, Early Warning and Prevention.* Williamsburg, VA: Association of Genocide Scholars, Department of Government, College of William and Mary, 1999.

Staub, Ervin. *The Roots of Evil: The Origins of Genocide and Other Group Violence.* New York: Cambridge University Press, 1992.

Steel, Ronald. "East Timor Isn't Kosovo." *New York Times*, September 12, 1999.

Steering Committee of Emergency Assistance to Rwanda. *The International Response to Conflict and Genocide: Lessons from the Rwandan Experience.* Danish Foreign Ministry, 1996.

Stremlau, John. *People in Peril: Human Rights, Humanitarian Action, and Preventing Deadly Conflict.* Report to the Carnegie Commission on Preventing Deadly Conflict. New York: Carnegie Corporation, May 1998.

Strobel, Warren P. *Late-Breaking Foreign Policy: The News Media's Influence on Peace Operations.* Washington, DC: United States Institute of Peace Press, 1997.

Strozier, Charles B., and Flynn, Michael, eds. *Genocide, War, and Human Survival.* Lanham, MD: Rowman & Littlefield, 1996.

Tesón, Fernando. *Humanitarian Intercession: An Inquiry into Law and Morality.* Dobbs Ferry, NY: Transnational Publishers, 1988.

Totten, Samuel. "Non-Governmental Organizations Working on the Issue of Genocide." In Israel W. Charney, ed., *The Widening Circle of Genocide.* New Brunswick, NJ: Transaction Publishers, 1994.

———, Parsons, Williams S., and Charny, Israel W. *Century of Genocide: Eyewitness Accounts and Critical Views.* New York: Garland, 1997.

Ullman, Richard H., ed. *The World and Yugoslavia's Wars.* New York: Council on Foreign Relations, 1996.

United Nations. *Supplement to an Agenda for Peace: Position Paper of the Secretary-General on the Occasion of the Fiftieth Anniversary of the United Nations.* New York: United Nations, 1995.

———. *Report to the Secretary-General on Humanitarian Needs in Kuwait and Iraq in the Immediate Post-Crisis Environment by a Mission to the Areas Led by Mr. Martti Athtisaari, Undersecretary-General for Administration and Management.* New York: United Nations, 1991.

———. *Revised and Updated Report on the Question of the Prevention and Punishment of the Crime of Genocide.* Prepared by Mr. Ben Whitaker. New York: United Nations, 1985.

United Nations High Commissioner for Refugees. *The State of the World's Refugees: The Challenge of Protection.* New York: United Nations, 1993.

United States Committee for Refugees. *Life after Death: Suspicion and Reintegration in Post-Genocide Rwanda.* Washington, DC: United States Committee for Refugees, 1998.

———. "Testimony of Jeff Drumtra, Africa Policy Analyst, USCR, on 'Rwanda: Genocide and the Continuing Cycle of Violence' " before the Subcommittee on International Operations and Human Rights, House Committee on International Relations." Washington, DC: United States Committee for Refugees, May 1998.

———. *1998 World Refugee Survey.* Washington, DC: United States Committee for Refugees, 1998.

U.S. Department of State. *Country Reports on Human Rights Practices.* Washington, DC: U.S. Government Printing Office, yearly.

U.S. Department of State Briefing, April 9, 1998. [http://www.un.org/ice/overview.htm].

U.S. General Accounting Office. *Economic Sanctions: Effectiveness as Tools of Foreign Policy.* Report for Chair, Committee on Foreign Relations, U.S. Senate, 102nd Cong., 2d sess. Washington, DC: U.S. Government Printing Office, 1992.

Urquart, Brian. "For a UN Volunteer Military Force." *New York Review of Books,* June 1993.

———. "Looking for the Sheriff." *New York Review of Books,* July 16, 1998.

Urvin, Peter. *Aiding Violence: The Development Enterprise in Rwanda.* West Hartford, CT: Kumarian Press, 1998.

Van Schaack, Beth. "The Crime of Political Genocide: Repairing the Genocide Convention's Blind Spot." *Yale Law Journal* 106, No. 7 (May) 1997.

Vincent, R. J. *Nonintervention and International Order*. Princeton, NJ: Princeton University Press, 1974.

———. *Human Rights and International Relations*. Cambridge, U.K.: Cambridge University Press, 1986.

Wallensteen, Peter, and Sollenberg, Margaret. "The End of International War? Armed Conflict 1989–1995." *Journal of Peace Research*, 33, No. 3 (August) 1996.

Waltz, Kenneth. *Theory of International Politics*. Reading, MA: Addison-Wesley, 1979.

———. "Realist Thought and Neorealist Theory." *Journal of International Affairs* 44 (Spring/Summer) 1990.

Walzer, Michael. *Just and Unjust Wars: A Moral Argument With Historical Illustrations*, 2d ed. New York: Basic Books, 1977, 1992.

Weart, Spencer R. *Never At War: Why Democracies Will Not Fight One Another*. New Haven, CT: Yale University Press, 1998.

Wedgwood, Ruth. "Fiddling in Rome: America and the International Criminal Court." *Foreign Affairs* 76, No. 6 (December 1998).

Weiss, Thomas, Cortright, David, Lopez, George, and Minear, Larry, eds. *Political Gain and Civilian Pain: Humanitarian Impacts of Economic Sanctions*. Lanham, MD: Rowman & Littlefield, 1997.

Weiss, Thomas G., and Collins, Cindy. *Humanitarian Challenges and Intervention: World Politics and the Dilemmas of Help*. Boulder, CO: Westview Press, 1996.

Wexler, Leila Sadat. "The Proposed International Criminal Court: An Appraisal." *Cornell International Law Journal* 29, (1996).

Wippman, David. "NATO Intervention in Kosovo and the Boundaries of International Law." Paper, African Society of International and Comparative Law Harare, Zimbabwe, August 3, 1999.

———, ed. *International Law and Ethnic Conflict*. Ithaca, NY: Cornell University Press, 1998.

Woodward, Susan L. *Balkan Tragedy*. Washington, DC: Brookings Institution, 1995.

Yoder, John Howard. *When War Is Unjust: Being Honest in Just-War Thinking* Minneapolis, MN: Augsburg, 1984.

Zaidi, Sarah, and Smith-Fazi, Mary C. "Health and Baghdad's Children." *The Lancet* 346, No. 8988 (December 2), 1995.

Zakaria, Fareed. "The Rise of Illiberal Democracy." *Foreign Affairs*, 76, No. 6 (November/December 1997).

Index

About the Editor and Contributors

HELEN FEIN, Ph.D., Sociology, Columbia University, is Director, Institute for the Study of Genocide and Associate, Kennedy School of Government of Harvard University. She has written several prize-winning publications on genocide, including *Accounting for Genocide: National Responses and Jewish Victimization during the Holocaust* (1979) and *Genocide: A Sociological Perspective* (1990). She served as editor and coauthor of *The Prevention of Genocide: Rwanda and Yugoslavia Reconsidered* (1994) and *Genocide Watch* (1992). Dr. Fein, a founder and first president of the International Association of Genocide Scholars, has lectured at leading universities in the United States and Europe.

JOHN FOUSEK, Ph.D., History, Cornell University, is Executive Director, World Order Models Project, and Associate Director, Center for Global Change and Governance, Rutgers University, Newark, NJ. He is the author of *To Lead the Free World: American Nationalism and the Ideological Origins of the Cold War* (1999). He is also coauthor with Saul Mendlovitz of "The Prevention and Punishment of the Crime of Genocide" in *Genocide, War, and Human Survival* (1996) and "Enforcing the Law on Genocide," in the journal *Alternatives*.

GEORGE A. LOPEZ, Ph.D., Syracuse University, Professor of Government, and faculty fellow, Joan B. Kroc Institute for International Peace Studies, University of Notre Dame, is coauthor/editor (with Thomas G. Weiss, David Cortright, and Larry Minear) of *Political Gain and Civilian*

Pain: Humanitarian Impacts of Economic Sanctions (1997); *Peace and Security: The Next Generation* (1997) (with Nancy Myers); and *Economic Sanctions: Panacea or Peacebuilding in a Post-Cold War World?* (1995) (with David Cortright). He serves on the editorial boards of *Bulletin of the Atomic Scientists, Human Rights Quarterly,* and *Mershon International Studies Review.* He is also Series Editor of *Dilemmas In World Politics.*

SAUL MENDLOVITZ, J. D., University of Chicago, is Dag Hammarskjold Professor of Peace and World Order Studies at the Rutgers University School of Law and Codirector of the World Order Models Project. He is the author of *On the Creation of a Just World Order* (1975) and "The Prevention and Punishment of the Crime of Genocide" (with John Fousek) in *Genocide, War, and Human Survival* (1996). He is also the editor and coauthor of such volumes as *Preferred Futures for the United Nations* (1995); *The United Nations and a Just World Order* (1991); *Contending Sovereignty* (1990); *Towards a Just World Peace* (1987); *International Law in a Contemporary Perspective* (1985); and *Strategy of World Order* (4 vols.) (1985).

NEAL RIEMER, Ph.D., Harvard University, is Andrew V. Stout Professor of Political Philosophy, Emeritus, Drew University. Among his books are *The New World of Politics* (with Douglas Simon) (1997); *Creative Breakthroughs in Politics* (1996); *Let Justice Roll: Prophetic Challenges in Religion, Politics, and Society* (editor and coauthor) (1996); *New Thinking and Developments in International Politics* (editor and coauthor) (1991); *Karl Marx and Prophetic Politics* (1987); *James Madison* (1968, 1986); *The Future of the Democratic Revolution: Toward a More Prophetic Politics* (1984); *The Democratic Experiment* (1967); *The Revival of Democratic Theory* (1962); *World Affairs: Problems and Prospects* (1958) (coauthor).

DOUGLAS W. SIMON, Ph.D., University of Oregon, is Professor of Political Science at Drew University, specializing in international affairs, U.S. foreign policy, international organization, and national security. He directed Drew University's Semester at the United Nations for fifteen years. In 1991 he was the first recipient of Drew's Presidential Distinguished Teaching Award. Professor Simon is coauthor (with Neal Riemer) of *The New World of Politics* (1997); coauthor of *New Thinking and Developments in International Politics* (1991); and has contributed scholarly articles to the *Harvard Journal of World Affairs, East Asia Survey, Comparative Political Studies,* and other journals.

MICHAEL JOSEPH SMITH, Ph.D., Harvard University, is Associate Professor of Government and Foreign Affairs and Director, Program in Political and Social Thought, at the University of Virginia. He is the author of *Realist*

Thought from Weber to Kissinger (1987, 1990); editor/coauthor of *Ideas and Ideals: Essays in Honor of Stanley Hoffmann* (1993); and coeditor of *Consensus: Issues and Problems* (1985). He has also written "Humanitarian Intervention: An Overview of the Ethical Issues," "Growing up with Just and Unjust Wars," and "American Realism and New Global Realities" in *Ethics and International Affairs*, and works in other journals and books. His current book project, undertaken with Stanley Hoffmann, is called "Taming Cold Monsters: Ethical Choice in the World of States."

DAVID WIPPMAN is Associate Professor of Law at Cornell Law School, where he teaches public international law and international human rights. Prior to joining the faculty at Cornell, Wippman practiced law in Washington, D.C., for nine years, specializing in the representation of developing countries in litigation, arbitration, and legislative lobbying. He is the editor/coauthor of *International Law and Ethnic Conflict* (1998), and the author of numerous articles on public international law issues. Professor Wippman spent the 1998–1999 academic year as Director for Multilateral and Humanitarian Affairs at the National Security Council. He is a graduate of Princeton and Yale Law School.

ISBN 0-275-96515-5